Who God Is -- Based on what He says about Himself in the Bible

The Character of God

STUDY MANUAL

Shepherd • Changeless • Father
Hiding Place • Impartial • King
Rock • Warrior • Compassionate
Deliverer • Judge • Righteous
Wonderful • Jealous • Shield
Truth • Light • Kind • Perfect
Blameless • Refuge • Faithful
Holy • Comforter • and more!

The Character of God
STUDY MANUAL

Table of Contents

STUDY MANUAL

<u>INTRODUCTION:</u>
WHO GOD IS -- BASED ON
WHAT HE SAYS ABOUT HIMSELF IN THE BIBLE

This book starts with the premise that **God wants us to know Him** and has revealed Himself to us through the Bible.

In fact, God has gone to great lengths in His Word to describe in human terms just who He is – using illustrative language that we can all relate to. For example, we see God as *Our Refuge* – a place to run and take shelter until trouble passes (Psalm 57:1); or *Our Guide* who leads us over dark, rough and unfamiliar roads (Isaiah 42:16); or *Our Majestic King* who is sovereign over all peoples and nations and has an eternal kingdom that far exceeds anything on earth (Daniel 7:14); or *Our Judge* who will one day judge every person's deeds (Revelation 20:12); or *Our Compassionate Father* who loves and disciplines His children (Psalm 103:13); or *Our Shepherd* who tenderly tends to his flock, carrying the lambs in His arms (Isaiah 40:11).

The Character of God Study Manual

We all have various and different concepts of God based on our backgrounds, what we've been taught, life experience -- and who knows what else! But why not just go to the source? Why not investigate what God actually tells us about Himself as revealed through the Bible? Once we start looking, we will find there is plenty God has told us about Himself.

This book has identified 48 names or character traits God has revealed about Himself in the Bible (Although there are certainly more!). At times these traits overlap while other times it may, perhaps, seem they contradict (such as, how can God be both loving and terrible?). Rather than try to dissect or answer any questions, this manual merely provides the study material for specified personal study into discovering who God is – again, based upon God's own Word.

Interestingly, of the 48 character traits, there was a definite "Top Ten" that emerged in terms of the quantity of times the trait was mentioned in the Bible. Here is a list of the Top Ten with the number of times the trait is mentioned: 1) King (558 times); 2) Powerful (290 times); 3) Love (266 times); 4) Holy (247 times); 5) Glorious (246 times); 6) Father (234 times); 7) Savior (234 times); 8) Great (192 times); 9) Righteous (141 times); and 10) Good (108 times).

The next page has a complete list of the 48 character traits found in this study manual with the corresponding number of times they are mentioned in the Bible (according to our research). However, this *does not* mean the trait may not be mentioned in *another way* (other than directly) in the Bible. For example, we found that God was referenced as "changeless" or "does not change" four times. But this would not take into consideration when God says in Exodus 3:14, "I AM WHO I AM" as it does not have the word "changeless" in the verse, although it most certainly refers to God as changeless. That could be a fun additional study, if so desired.

Name or Character Trait	Number of Times Referred to in Bible	Name or Character Trait	Number of Times Referred to in Bible
KING	558	ROCK	40
POWERFUL	290	CREATOR	37
LOVE	266	GRACIOUS	34
HOLY	247	SHIELD	31
GLORIOUS	246	KIND	30
FATHER	234	SHEPHERD	26
SAVIOR	234	FORTRESS	25
GREAT	192	PROVIDER	25
RIGHTEOUS	141	JEALOUS	24
GOOD	108	PERFECT	23
MERCIFUL	92	TRUTH	23
PEACE	92	GUIDE	21
JUDGE	88	COMFORTER	17
TERRIBLE	88	PATIENT	17
DELIVERER	83	DEFENDER	16
LIGHT	81	FRIEND	13
HEALER	77	COUNSELOR	10
JUST	71	BLAMELESS	9
FAITHFUL	69	TRUSTWORTHY	7
REDEEMER	61	GENTLE	5
COMPASSIONATE	58	CHANGELESS	4
REFUGE	58	WARRIOR	4
FORGIVING	52	IMPARTIAL	2
WONDERFUL	49	HIDING PLACE	2

The Character of God Study Manual

Another interesting thing that emerged was the consistency of God throughout both the Old and New Testaments. In other words, the Bible shows a God who retains the same character throughout the span of history. The same God who Moses proclaims is "compassionate and gracious ... slow to anger, abounding in love and faithfulness" (Exodus 34:6) is seen fleshed out as Jesus having compassion over the crowds that gathered to see Him and later in God's love for us through Jesus' death on the cross (Matthew 9:36; John 3:16). There is no evidence in the Bible that there is a different God from the Old Testament to the New Testament. In fact, the evidence is quite the opposite.

GOD'S CHARACTER SPANNING OLD & NEW TESTAMENTS

Name or Character Trait	Verses in Old Testament showing this Character Trait	Verses in New Testament showing this Character Trait
Compassionate	Exodus 34:6; Jeremiah 33:26; Lamentations 3:22, 32	Matthew 9:36; II Corinthians 1:3; James 5:11
Savior	Exodus 15:2; II Samuel 22:47; Psalm 18:46; Isaiah 43:3; Jeremiah 14:8; Ezekiel 37:23	Matthew 1:21; John 4:42; Titus 2:13; Hebrews 7:25; Revelation 7:10, 12:10, 19:1
Love (Abounding)	Exodus 34:6; II Samuel 12:24; Nehemiah 13:26; Daniel 9:4	Mark 10:21; John 3:16; John 15:9; I John 4:19
Faithful	Deuteronomy 32:4; Psalm 33:4 Lamentations 3:23	I Corinthians 1:9 and 10:13; Hebrews 10:23; I John 1:9
Powerful / Mighty	I Chronicles 29:11-12; Jeremiah 10:6	Matthew 26:64; Luke 4:36; Ephesians 1:18-20
Good	Exodus 33:19; Joshua 21:45; Psalm 13:6; Nahum 1:7	Mark 10:18; Romans 8:28; Philippians 2:13; James 1:17
Shepherd	Genesis 48:15; Psalm 23:1; Jeremiah 31:10; Ezekiel 34:16	John 10:11 & 14; Hebrews 13:20; I Peter 5:4; Revelation 7:17
Terrible / A Consuming Fire	Exodus 24:17; Deuteronomy 4:24; Isaiah 30:27; Malachi 1:14	Hebrews 10:31 and 12:29; Revelation 6:16
King / Sovereign	Psalm 103:19; Daniel 6:26; Zechariah 14:9; Malachi 1:14	John 18:36; Hebrews 1:8; II Peter 1:11; Revelation 19:16

God's desire for us to know – or seek -- Him has been a constant as well. We see in Deuteronomy 4:29, "But if ... you s**eek the LORD your God, you will find him** if you seek him with all your heart and with all your soul." Then in Psalm 53:2, "God looks down from heaven on all mankind to see if there are any who understand, **any who seek God**." And in Hebrews 11:6, "And without faith it is impossible to please God, because anyone who comes to him must believe that he exists and that he rewards those **who earnestly seek him**."

Perhaps the saddest verses in the Bible are those of God reflecting on how mankind not only rejects Him, but even forgets Him. It seems rather ironic that we could or would forget God our Creator. Unfortunately, this is the very picture history too often reveals (Deuteronomy 32:18; Judges 3:7; I Samuel 12:9; Psalm 78:11; Psalm 106:13; Psalm 106:21; Isaiah 17:10; Jeremiah 2:32; Jeremiah 13:25; Jeremiah 18:15; Ezekiel 22:12; Ezekiel 23:35; Hosea 8:14 and Zephaniah 1:6). We also see God lament that his people "**do not know me**" (Jeremiah 4:22) and that there is "no love, **no acknowledgment of God** in the land" (Hosea 4:1).

The Bible serves many purposes. But perhaps the most important purpose was that God wanted to use His Word to reveal Himself to us in order for us to know Him – that we would have evidence of the way God has dealt with mankind throughout history. We can actually know and commune with God our Creator! God doesn't want religion, He wants *relationship* – and there is a very big difference! Jesus spoke to the religious leaders of His day about this very thing saying, "You study the Scriptures diligently because you think that in them you have eternal life. These are the very Scriptures that testify about me, *yet you refuse to come to me to have life*." (John 5:39-40)

So let's start our journey to gain a greater understanding of God – who He is and what He has revealed about Himself through His Word.

The Character of God Study Manual

About the Book Format:

The *New International Version* (NIV) of the Bible was used throughout this book. The format goes as follows: A Name or Character Trait (alphabetically) is introduced with Definition, followed by Question and Personal Study Notes Pages. Lastly, are the Biblical References (we wanted to include each Biblical reference to give quick access to what is stated in each verse and to make for easier studying) with character trait emphasized in bold lettering.

Dedication:

This book is dedicated to real life examples found throughout the Bible of people who knew their God -- and to all those who desire to be like them.

- Those who desire, like both Abraham and Moses, to be called friends of God. (Exodus 33:11; Isaiah 41:8; James 2:23)

- Those who, like David, earnestly seek God and have a thirst to know Him better. (Psalm 63:1)

- Those who, like Moses, are not satisfied to see only God's actions but want to also understand His ways. (Psalm 103:7)

- Those who want to be like Phineas who "was zealous for the honor of his God". (Numbers 25:10-13)

- Those who desire to be like the three friends: Shadrach, Meshach and Abednego who were so confident they could trust God -- they bet their lives on it. (Daniel 3:8-27)

- Those who want to be like Job who chose to trust and defend God's character even when not understanding God's actions. (Job 1:22; Job 2:10)

God is Blameless
Does No Wrong
No Deceit; Innocent

Blameless:
Deserving no blame; Innocent.

*He committed **no sin**, and **no deceit** was found in his mouth.*

- I Peter 2:22

God is Blameless

1. DEFINE BLAMELESS USING YOUR OWN WORDS, SYNONYMS, OR DESCRIPTIONS:

_____

_____

_____

2. WHY WAS IT SO IMPORTANT THAT JESUS BE BLAMELESS OR INNOCENT?

_____

_____

_____

3. DO YOU HAVE ANY OBSERVATIONS ABOUT THIS CHARACTER TRAIT OF GOD OR WHY HE WANTS US TO KNOW THAT HE IS BLAMELESS, INNOCENT, OR WITHOUT DECEIT?

_____

_____

_____

_____

_____

_____

O Love divine, what hast Thou done!
Th' incarnate God hath died for me!
The Father's co-eternal Son
Bore all my sins upon the tree!
The Son of God for me that died:
My Lord, My love, is crucified.
— _Charles Wesley_

NOTES:

God is Blameless

Deuteronomy 32:4
He is the Rock, his works are perfect, and all his ways are just. A faithful God who **does no wrong**, upright and just is he.

Job 1:22
In all this, Job did not sin by charging God with **wrongdoing**.

Psalm 18:25
To the faithful you show yourself faithful, to the blameless you show yourself **blameless**,

Isaiah 53:9
He was assigned a grave with the wicked, and with the rich in his death, though he had done no violence, **nor was any deceit** in his mouth.

Zephaniah 3:5
The LORD within her is righteous; he **does no wrong**.

Matthew 27:4
[*Judas after betraying Jesus*] "I have sinned," he said, "for I have betrayed **innocent** blood."

Luke 23:41
[*Thief on cross next to Jesus*] We are punished justly, for we are getting what our deeds deserve. But this man has **done nothing wrong**."

Hebrews 7:26
Such a high priest truly meets our need—one who is holy, **blameless**, pure, set apart from sinners, exalted above the heavens.

I Peter 2:22
He committed no sin, and **no deceit** was found in his mouth.

God is Changeless
Does Not Change

Changeless:
Having no change or alteration; Unable to do something against ones' inherent nature; No substitution of one thing for another.

*I the LORD **do not change**.*

- Malachi 3:6

God is Changeless

1. DEFINE CHANGELESS USING YOUR OWN WORDS, SYNONYMS, OR DESCRIPTIONS:

_____

_____

_____

2. EXODUS 3:14, "GOD SAID TO MOSES, 'I AM WHO I AM. THIS IS WHAT YOU ARE TO SAY TO THE ISREALITES: I AM HAS SENT ME TO YOU.'" WAS THIS ANTOHER WAY OF GOD SAYING HE WAS CHANGELESS? EXPLAIN.

_____

_____

_____

3. THERE ARE INSTANCES WHERE GOD SAYS HE RELENTS FROM AN ACTION OR CHANGES WHAT HE PLANNED TO DO BECAUSE HE CHOOSES TO BE MERCIFUL (Deuteronomy 9:13-20; Jonah 3:1-10; I Chronicles 21:14-16). HOW THEN CAN GOD SAY HE DOES NOT CHANGE HIS MIND?

_____

_____

_____

4. DO YOU HAVE ANY OBSERVATIONS ABOUT THIS CHARACTER TRAIT OF GOD OR WHY HE WANTS US TO KNOW THAT HE IS CHANGELESS OR DOES NOT CHANGE?

_____

_____

_____

_____

_____

I can see how it might be possible for a man to look down upon the earth and be an atheist, but I cannot conceive how he could look up into the heavens and say there is no God.
- Abraham Lincoln

Let nothing disturb you, let nothing frighten you,
* All things are passing away: God never changes.*
Patience obtains all things, whoever has God lacks nothing;
* God alone suffices.*
- Santa Teresa de Jesus

NOTES:

God is Changeless

Numbers 23:19
God is not human, that he should lie, not a human being, **that he should change his mind**. Does he speak and then not act? Does he promise and not fulfill?

Malachi 3:6
I the LORD **do not change**.

II Timothy 2:13
If we are faithless, he remains faithful, for **he cannot disown himself**.

James 1:17
Every good and perfect gift is from above, coming down from the Father of the heavenly lights, who **does not change** like shifting shadows.

God Our Comforter
Gives Comfort

Comforter:
One who comforts; One who relieves grief or suffering.

*As a mother comforts her child, so will I **comfort** you; and you will be **comforted** over Jerusalem.*

- Isaiah 66:13

God Our Comforter

1. DEFINE COMFORTER USING YOUR OWN WORDS, SYNONYMS, OR DESCRIPTIONS:

_____

_____

_____

2. HOW IS GIVING COMFORT DIFFERENT THAT BEING COMPASSIONATE?

_____

_____

_____

3. DO YOU HAVE ANY OBSERVATIONS ABOUT THIS CHARACTER TRAIT OF GOD OR WHY GOD WANTS US TO KNOW THAT HE IS OUR COMFORTER?

_____

_____

_____

_____

_____

Earth has no sorrow that heaven cannot heal.
- Thomas Moore

The Lord gets His best soldiers out of the hightlights of affliction.
- Charles Spurgeon

NOTES:

God Our Comforter

Psalm 23:4
Even though I walk through the darkest valley, I will fear no evil, for you are with me; your rod and your staff, they **comfort** me.

Psalm 71:21
You will increase my honor and **comfort** me once more.

Psalm 86:17
Give me a sign of your goodness, that my enemies may see it and be put to shame, for you, LORD, have helped me and **comforted** me.

Psalm 119:76
May your unfailing love be my **comfort**, according to your promise to your servant.

Isaiah 12:1
In that day you will say: "I will praise you, LORD. Although you were angry with me, your anger has turned away and you have **comforted** me."

Isaiah 49:13
Shout for joy, you heavens; rejoice, you earth; burst into song, you mountains! For the LORD **comforts** his people and will have compassion on his afflicted ones.

Isaiah 51:3
The LORD will surely **comfort** Zion and will look with compassion on all her ruins; he will make her deserts like Eden, her wastelands like the garden of the LORD.

Isaiah 51:12
I, even I, am he who **comforts** you.

Isaiah 52:9
Burst into songs of joy together, you ruins of Jerusalem, for the LORD has **comforted** his people, he has redeemed Jerusalem.

Isaiah 57:18
I have seen their ways, but I will heal them; I will guide them and restore **comfort** to Israel's mourners,

Isaiah 66:13
As a mother comforts her child, so will I **comfort** you; and you will be **comforted** over Jerusalem.

Jeremiah 31:13
Then young women will dance and be glad, young men and old as well. I will turn their mourning into gladness; I will give them **comfort** and joy instead of sorrow.

Zechariah 1:13
So the LORD spoke kind and **comforting** words to the angel who talked with me.

Zechariah 1:17
Proclaim further: This is what the LORD Almighty says: "My towns will again overflow with prosperity, and the LORD will again **comfort** Zion and choose Jerusalem."

Matthew 5:4
Blessed are those who mourn, for they will be **comforted**.

2 Corinthians 1:3-5
Praise be to the God and Father of our Lord Jesus Christ, the Father of compassion and the God of all **comfort**, who **comforts** us in all our troubles, so that we can comfort those in any trouble with the **comfort** we ourselves receive from God. For just as we share abundantly in the sufferings of Christ, so also our **comfort** abounds through Christ.

2 Corinthians 7:6
But God, who **comforts** the downcast, **comforted** us by the coming of Titus,

God is Compassionate
Shows Compassion

Compassionate:
Sympathetic consciousness of anothers' distress together with a desire to alleviate it.

*As a father has compassion on his children, so the Lord has **compassion** on those who fear him;*

- Psalm 103:13

God is Compassionate

1. DEFINE COMPASSIONATE USING YOUR OWN WORDS, SYNONYMS, OR DESCRIPTIONS:

_____

_____

_____

2. ISAIAH 54:7-8, SHOWS A PATTERN OF GOD'S ANGER/DISCIPLINE FOLLOWED WITH GREAT COMPASSION. CAN YOU FIND OTHER SCRIPTURES THAT SHOW THIS PATTERN?

_____

_____

_____

_____

_____

3. DO YOU HAVE ANY OBSERVATIONS ABOUT THIS CHARACTER TRAIT OF GOD OR WHY GOD WANTS US TO KNOW THAT HE IS COMPASSIONATE?

_____

_____

_____

_____

_____

_____

Pity weeps and runs away; Compassion comes to help and stay.
- Janet Curtis O'Leary

God giveth the shoulder according to the burden.

NOTES:

God is Compassionate

Exodus 22:27
When they cry out to me, I will hear, for I am **compassionate**.

Exodus 33:19
And the LORD said, "I will cause all my goodness to pass in front of you, and I will proclaim my name, the LORD, in your presence. I will have mercy on whom I will have mercy, and I will have compassion on whom I will have **compassion**."

Exodus 34:6
And he passed in front of Moses, proclaiming, "The LORD, the LORD, the **compassionate** and gracious God, slow to anger, abounding in love and faithfulness,"

Deuteronomy 13:17
Then the LORD will turn from his fierce anger, will show you mercy, and will have **compassion** on you.

Deuteronomy 30:3
then the LORD your God will restore your fortunes and have **compassion** on you and gather you again from all the nations where he scattered you.

2 Kings 13:23
But the LORD was gracious to them and had **compassion** and showed concern for them because of his covenant with Abraham, Isaac and Jacob. To this day he has been unwilling to destroy them or banish them from his presence.

2 Chronicles 30:9
If you return to the LORD, then your fellow Israelites and your children will be shown **compassion** by their captors and will return to this land, for the LORD your God is gracious and **compassionate**.

Nehemiah 9:17
But you are a forgiving God, gracious and **compassionate**, slow to anger and abounding in love.

Nehemiah 9:19
Because of your great **compassion** you did not abandon them in the wilderness.

Nehemiah 9:27
From heaven you heard them, and in your great **compassion** you gave them deliverers, who rescued them from the hand of their enemies.

Nehemiah 9:28
And when they cried out to you again, you heard from heaven, and in your **compassion** you delivered them time after time.

Psalm 51:1
Have mercy on me, O God, according to your unfailing love; according to your great **compassion** blot out my transgressions.

Psalm 86:15
But you, Lord, are a **compassionate** and gracious God, slow to anger, abounding in love and faithfulness.

Psalm 103:4
who redeems your life from the pit and crowns you with love and **compassion**,

Psalm 103:8
The LORD is **compassionate** and gracious, slow to anger, abounding in love.

Psalm 103:13
As a father has **compassion** on his children, so the LORD has **compassion** on those who fear him;

Psalm 111:4
He has caused his wonders to be remembered; the LORD is gracious and **compassionate**.

Psalm 116:5
The LORD is gracious and righteous; our God is full of **compassion**.

Psalm 119:77
Let your **compassion** come to me that I may live, for your law is my delight.

God is Compassionate

Psalm 119:156
Your **compassion**, LORD, is great; preserve my life according to your laws.

Psalm 135:14
For the LORD will vindicate his people and have **compassion** on his servants.

Psalm 145:8
The LORD is gracious and **compassionate**, slow to anger and rich in love.

Psalm 145:9
The LORD is good to all; he has **compassion** on all he has made.

Isaiah 14:1
The LORD will have **compassion** on Jacob; once again he will choose Israel and will settle them in their own land.

Isaiah 30:18
Yet the LORD longs to be gracious to you; therefore he will rise up to show you **compassion**.

Isaiah 49:10
He who has **compassion** on them will guide them and lead them beside springs of water.

Isaiah 49:13
For the LORD comforts his people and will have **compassion** on his afflicted ones.

Isaiah 49:15
Can a mother forget the baby at her breast and have no **compassion** on the child she has borne? Though she may forget, I will not forget you!

Isaiah 51:3
The LORD will surely comfort Zion and will look with **compassion** on all her ruins; he will make her deserts like Eden, her wastelands like the garden of the LORD. Joy and gladness will be found in her, thanksgiving and the sound of singing.

Isaiah 54:7
For a brief moment I abandoned you, but with deep **compassion** I will bring you back.

Isaiah 54:8
"In a surge of anger I hid my face from you for a moment, but with everlasting kindness I will have **compassion** on you," says the LORD your Redeemer.

Isaiah 54:10
"Though the mountains be shaken and the hills be removed, yet my unfailing love for you will not be shaken nor my covenant of peace be removed," says the LORD, who has **compassion** on you.

Isaiah 60:10
Though in anger I struck you, in favor I will show you **compassion**.

Isaiah 63:7
I will tell of the kindnesses of the LORD, the deeds for which he is to be praised, according to all the LORD has done for us— yes, the many good things he has done for Israel, according to his **compassion** and many kindnesses.

Jeremiah 12:15
But after I uproot them, I will again have **compassion** and will bring each of them back to their own inheritance and their own country.

Jeremiah 30:18
This is what the LORD says: "'I will restore the fortunes of Jacob's tents and have **compassion** on his dwellings;"

Jeremiah 31:20
"Is not Ephraim my dear son, the child in whom I delight? Though I often speak against him, I still remember him. Therefore my heart yearns for him; I have great **compassion** for him," declares the LORD.

Jeremiah 33:26
For I will restore their fortunes and have **compassion** on them.

God is Compassionate

Lamentations 3:22
Because of the LORD's great love we are not consumed, for his **compassions** never fail.

Lamentations 3:32
Though he brings grief, he will show **compassion**, so great is his unfailing love.

Ezekiel 39:25
Therefore this is what the Sovereign LORD says: "I will now restore the fortunes of Jacob and will have **compassion** on all the people of Israel, and I will be zealous for my holy name."

Hosea 2:19
I will betroth you to me forever; I will betroth you in righteousness and justice, in love and **compassion**.

Hosea 11:8
"How can I give you up, Ephraim? How can I hand you over, Israel? How can I treat you like Admah? How can I make you like Zeboyim? My heart is changed within me; all my **compassion** is aroused.

Hosea 14:3
We will never again say 'Our gods' to what our own hands have made, for in you the fatherless find **compassion**.

Joel 2:13
Rend your heart and not your garments. Return to the LORD your God, for he is gracious and **compassionate**, slow to anger and abounding in love, and he relents from sending calamity.

Jonah 3:9
Who knows? God may yet relent and with **compassion** turn from his fierce anger so that we will not perish.

Jonah 4:2
[*Jonah speaking to God*] I knew that you are a gracious and **compassionate** God, slow to anger and abounding in love, a God who relents from sending calamity.

Zechariah 10:6
I will strengthen Judah and save the tribes of Joseph. I will restore them because I have **compassion** on them. They will be as though I had not rejected them, for I am the LORD their God and I will answer them.

Malachi 3:17
"On the day when I act," says the LORD Almighty, "they will be my treasured possession. I will spare them, just as a father has **compassion** and spares his son who serves him."

Matthew 9:36
When he saw the crowds, he had **compassion** on them, because they were harassed and helpless, like sheep without a shepherd.

Matthew 14:14
When Jesus landed and saw a large crowd, he had **compassion** on them and healed their sick.

Matthew 15:32
Jesus called his disciples to him and said, "I have **compassion** for these people; they have already been with me three days and have nothing to eat. I do not want to send them away hungry, or they may collapse on the way."

Matthew 20:34
Jesus had **compassion** on them and touched their eyes. Immediately they received their sight and followed him.

Mark 6:34
When Jesus landed and saw a large crowd, he had **compassion** on them, because they were like sheep without a shepherd.

Mark 8:2
I have **compassion** for these people; they have already been with me three days and have nothing to eat.

Romans 9:15
For he says to Moses, "I will have mercy on whom I have mercy, and I will have **compassion** on whom I have **compassion**."

2 Corinthians 1:3
Praise be to the God and Father of our Lord Jesus Christ, the Father of **compassion** and the God of all comfort,

James 5:11
The Lord is full of **compassion** and mercy.

God Our Counselor
Able to Give Counsel

Counselor:
One who shows good judgment by giving good advice or guidance; One who has greater understanding than the one being counseled.

*I will instruct you and teach you in the way you should go; I will **counsel** you with my loving eye on you.*

- Psalm 32:8

God Our Counselor

1. DEFINE COUNSELOR USING YOUR OWN WORDS, SYNONYMS, OR DESCRIPTIONS:

_____

_____

_____

2. IN 2 CHRONICLES 18:4, KING JEHOSHAPHAT TELLS KING AHAB TO SEEK GOD'S COUNSEL *FIRST*. DOESN'T IT SEEM THAT WE OFTEN SEEK EVERYONE ELSE'S COUNSEL AND THEN AS LAST RESORT SEEK GOD'S? READ THIS INTERESTING STORY IN 2 CHRONICLES 18 OF HOW KING AHAB DECIDED TO LISTEN TO THE COUNSEL HE WANTED TO HEAR INSTEAD OF GOD'S COUNSEL AND HOW IT COST HIM HIS LIFE.

_____

_____

_____

3. DO YOU HAVE ANY OBSERVATIONS ABOUT THIS CHARACTER TRAIT OF GOD OR WHY HE WANTS US TO KNOW THAT HE IS OUR COUNSELOR AND ABLE TO GIVE COUNSEL?

_____

_____

_____

_____

_____

Is God your refuge, your hiding place, your stronghold, your shepherd, your counselor, your friend, your redeemer, your saviour, your guide? If He is, you don't need to search any further for security.
- Elizabeth Elliot

Sometimes God calms the storm and sometimes He calms His child.
- John Groberg

NOTES:

God Our Counselor

2 Chronicles 18:4
But Jehoshaphat also said to the king of Israel, "First seek the **counsel** of the LORD."

Job 12:13
"To God belong wisdom and power; **counsel** and understanding are his.

Psalm 16:7
I will praise the LORD, who **counsels** me; even at night my heart instructs me.

Psalm 32:8
I will instruct you and teach you in the way you should go; I will **counsel** you with my loving eye on you.

Psalm 73:24
You guide me with your **counsel**, and afterward you will take me into glory.

Psalm 119:24
Your statutes are my delight; they are my **counselors**.

Isaiah 9:6
For to us a child is born, to us a son is given, and the government will be on his shoulders. And he will be called Wonderful **Counselor**, Mighty God, Everlasting Father, Prince of Peace.

Isaiah 11:2
The Spirit of the LORD will rest on him—the Spirit of wisdom and of understanding, the Spirit of **counsel** and of might, the Spirit of the knowledge and fear of the LORD—

Isaiah 40:13
Who can fathom the Spirit of the LORD, or instruct the LORD as his **counselor**?

Romans 11:34
"Who has known the mind of the Lord? Or who has been his **counselor**?"

God Our Creator
Our Maker

Creator:
One who brings something into existence;
Originator of life.

*This is what God the Lord says -- the **Creator** of the
heavens, who stretches them out, who spreads out
the earth with all that springs from it, who gives
breath to its people, and life to those who walk on it.*

- Isaiah 42:5

God Our Creator

1. DEFINE CREATOR USING YOUR OWN WORDS, SYNONYMS, OR DESCRIPTIONS:

_____

_____

_____

2. ROMANS 1:25, "THEY EXCHANGED THE TRUTH ABOUT GOD FOR A LIE, AND WORSHIPED AND SERVED CREATED THINGS RATHER THAN THE CREATOR -- WHO IS FOREVER PRAISED." WHAT "CREATED" THINGS DO WE SERVE?

_____

_____

_____

3. DO YOU HAVE ANY OBSERVATIONS ABOUT THIS CHARACTER TRAIT OF GOD OR WHY GOD WANTS US TO KNOW THAT HE IS OUR CREATOR?

_____

_____

_____

_____

_____

_____

I think that I shall never see
  A poem lovely as a tree.
A tree whose hungry mouth is pressed
  Against the earth's sweet flowing breast;
A tree that looks at God all day
  And lifts her leafy arms to pray;
A tree may in summer wear
  A nest of robins in her hair;
Upon whose bosom snow has lain;
  Who intimately lives with rain.
Poems are made by fools like me,
  But only God can make a tree.
                    - Joyce Kilmer

NOTES:

God Our Creator

Genesis 14:19
and he blessed Abram, saying, "Blessed be Abram by God Most High, **Creator** of heaven and earth.

Genesis 14:22
But Abram said . . . I have sworn an oath to the LORD, God Most High, **Creator** of heaven and earth,

Deuteronomy 32:6
Is this the way you repay the LORD, you foolish and unwise people? Is he not your Father, your **Creator**, who made you and formed you?

Job 4:17
'Can a mortal be more righteous than God? Can even a strong man be more pure than his **Maker**?

Job 9:9
He is the **Maker** of the Bear and Orion, the Pleiades and the constellations of the south.

Job 35:10
But no one says, 'Where is God my **Maker**, who gives songs in the night,

Job 36:3
I get my knowledge from afar; I will ascribe justice to my **Maker**.

Job 40:19
It ranks first among the works of God, yet its **Maker** can approach it with his sword.

Psalm 95:6
Come, let us bow down in worship, let us kneel before the LORD our **Maker**;

Psalm 115:15
May you be blessed by the LORD, the **Maker** of heaven and earth.

Psalm 121:2
My help comes from the LORD, the **Maker** of heaven and earth.

Psalm 124:8
Our help is in the name of the LORD, the **Maker** of heaven and earth.

Psalm 134:3
May the LORD bless you from Zion, he who is the **Maker** of heaven and earth.

Psalm 146:6
He is the **Maker** of heaven and earth, the sea, and everything in them— he remains faithful forever.

Psalm 149:2
Let Israel rejoice in their **Maker**; let the people of Zion be glad in their King.

Proverbs 14:31
Whoever oppresses the poor shows contempt for their **Maker**, but whoever is kind to the needy honors God.

Proverbs 17:5
Whoever mocks the poor shows contempt for their **Maker**; whoever gloats over disaster will not go unpunished.

Proverbs 22:2
Rich and poor have this in common: The LORD is the **Maker** of them all.

Ecclesiastes 11:5
As you do not know the path of the wind, or how the body is formed in a mother's womb, so you cannot understand the work of God, the **Maker** of all things.

Ecclesiastes 12:1
Remember your **Creator** in the days of your youth,

Isaiah 17:7
In that day people will look to their **Maker** and turn their eyes to the Holy One of Israel.

Isaiah 27:11
For this is a people without understanding; so their Maker has no compassion on them, and their **Creator** shows them no favor.

Isaiah 40:28
Do you not know? Have you not heard? The LORD is the everlasting God, the **Creator** of the ends of the earth. He will not grow tired or weary, and his understanding no one can fathom.

Isaiah 42:5
This is what God the LORD says— the **Creator** of the heavens, who stretches them out, who spreads out the earth with all that springs from it, who gives breath to its people, and life to those who walk on it:

Isaiah 43:15
I am the LORD, your Holy One, Israel's **Creator**, your King."

Isaiah 44:24
"This is what the LORD says— your Redeemer, who formed you in the womb: I am the LORD, the **Maker** of all things, who stretches out the heavens, who spreads out the earth by myself,

Isaiah 45:9
"Woe to those who quarrel with their **Maker**, those who are nothing but potsherds among the potsherds on the ground. Does the clay say to the potter, 'What are you making?' Does your work say, 'The potter has no hands'?

Isaiah 45:11
"This is what the LORD says— the Holy One of Israel, and its **Maker**: Concerning things to come, do you question me about my children, or give me orders about the work of my hands?

Isaiah 51:13
that you forget the LORD your **Maker**, who stretches out the heavens and who lays the foundations of the earth, that you live in constant terror every day because of the wrath of the oppressor, who is bent on destruction?

Isaiah 54:5
For your **Maker** is your husband— the LORD Almighty is his name— the Holy One of Israel is your Redeemer; he is called the God of all the earth.

Jeremiah 10:16
He who is the Portion of Jacob is not like these, for he is the **Maker** of all things, including Israel, the people of his inheritance— the LORD Almighty is his name.

Jeremiah 51:19
He who is the Portion of Jacob is not like these, for he is the **Maker** of all things, including the people of his inheritance— the LORD Almighty is his name.

Hosea 8:14
Israel has forgotten their **Maker** and built palaces; Judah has fortified many towns. But I will send fire on their cities that will consume their fortresses."

Matthew 19:4
"Haven't you read," he replied, "that at the beginning the **Creator** 'made them male and female,'

Romans 1:25
They exchanged the truth about God for a lie, and worshiped and served created things rather than the **Creator**—who is forever praised.

God Our Creator

Colossians 3:10
and have put on the new self, which is being renewed in knowledge in the image of its **Creator**.

1 Peter 4:19
So then, those who suffer according to God's will should commit themselves to their faithful **Creator** and continue to do good.

God Our Defender
Able to Defend
Our Defense

Defender:
One who defends or protects against all attacks.

*The Lord is my strength and my **defense**; he has become my salvation.*

- Exodus 15:2

God Our Defender

1. DEFINE DEFENDER USING YOUR OWN WORDS, SYNONYMS, OR DESCRIPTIONS:

_____

_____

_____

2. GOD MENTIONS SEVERAL TIMES THAT HE IS THE DEFENDER TO THE FATHERLESS/ORPHANED, WIDOWS AND THOSE OPPRESSED. WHY DO YOU THINK HE MENTIONS THESE GROUPS ESPECIALLY?

_____

_____

_____

3. DO YOU HAVE ANY OBSERVATIONS ABOUT THIS CHARACTER TRAIT OF GOD OR WHY HE WANTS US TO KNOW THAT HE IS OUR DEFENDER OR DEFENSE?

_____

_____

_____

_____

_____

The plant protected by God is never hurt by the wind.
- African Proverb

Think of God and not religion, of ecstacy and not mysticism. The difference between the theoretician of faith and the believer is as great as between the psychiatrist and the psychotic.
- Emil Cioran

NOTES:

God Our Defender

Exodus 15:2
"The LORD is my strength and my **defense**; he has become my salvation.

Deuteronomy 10:18
He **defends** the cause of the fatherless and the widow,

2 Kings 19:34
I will **defend** this city and save it, for my sake and for the sake of David my servant.

2 Kings 20:6
I will **defend** this city for my sake and for the sake of my servant David.

Psalm 10:18
defending the fatherless and the oppressed, so that mere earthly mortals will never again strike terror.

Psalm 35:23
Awake, and rise to my **defense**! Contend for me, my God and Lord.

Psalm 68:5
A father to the fatherless, a **defender** of widows, is God in his holy dwelling.

Psalm 118:14
The LORD is my strength and my **defense**; he has become my salvation.

Proverbs 23:11
for their **Defender** is strong; he will take up their case against you.

Isaiah 12:2
The LORD, the LORD himself, is my strength and my **defense**; he has become my salvation."

Isaiah 19:20
It will be a sign and witness to the LORD Almighty in the land of Egypt. When they cry out to the LORD because of their oppressors, he will send them a savior and **defender**, and he will rescue them.

Isaiah 37:35
I will **defend** this city and save it, for my sake and for the sake of David my servant!

Isaiah 38:6
And I will deliver you and this city from the hand of the king of Assyria. I will **defend** this city.

Isaiah 51:22
This is what your Sovereign LORD says, your God, who **defends** his people: "See, I have taken out of your hand the cup that made you stagger; from that cup, the goblet of my wrath, you will never drink again."

Jeremiah 50:34
Yet their Redeemer is strong; the LORD Almighty is his name. He will vigorously **defend** their cause so that he may bring rest to their land, but unrest to those who live in Babylon.

Jeremiah 51:36
Therefore this is what the LORD says: "See, I will **defend** your cause and avenge you;

God Our Deliverer
Giving Deliverance

Deliverer:
One who rescues, saves or sets free.

*The Lord helps them and **delivers** them; he **delivers** them from the wicked and saves them, because they take refuge in him.*

- Psalm 37:40

God Our Deliverer

1. DEFINE DELIVERER USING YOUR OWN WORDS, SYNONYMS, OR DESCRIPTIONS:

_____

_____

_____

2. LOOK AT THE AMAZING STORY OF GOD'S DELIVERENCE IN DANIEL CHAPTER 3 OF THREE MEN WHO REFUSED TO WORSHIP ANYONE OTHER THAN GOD. HOW DID GOD DELIVER THEM?

_____

_____

_____

3. DO YOU HAVE ANY OBSERVATIONS ABOUT THIS CHARACTER TRAIT OF GOD OR WHY GOD WANTS US TO KNOW THAT HE IS OUR DELIVERER AND GIVES DELIVERANCE?

_____

_____

_____

_____

_____

Bare heights of loneliness . . . a wilderness whose burning winds sweep over glowing sands, what are they to Him? Even there He can refresh us, even there He can renew us.
- Amy Wilson-Carmichael

NOTES:

God Our Deliverer

Genesis 14:20
And praise be to God Most High, who **delivered** your enemies into your hand.

Genesis 45:7
[*Joseph speaking to his brothers*] But God sent me ahead of you to preserve for you a remnant on earth and to save your lives by a great **deliverance**.

Genesis 49:18
I look for your **deliverance**, LORD.

Exodus 14:13
Moses answered the people, "Do not be afraid. Stand firm and you will see the **deliverance** the LORD will bring you today. The Egyptians you see today you will never see again."

Numbers 21:34
The LORD said to Moses, "Do not be afraid of him, for I have **delivered** him into your hands, along with his whole army and his land."

Deuteronomy 2:33
the LORD our God **delivered** him over to us

Deuteronomy 3:2
The LORD said to me, "Do not be afraid of him, for I have **delivered** him into your hands, along with his whole army and his land."

Deuteronomy 7:23
But the LORD your God will **deliver** them over to you, throwing them into great confusion until they are destroyed.

Deuteronomy 23:14
For the LORD your God moves about in your camp to protect you and to **deliver** your enemies to you.

Deuteronomy 31:5
The LORD will **deliver** them to you,

Deuteronomy 32:39
See now that I myself am he! There is no god besides me. I put to death and I bring to life, I have wounded and I will heal, and no one can **deliver** out of my hand.

Joshua 6:2
Then the LORD said to Joshua, "See, I have **delivered** Jericho into your hands, along with its king and its fighting men."

Joshua 8:1
Then the LORD said to Joshua, "Do not be afraid; do not be discouraged. Take the whole army with you, and go up and attack Ai. For I have **delivered** into your hands the king of Ai, his people, his city and his land."

Joshua 8:18
Then the LORD said to Joshua, "Hold out toward Ai the javelin that is in your hand, for into your hand I will **deliver** the city."

Judges 4:9
"Certainly I will go with you," said Deborah. "But because of the course you are taking, the honor will not be yours, for the LORD will **deliver** Sisera into the hands of a woman." So Deborah went with Barak to Kedesh.

Judges 6:9
I rescued you from the hand of the Egyptians. And I **delivered** you from the hand of all your oppressors; I drove them out before you and gave you their land.

1 Samuel 2:1
Then Hannah prayed and said: "My heart rejoices in the LORD; in the LORD my horn is lifted high. My mouth boasts over my enemies, for I delight in your **deliverance**."

God Our Deliverer

1 Samuel 7:3
So Samuel said to all the Israelites, "If you are returning to the LORD with all your hearts, then rid yourselves of the foreign gods and the Ashtoreths and commit yourselves to the LORD and serve him only, and he will **deliver** you out of the hand of the Philistines."

1 Samuel 9:16
About this time tomorrow I will send you a man from the land of Benjamin. Anoint him ruler over my people Israel; he will **deliver** them from the hand of the Philistines. I have looked on my people, for their cry has reached me.

1 Samuel 10:18
and said to them, "This is what the LORD, the God of Israel, says: 'I brought Israel up out of Egypt, and I **delivered** you from the power of Egypt and all the kingdoms that oppressed you.'"

1 Samuel 12:11
Then the LORD sent Jerub-Baal, Barak, Jephthah and Samuel, and he **delivered** you from the hands of your enemies all around you, so that you lived in safety.

1 Samuel 17:46
[*David speaking to Goliath*] This day the LORD will **deliver** you into my hands, and I'll strike you down and cut off your head. This very day I will give the carcasses of the Philistine army to the birds and the wild animals, and the whole world will know that there is a God in Israel.

2 Samuel 4:9
David answered Rekab, "As surely as the LORD lives, who has **delivered** me out of every trouble,"

2 Samuel 12:7
Then Nathan said to David, "You are the man! This is what the LORD, the God of Israel, says: 'I anointed you king over Israel, and I **delivered** you from the hand of Saul."

2 Samuel 18:31
Then the Cushite arrived and said, "My lord the king, hear the good news! The LORD has vindicated you today by **delivering** you from the hand of all who rose up against you."

2 Samuel 22:1
David sang to the LORD the words of this song when the LORD **delivered** him from the hand of all his enemies and from the hand of Saul.

2 Samuel 22:2
He said: "The LORD is my rock, my fortress and my **deliverer**;"

2 Samuel 22:44
You have **delivered** me from the attacks of the peoples; you have preserved me as the head of nations.

1 Kings 1:29
The king then took an oath: "As surely as the LORD lives, who has **delivered** me out of every trouble,"

1 Kings 20:28
The man of God came up and told the king of Israel, "This is what the LORD says: 'Because the Arameans think the LORD is a god of the hills and not a god of the valleys, I will **deliver** this vast army into your hands, and you will know that I am the LORD.'"

2 Kings 3:18
This is an easy thing in the eyes of the LORD; he will also **deliver** Moab into your hands.

2 Kings 17:39
Rather, worship the LORD your God; it is he who will **deliver** you from the hand of all your enemies.

Nehemiah 9:28
"But as soon as they were at rest, they again did what was evil in your sight. Then you abandoned them to the hand of their enemies so that they ruled over them. And when they cried out to you again, you heard from heaven, and in your compassion you **delivered** them time after time.

God Our Deliverer

Psalm 3:8
From the LORD comes **deliverance**.

Psalm 18:2
The LORD is my rock, my fortress and my **deliverer**; my God is my rock, in whom I take refuge, my shield and the horn of my salvation, my stronghold.

Psalm 18:43
You have **delivered** me from the attacks of the people;

Psalm 22:4
In you our ancestors put their trust; they trusted and you **delivered** them.

Psalm 32:7
You are my hiding place; you will protect me from trouble and surround me with songs of **deliverance**.

Psalm 33:19
to **deliver** them from death and keep them alive in famine.

Psalm 34:4
I sought the LORD, and he answered me; he **delivered** me from all my fears.

Psalm 34:7
The angel of the LORD encamps around those who fear him, and he **delivers** them.

Psalm 34:17
The righteous cry out, and the LORD hears them; he **delivers** them from all their troubles.

Psalm 34:19
The righteous person may have many troubles, but the LORD **delivers** him from them all;

Psalm 37:40
The LORD helps them and **delivers** them; he **delivers** them from the wicked and saves them, because they take refuge in him.

Psalm 40:17
But as for me, I am poor and needy; may the Lord think of me. You are my help and my **deliverer**; you are my God, do not delay.

Psalm 41:1
Blessed are those who have regard for the weak; the LORD **delivers** them in times of trouble.

Psalm 50:15
and call on me in the day of trouble; I will **deliver** you, and you will honor me.

Psalm 54:7
You have **delivered** me from all my troubles, and my eyes have looked in triumph on my foes.

Psalm 56:13
For you have **delivered** me from death and my feet from stumbling, that I may walk before God in the light of life.

Psalm 70:5
But as for me, I am poor and needy; come quickly to me, O God. You are my help and my **deliverer**; LORD, do not delay.

Psalm 71:23
My lips will shout for joy when I sing praise to you— I whom you have **delivered**.

Psalm 78:22
for they did not believe in God or trust in his **deliverance**.

God Our Deliverer

Psalm 86:13
For great is your love toward me; you have **delivered** me from the depths, from the realm of the dead.

Psalm 91:15
He will call on me, and I will answer him; I will be with him in trouble, I will **deliver** him and honor him.

Psalm 97:10
Let those who love the LORD hate evil, for he guards the lives of his faithful ones and **delivers** them from the hand of the wicked.

Psalm 106:43
Many times he **delivered** them, but they were bent on rebellion and they wasted away in their sin.

Psalm 107:6
Then they cried out to the LORD in their trouble, and he **delivered** them from their distress.

Psalm 116:8
For you, LORD, have **delivered** me from death, my eyes from tears, my feet from stumbling,

Psalm 140:7
Sovereign LORD, my strong **deliverer**, you shield my head in the day of battle.

Psalm 144:2
He is my loving God and my fortress, my stronghold and my **deliverer**, my shield, in whom I take refuge,

Psalm 144:10
to the One who gives victory to kings, who **delivers** his servant David. From the deadly sword

Isaiah 31:5
Like birds hovering overhead, the LORD Almighty will shield Jerusalem; he will shield it and **deliver** it, he will 'pass over' it and will rescue it.

Isaiah 38:6
And I will **deliver** you and this city from the hand of the king of Assyria. I will defend this city.

Isaiah 45:24
They will say of me, 'In the LORD alone are **deliverance** and strength.' All who have raged against him will come to him and be put to shame.

Isaiah 45:25
But all the descendants of Israel will find **deliverance** in the LORD and will make their boast in him.

Isaiah 50:2
When I came, why was there no one? When I called, why was there no one to answer? Was my arm too short to **deliver** you? Do I lack the strength to rescue you? By a mere rebuke I dry up the sea, I turn rivers into a desert; their fish rot for lack of water and die of thirst.

Jeremiah 15:11
The LORD said, "Surely I will **deliver** you for a good purpose; surely I will make your enemies plead with you in times of disaster and times of distress.

Jeremiah 15:21
"I will save you from the hands of the wicked and **deliver** you from the grasp of the cruel."

Jeremiah 31:11
For the LORD will **deliver** Jacob and redeem them from the hand of those stronger than they.

Jeremiah 42:11
Do not be afraid of the king of Babylon, whom you now fear. Do not be afraid of him, declares the LORD, for I am with you and will save you and **deliver** you from his hands.

God Our Deliverer

Daniel 3:17
If we are thrown into the blazing furnace, the God we serve is able to **deliver** us from it, and he will **deliver** us from your Majesty's hand.

Daniel 12:1
[*The End Times*] "At that time Michael, the great prince who protects your people, will arise. There will be a time of distress such as has not happened from the beginning of nations until then. But at that time your people—everyone whose name is found written in the book—will be **delivered**.

Hosea 13:14
"I will **deliver** this people from the power of the grave; I will redeem them from death. Where, O death, are your plagues? Where, O grave, is your destruction? "

Joel 2:32
And everyone who calls on the name of the LORD will be saved; for on Mount Zion and in Jerusalem there will be **deliverance**, as the LORD has said, even among the survivors whom the LORD calls.

Obadiah 1:17
But on Mount Zion will be **deliverance**; it will be holy, and Jacob will possess his inheritance.

Micah 2:12
[*Deliverance Promised*] "I will surely gather all of you, Jacob; I will surely bring together the remnant of Israel. I will bring them together like sheep in a pen, like a flock in its pasture; the place will throng with people.

Habakkuk 3:13
You came out to **deliver** your people, to save your anointed one. You crushed the leader of the land of wickedness, you stripped him from head to foot.

Matthew 6:13
And lead us not into temptation, but **deliver** us from the evil one.

Romans 7:25
Thanks be to God, who **delivers** me through Jesus Christ our Lord!

Romans 11:26
As it is written: "The **deliverer** will come from Zion; he will turn godlessness away from Jacob.

2 Corinthians 1:10
He has **delivered** us from such a deadly peril, and he will **deliver** us again. On him we have set our hope that he will continue to **deliver** us,

2 Timothy 4:17
But the Lord stood at my side and gave me strength, so that through me the message might be fully proclaimed and all the Gentiles might hear it. And I was **delivered** from the lion's mouth.

Jude 1:5
Though you already know all this, I want to remind you that the Lord at one time **delivered** his people out of Egypt, but later destroyed those who did not believe.

God is Faithful
Acting Faithfully
Showing Faithfulness

Faithful:
One who is loyal and trustworthy.

*I saw heaven standing open and there before me was a white horse, whose rider is called **Faithful** and True.*

- Revelation 19:11

God is Faithful

1. DEFINE FAITHFUL USING YOUR OWN WORDS, SYNONYMS, OR DESCRIPTIONS:

_____

_____

_____

2. GOD'S FAITHFULNESS IS OFTEN MENTIONED IN CONNECTION WITH HIS LOVE. WHY DO YOU THINK THIS IS?

_____

_____

_____

3. DO YOU HAVE ANY OBSERVATIONS ABOUT THIS CHARACTER TRAIT OF GOD OR WHY GOD WANTS US TO KNOW THAT HE IS FAITHFUL AND ACTS FAITHFULLY?

_____

_____

_____

_____

_____

It is love that asks, that seeks, that knocks,
that finds, and is faithful to what it finds.
- Augustine

NOTES:

God is Faithful

Genesis 24:27
"Praise be to the LORD, the God of my master Abraham, who has not abandoned his kindness and **faithfulness** to my master. As for me, the LORD has led me on the journey to the house of my master's relatives."

Exodus 34:6
And he passed in front of Moses, proclaiming, "The LORD, the LORD, the compassionate and gracious God, slow to anger, abounding in love and **faithfulness**,

Deuteronomy 32:4
He is the Rock, his works are perfect, and all his ways are just. A **faithful** God who does no wrong, upright and just is he.

2 Samuel 22:26
To the faithful you show yourself **faithful**, to the blameless you show yourself blameless,

Nehemiah 9:33
In all that has happened to us, you have remained righteous; you have acted **faithfully**, while we acted wickedly.

Psalm 18:25
To the faithful you show yourself **faithful**, to the blameless you show yourself blameless,

Psalm 25:10
All the ways of the LORD are loving and **faithful** toward those who keep the demands of his covenant.

Psalm 26:3
for I have always been mindful of your unfailing love and have lived in reliance on your **faithfulness**.

Psalm 30:9
What is gained if I am silenced, if I go down to the pit? Will the dust praise you? Will it proclaim your **faithfulness**?

Psalm 31:5
Into your hands I commit my spirit; deliver me, LORD, my **faithful** God.

Psalm 33:4
For the word of the LORD is right and true; he is **faithful** in all he does.

Psalm 36:5
Your love, LORD, reaches to the heavens, your **faithfulness** to the skies.

Psalm 40:10
I do not hide your righteousness in my heart; I speak of your **faithfulness** and your saving help. I do not conceal your love and your **faithfulness** from the great assembly.

Psalm 40:11
Do not withhold your mercy from me, LORD; may your love and **faithfulness** always protect me.

Psalm 43:3
Send me your light and your **faithful** care, let them lead me; let them bring me to your holy mountain, to the place where you dwell.

Psalm 57:3
He sends from heaven and saves me, rebuking those who hotly pursue me—God sends forth his love and his **faithfulness**.

Psalm 57:10
For great is your love, reaching to the heavens; your **faithfulness** reaches to the skies.

Psalm 71:22
I will praise you with the harp for your **faithfulness**, my God;

Psalm 85:10-11
Love and **faithfulness** meet together; righteousness and peace kiss each other. **Faithfulness** springs forth from the earth, and righteousness looks down from heaven.

Psalm 86:11
Teach me your way, LORD, that I may rely on your **faithfulness**; give me an undivided heart, that I may fear your name.

Psalm 86:15
But you, Lord, are a compassionate and gracious God, slow to anger, abounding in love and **faithfulness**.

Psalm 89:2
I will declare that your love stands firm forever, that you have established your **faithfulness** in heaven itself.

Psalm 89:5
The heavens praise your wonders, LORD, your **faithfulness** too, in the assembly of the holy ones.

Psalm 89:8
Who is like you, LORD God Almighty? You, LORD, are mighty, and your **faithfulness** surrounds you.

Psalm 89:14
Righteousness and justice are the foundation of your throne; love and **faithfulness** go before you.

Psalm 89:33
but I will not take my love from him, nor will I ever betray my **faithfulness**.

Psalm 91:4
He will cover you with his feathers, and under his wings you will find refuge; his **faithfulness** will be your shield and rampart.

Psalm 92:2
proclaiming your love in the morning and your **faithfulness** at night,

Psalm 96:13
Let all creation rejoice before the LORD, for he comes, he comes to judge the earth. He will judge the world in righteousness and the peoples in his **faithfulness**.

Psalm 98:3
He has remembered his love and his **faithfulness** to Israel; all the ends of the earth have seen the salvation of our God.

Psalm 100:5
For the LORD is good and his love endures forever; his **faithfulness** continues through all generations.

Psalm 108:4
For great is your love, higher than the heavens; your **faithfulness** reaches to the skies.

Psalm 111:8
They are established for ever and ever, enacted in **faithfulness** and uprightness.

Psalm 115:1
Not to us, LORD, not to us but to your name be the glory, because of your love and **faithfulness**.

Psalm 117:2
For great is his love toward us, and the **faithfulness** of the LORD endures forever. Praise the LORD.

Psalm 145:13
Your kingdom is an everlasting kingdom, and your dominion endures through all generations. The LORD is trustworthy in all he promises and **faithful** in all he does.

God is Faithful

Psalm 145:17
The LORD is righteous in all his ways and **faithful** in all he does.

Psalm 146:6
He is the Maker of heaven and earth, the sea, and everything in them— he remains **faithful** forever.

Isaiah 11:5
Righteousness will be his belt and **faithfulness** the sash around his waist.

Isaiah 25:1
LORD, you are my God; I will exalt you and praise your name, for in perfect **faithfulness** you have done wonderful things, things planned long ago.

Isaiah 38:18
For the grave cannot praise you, death cannot sing your praise; those who go down to the pit cannot hope for your **faithfulness.**

Isaiah 38:19
The living, the living—they praise you, as I am doing today; parents tell their children about your **faithfulness.**

Isaiah 42:3
A bruised reed he will not break, and a smoldering wick he will not snuff out. In **faithfulness** he will bring forth justice;

Isaiah 49:7
This is what the LORD says— the Redeemer and Holy One of Israel— to him who was despised and abhorred by the nation, to the servant of rulers: "Kings will see you and stand up, princes will see and bow down, because of the LORD, who is **faithful**, the Holy One of Israel, who has chosen you."

Isaiah 55:3
Give ear and come to me; listen, that you may live. I will make an everlasting covenant with you, my **faithful** love promised to David.

Isaiah 61:8
"For I, the LORD, love justice; I hate robbery and wrongdoing. In my **faithfulness** I will reward my people and make an everlasting covenant with them.

Jeremiah 3:12
Go, proclaim this message toward the north: "'Return, faithless Israel,' declares the LORD, 'I will frown on you no longer, for I am **faithful**,' declares the LORD, 'I will not be angry forever.

Lamentations 3:23
They are new every morning; great is your **faithfulness.**

Hosea 2:20
I will betroth you in **faithfulness**, and you will acknowledge the LORD.

Hosea 11:12
[*Israel's Sin*] Ephraim has surrounded me with lies, Israel with deceit. And Judah is unruly against God, even against the **faithful** Holy One.

Joel 2:23
Be glad, people of Zion, rejoice in the LORD your God, for he has given you the autumn rains because he is **faithful**. He sends you abundant showers, both autumn and spring rains, as before.

God is Faithful

Micah 7:20
You will be **faithful** to Jacob, and show love to Abraham, as you pledged on oath to our ancestors in days long ago.

Zechariah 8:8
I will bring them back to live in Jerusalem; they will be my people, and I will be **faithful** and righteous to them as their God."

Romans 3:3
What if some were unfaithful? Will their unfaithfulness nullify God's **faithfulness**?

1 Corinthians 1:9
God is **faithful**, who has called you into fellowship with his Son, Jesus Christ our Lord.

1 Corinthians 10:13
No temptation has overtaken you except what is common to mankind. And God is **faithful**; he will not let you be tempted beyond what you can bear. But when you are tempted, he will also provide a way out so that you can endure it.

2 Corinthians 1:18
But as surely as God is **faithful**, our message to you is not "Yes" and "No."

Galatians 5:22
But the fruit of the Spirit is love, joy, peace, forbearance, kindness, goodness, **faithfulness**,

1 Thessalonians 5:24
The one who calls you is **faithful**, and he will do it.

2 Thessalonians 3:3
But the Lord is **faithful**, and he will strengthen you and protect you from the evil one.

2 Timothy 2:13
if we are faithless, he remains **faithful**, for he cannot disown himself.

Hebrews 2:17
For this reason he had to be made like them, fully human in every way, in order that he might become a merciful and **faithful** high priest in service to God, and that he might make atonement for the sins of the people.

Hebrews 3:2
He was **faithful** to the one who appointed him, just as Moses was faithful in all God's house.

Hebrews 10:23
Let us hold unswervingly to the hope we profess, for he who promised is **faithful**.

Hebrews 11:11
And by faith even Sarah, who was past childbearing age, was enabled to bear children because she considered him **faithful** who had made the promise.

1 Peter 4:19
So then, those who suffer according to God's will should commit themselves to their **faithful** Creator and continue to do good.

1 John 1:9
If we confess our sins, he is **faithful** and just and will forgive us our sins and purify us from all unrighteousness.

Revelation 1:5
and from Jesus Christ, who is the **faithful** witness, the firstborn from the dead, and the ruler of the kings of the earth.

God is Faithful

Revelation 19:11
I saw heaven standing open and there before me was a white horse, whose rider is called **Faithful** and True. With justice he judges and wages war.

God Our Father

Father:
A male parent or ancestor; One who begets;
Founder and originator.

*Yet you, Lord, are our **Father**. We are the clay, you
are the potter; we are all the work of your hand.*
- Isaiah 64:8

God Our Father

1. DEFINE FATHER USING YOUR OWN WORDS, SYNONYMS, OR DESCRIPTIONS:

_____

_____

_____

2. FOR GOD TO DESCRIBE HIMSELF AS OUR FATHER IS PROBABLY THE BEST EXAMPLE, IN HUMAN TERMS, TO DESCRIBE HIS POSITION OF AUTHORITY WITH A DESIRE FOR A RELATIONSHIP IN OUR LIVES. ALSO, FOR GOD TO BE OUR FATHER, WE ARE HIS SONS AND DAUGHTERS -- WE HOLD A POSITION OF CLOSENESS TO HIM. WHAT DOES THIS MEAN TO YOU?

_____

_____

_____

3. "FATHER" IS THE CHOSEN NAME JESUS USES WHEN REFERRING TO GOD. HE OFTEN TALKED ABOUT THE LOVE AND RESPECT THEY HAVE FOR EACH OTHER. FIND SOME EXAMPLES OF THIS.

_____

_____

_____

_____

_____

4. DO YOU HAVE ANY OBSERVATIONS ABOUT THIS CHARACTER TRAIT OF GOD OR WHY GOD WANTS US TO KNOW THAT HE OUR FATHER?

_____

_____

_____

_____

_____

_G_od became a man to turn creatures into sons._
- C. S. Lewis_

The very center of the Christian belief is the approachability of God. We are told of a little boy whose father was promoted to the exalted rank of Brigadier. When the little lad heard the news, he was silent for a moment, and then said, "Do you think he will mind if I still call him Daddy?"
- William Barclay_

NOTES:

God Our Father

Deuteronomy 32:6
Is this the way you repay the LORD, you foolish and unwise people? Is he not your **Father**, your Creator, who made you and formed you?

1 Chronicles 22:10
He is the one who will build a house for my Name. He will be my son, and I will be his **father**. And I will establish the throne of his kingdom over Israel forever.

1 Chronicles 28:6
He said to me: 'Solomon your son is the one who will build my house and my courts, for I have chosen him to be my son, and I will be his **father**.

Psalm 2:7
I will proclaim the LORD's decree: He said to me, "You are my son; today I have become your **father**.

Psalm 68:5
A **father** to the fatherless, a defender of widows, is God in his holy dwelling.

Psalm 89:26
He will call out to me, 'You are my **Father**, my God, the Rock my Savior.'

Psalm 103:13
As a **father** has compassion on his children, so the LORD has compassion on those who fear him;

Proverbs 3:12
because the LORD disciplines those he loves, as a **father** the son he delights in.

Isaiah 9:6
For to us a child is born, to us a son is given, and the government will be on his shoulders. And he will be called Wonderful Counselor, Mighty God, Everlasting **Father**, Prince of Peace.

Isaiah 63:16
But you are our **Father**, though Abraham does not know us or Israel acknowledge us; you, LORD, are our **Father**, our Redeemer from of old is your name.

Isaiah 64:8
Yet you, LORD, are our **Father**. We are the clay, you are the potter; we are all the work of your hand.

Matthew 5:45
that you may be children of your **Father** in heaven.

Matthew 5:48
Be perfect, therefore, as your heavenly **Father** is perfect.

Matthew 6:1
Be careful not to practice your righteousness in front of others to be seen by them. If you do, you will have no reward from your **Father** in heaven.

Matthew 6:4
so that your giving may be in secret. Then your **Father**, who sees what is done in secret, will reward you.

Matthew 6:6
But when you pray, go into your room, close the door and pray to your **Father**, who is unseen. Then your **Father**, who sees what is done in secret, will reward you.

Matthew 6:8
Do not be like them, for your **Father** knows what you need before you ask him.

Matthew 6:9
"This, then, is how you should pray: "'Our **Father** in heaven, hallowed be your name,

Matthew 6:14
For if you forgive other people when they sin against you, your heavenly **Father** will also forgive you.

Matthew 6:15
But if you do not forgive others their sins, your **Father** will not forgive your sins.

Matthew 6:26
Look at the birds of the air; they do not sow or reap or store away in barns, and yet your heavenly **Father** feeds them. Are you not much more valuable than they?

Matthew 6:32
For the pagans run after all these things, and your heavenly **Father** knows that you need them.

Matthew 7:11
If you, then, though you are evil, know how to give good gifts to your children, how much more will your **Father** in heaven give good gifts to those who ask him!

Matthew 7:21
Not everyone who says to me, 'Lord, Lord,' will enter the kingdom of heaven, but only the one who does the will of my **Father** who is in heaven.

Matthew 10:20
for it will not be you speaking, but the Spirit of your **Father** speaking through you.

Matthew 10:29
Are not two sparrows sold for a penny? Yet not one of them will fall to the ground outside your **Father's** care.

Matthew 10:32
"Whoever acknowledges me before others, I will also acknowledge before my **Father** in heaven.

Matthew 11:25
At that time Jesus said, "I praise you, **Father**, Lord of heaven and earth, because you have hidden these things from the wise and learned, and revealed them to little children.

Matthew 11:27
"All things have been committed to me by my **Father**. No one knows the Son except the **Father**, and no one knows the **Father** except the Son and those to whom the Son chooses to reveal him.

Matthew 12:50
For whoever does the will of my **Father** in heaven is my brother and sister and mother.

Matthew 13:43
Then the righteous will shine like the sun in the kingdom of their **Father**. Whoever has ears, let them hear.

Matthew 15:13
He replied, "Every plant that my heavenly **Father** has not planted will be pulled up by the roots.

Matthew 16:17
Jesus replied, "Blessed are you, Simon son of Jonah, for this was not revealed to you by flesh and blood, but by my **Father** in heaven.

Matthew 16:27
For the Son of Man is going to come in his **Father's** glory with his angels, and then he will reward each person according to what they have done.

Matthew 18:14
In the same way your **Father** in heaven is not willing that any of these little ones should perish.

Matthew 18:19
"Again, truly I tell you that if two of you on earth agree about anything they ask for, it will be done for them by my **Father** in heaven.

God Our Father

Matthew 18:35
"This is how my heavenly **Father** will treat each of you unless you forgive your brother or sister from your heart."

Matthew 20:23
Jesus said to them, "You will indeed drink from my cup, but to sit at my right or left is not for me to grant. These places belong to those for whom they have been prepared by my **Father**."

Matthew 24:36
But about that day or hour no one knows, not even the angels in heaven, nor the Son, but only the **Father**.

Matthew 25:34
"Then the King will say to those on his right, 'Come, you who are blessed by my **Father**; take your inheritance, the kingdom prepared for you since the creation of the world.

Matthew 26:29
I tell you, I will not drink from this fruit of the vine from now on until that day when I drink it new with you in my **Father's** kingdom."

Matthew 26:39
Going a little farther, he fell with his face to the ground and prayed, "My **Father**, if it is possible, may this cup be taken from me. Yet not as I will, but as you will."

Matthew 26:42
He went away a second time and prayed, "My **Father**, if it is not possible for this cup to be taken away unless I drink it, may your will be done."

Matthew 26:53
Do you think I cannot call on my **Father**, and he will at once put at my disposal more than twelve legions of angels?

Matthew 28:19
Therefore go and make disciples of all nations, baptizing them in the name of the **Father** and of the Son and of the Holy Spirit,

Mark 8:38
If anyone is ashamed of me and my words in this adulterous and sinful generation, the Son of Man will be ashamed of them when he comes in his **Father's** glory with the holy angels."

Mark 11:25
And when you stand praying, if you hold anything against anyone, forgive them, so that your **Father** in heaven may forgive you your sins."

Mark 13:32
"But about that day or hour no one knows, not even the angels in heaven, nor the Son, but only the **Father**.

Mark 14:36
"Abba, **Father**," he said, "everything is possible for you. Take this cup from me. Yet not what I will, but what you will."

Luke 2:49
"Why were you searching for me?" he asked. "Didn't you know I had to be in my **Father's** house?"

Luke 6:36
Be merciful, just as your **Father** is merciful.

Luke 9:26
Whoever is ashamed of me and my words, the Son of Man will be ashamed of them when he comes in his glory and in the glory of the **Father** and of the holy angels.

Luke 10:21
At that time Jesus, full of joy through the Holy Spirit, said, "I praise you, **Father**, Lord of heaven and earth, because you have hidden these things from the wise and learned, and revealed them to little children. Yes, **Father**, for this is what you were pleased to do.

Luke 10:22
"All things have been committed to me by my **Father**. No one knows who the Son is except the **Father**, and no one knows who the **Father** is except the Son and those to whom the Son chooses to reveal him."

Luke 11:2
He said to them, "When you pray, say: "'**Father**, hallowed be your name, your kingdom come.

Luke 11:13
If you then, though you are evil, know how to give good gifts to your children, how much more will your **Father** in heaven give the Holy Spirit to those who ask him!"

Luke 12:30
For the pagan world runs after all such things, and your **Father** knows that you need them.

Luke 12:32
"Do not be afraid, little flock, for your **Father** has been pleased to give you the kingdom.

Luke 22:29
And I confer on you a kingdom, just as my **Father** conferred one on me,

Luke 22:42
"**Father**, if you are willing, take this cup from me; yet not my will, but yours be done."

Luke 23:34
Jesus said, "**Father**, forgive them, for they do not know what they are doing." And they divided up his clothes by casting lots.

Luke 23:46
Jesus called out with a loud voice, "**Father**, into your hands I commit my spirit." When he had said this, he breathed his last.

Luke 24:49
I am going to send you what my **Father** has promised; but stay in the city until you have been clothed with power from on high."

John 1:14
The Word became flesh and made his dwelling among us. We have seen his glory, the glory of the one and only Son, who came from the **Father**, full of grace and truth.

John 1:18
No one has ever seen God, but the one and only Son, who is himself God and is in closest relationship with the **Father**, has made him known.

John 2:16
To those who sold doves he said, "Get these out of here! Stop turning my **Father's** house into a market!"

John 3:35
The **Father** loves the Son and has placed everything in his hands.

John 4:21
"Woman," Jesus replied, "believe me, a time is coming when you will worship the **Father** neither on this mountain nor in Jerusalem.

John 4:23
Yet a time is coming and has now come when the true worshipers will worship the **Father** in the Spirit and in truth, for they are the kind of worshipers the **Father** seeks.

John 5:17
In his defense Jesus said to them, "My **Father** is always at his work to this very day, and I too am working."

John 5:18
For this reason they tried all the more to kill him; not only was he breaking the Sabbath, but he was even calling God his own **Father**, making himself equal with God.

God Our Father

John 5:19
Jesus gave them this answer: "Very truly I tell you, the Son can do nothing by himself; he can do only what he sees his **Father** doing, because whatever the **Father** does the Son also does.

John 5:20
For the **Father** loves the Son and shows him all he does. Yes, and he will show him even greater works than these, so that you will be amazed.

John 5:21
For just as the **Father** raises the dead and gives them life, even so the Son gives life to whom he is pleased to give it.

John 5:22
Moreover, the **Father** judges no one, but has entrusted all judgment to the Son,

John 5:23
that all may honor the Son just as they honor the **Father**. Whoever does not honor the Son does not honor the **Father**, who sent him.

John 5:26
For as the **Father** has life in himself, so he has granted the Son also to have life in himself.

John 5:36
"I have testimony weightier than that of John. For the works that the **Father** has given me to finish—the very works that I am doing—testify that the **Father** has sent me.

John 5:37
And the **Father** who sent me has himself testified concerning me. You have never heard his voice nor seen his form,

John 5:43
I have come in my **Father's** name, and you do not accept me; but if someone else comes in his own name, you will accept him.

John 5:45
"But do not think I will accuse you before the **Father**. Your accuser is Moses, on whom your hopes are set.

John 6:27
Do not work for food that spoils, but for food that endures to eternal life, which the Son of Man will give you. For on him God the **Father** has placed his seal of approval."

John 6:32
Jesus said to them, "Very truly I tell you, it is not Moses who has given you the bread from heaven, but it is my **Father** who gives you the true bread from heaven.

John 6:37
All those the **Father** gives me will come to me, and whoever comes to me I will never drive away.

John 6:40
For my **Father's** will is that everyone who looks to the Son and believes in him shall have eternal life, and I will raise them up at the last day."

John 6:44
"No one can come to me unless the **Father** who sent me draws them, and I will raise them up at the last day.

John 6:45
It is written in the Prophets: 'They will all be taught by God.' Everyone who has heard the **Father** and learned from him comes to me.

John 6:46
No one has seen the **Father** except the one who is from God; only he has seen the **Father**.

John 6:57
Just as the living **Father** sent me and I live because of the **Father**, so the one who feeds on me will live because of me.

John 6:65
He went on to say, "This is why I told you that no one can come to me unless the **Father** has enabled them."

John 8:16
But if I do judge, my decisions are true, because I am not alone. I stand with the **Father**, who sent me.

John 8:18
I am one who testifies for myself; my other witness is the **Father**, who sent me."

John 8:19
Then they asked him, "Where is your father?" "You do not know me or my **Father**," Jesus replied. "If you knew me, you would know my **Father** also."

John 8:27
They did not understand that he was telling them about his **Father**.

John 8:28
So Jesus said, "When you have lifted up the Son of Man, then you will know that I am he and that I do nothing on my own but speak just what the **Father** has taught me.

John 8:38
I am telling you what I have seen in the **Father's** presence, and you are doing what you have heard from your father."

John 8:41
You are doing the works of your own father." "We are not illegitimate children," they protested. "The only **Father** we have is God himself."

John 8:42
Jesus said to them, "If God were your **Father**, you would love me, for I have come here from God. I have not come on my own; God sent me.

John 8:49
"I am not possessed by a demon," said Jesus, "but I honor my **Father** and you dishonor me.

John 8:54
Jesus replied, "If I glorify myself, my glory means nothing. My **Father**, whom you claim as your God, is the one who glorifies me.

John 10:15
just as the **Father** knows me and I know the **Father**—and I lay down my life for the sheep.

John 10:17
The reason my **Father** loves me is that I lay down my life—only to take it up again.

John 10:18
No one takes it from me, but I lay it down of my own accord. I have authority to lay it down and authority to take it up again. This command I received from my **Father**."

John 10:25
Jesus answered, "I did tell you, but you do not believe. The works I do in my **Father's** name testify about me,

John 10:29
My **Father**, who has given them to me, is greater than all ; no one can snatch them out of my **Father's** hand.

John 10:30
I and the **Father** are one."

John 10:32
but Jesus said to them, "I have shown you many good works from the **Father**. For which of these do you stone me?"

God Our Father

John 10:37
Do not believe me unless I do the works of my **Father**.

John 10:38
But if I do them, even though you do not believe me, believe the works, that you may know and understand that the **Father** is in me, and I in the **Father**."

John 11:41
So they took away the stone. Then Jesus looked up and said, "**Father**, I thank you that you have heard me.

John 12:26
Whoever serves me must follow me; and where I am, my servant also will be. My **Father** will honor the one who serves me.

John 12:27
"Now my soul is troubled, and what shall I say? '**Father**, save me from this hour'? No, it was for this very reason I came to this hour.

John 12:28
Father, glorify your name!" Then a voice came from heaven, "I have glorified it, and will glorify it again."

John 12:49
For I did not speak on my own, but the **Father** who sent me commanded me to say all that I have spoken.

John 12:50
I know that his command leads to eternal life. So whatever I say is just what the **Father** has told me to say."

John 13:1
It was just before the Passover Festival. Jesus knew that the hour had come for him to leave this world and go to the **Father**. Having loved his own who were in the world, he loved them to the end.

John 13:3
Jesus knew that the **Father** had put all things under his power, and that he had come from God and was returning to God;

John 14:2
My **Father's** house has many rooms; if that were not so, would I have told you that I am going there to prepare a place for you?

John 14:6
Jesus answered, "I am the way and the truth and the life. No one comes to the **Father** except through me.

John 14:7
If you really know me, you will know my **Father** as well. From now on, you do know him and have seen him."

John 14:9
Jesus answered: "Don't you know me, Philip, even after I have been among you such a long time? Anyone who has seen me has seen the **Father**. How can you say, 'Show us the **Father**'?

John 14:10
Don't you believe that I am in the **Father**, and that the **Father** is in me? The words I say to you I do not speak on my own authority. Rather, it is the **Father**, living in me, who is doing his work.

John 14:11
Believe me when I say that I am in the **Father** and the **Father** is in me; or at least believe on the evidence of the works themselves.

John 14:12
Very truly I tell you, whoever believes in me will do the works I have been doing, and they will do even greater things than these, because I am going to the **Father**.

John 14:13
And I will do whatever you ask in my name, so that the **Father** may be glorified in the Son.

John 14:16
And I will ask the **Father**, and he will give you another advocate to help you and be with you forever—

John 14:20
On that day you will realize that I am in my **Father**, and you are in me, and I am in you.

John 14:21
Whoever has my commands and keeps them is the one who loves me. The one who loves me will be loved by my **Father**, and I too will love them and show myself to them."

John 14:23
Jesus replied, "Anyone who loves me will obey my teaching. My **Father** will love them, and we will come to them and make our home with them.

John 14:24
Anyone who does not love me will not obey my teaching. These words you hear are not my own; they belong to the **Father** who sent me.

John 14:26
But the Advocate, the Holy Spirit, whom the **Father** will send in my name, will teach you all things and will remind you of everything I have said to you.

John 14:28
"You heard me say, 'I am going away and I am coming back to you.' If you loved me, you would be glad that I am going to the **Father**, for the **Father** is greater than I.

John 14:31
but he comes so that the world may learn that I love the **Father** and do exactly what my **Father** has commanded me. "Come now; let us leave.

John 15:1
I am the true vine, and my **Father** is the gardener.

John 15:8
This is to my **Father's** glory, that you bear much fruit, showing yourselves to be my disciples.

John 15:9
"As the **Father** has loved me, so have I loved you. Now remain in my love.

John 15:10
If you keep my commands, you will remain in my love, just as I have kept my **Father's** commands and remain in his love.

John 15:15
I no longer call you servants, because a servant does not know his master's business. Instead, I have called you friends, for everything that I learned from my **Father** I have made known to you.

John 15:16
You did not choose me, but I chose you and appointed you so that you might go and bear fruit—fruit that will last—and so that whatever you ask in my name the **Father** will give you.

John 15:23
Whoever hates me hates my **Father** as well.

John 15:24
If I had not done among them the works no one else did, they would not be guilty of sin. As it is, they have seen, and yet they have hated both me and my **Father**.

John 15:26
[*The Work of the Holy Spirit*] "When the Advocate comes, whom I will send to you from the **Father**—the Spirit of truth who goes out from the **Father**—he will testify about me.

God Our Father

John 16:3
They will do such things because they have not known the **Father** or me.

John 16:10
about righteousness, because I am going to the **Father**, where you can see me no longer;

John 16:15
All that belongs to the **Father** is mine. That is why I said the Spirit will receive from me what he will make known to you."

John 16:17
At this, some of his disciples said to one another, "What does he mean by saying, 'In a little while you will see me no more, and then after a little while you will see me,' and 'Because I am going to the **Father**'?"

John 16:23
In that day you will no longer ask me anything. Very truly I tell you, my **Father** will give you whatever you ask in my name.

John 16:25
"Though I have been speaking figuratively, a time is coming when I will no longer use this kind of language but will tell you plainly about my **Father**.

John 16:26
In that day you will ask in my name. I am not saying that I will ask the **Father** on your behalf.

John 16:27
No, the **Father** himself loves you because you have loved me and have believed that I came from God.

John 16:28
I came from the **Father** and entered the world; now I am leaving the world and going back to the **Father**."

John 16:32
"A time is coming and in fact has come when you will be scattered, each to your own home. You will leave me all alone. Yet I am not alone, for my **Father** is with me.

John 17:1
After Jesus said this, he looked toward heaven and prayed: "**Father**, the hour has come. Glorify your Son, that your Son may glorify you.

John 17:5
And now, **Father**, glorify me in your presence with the glory I had with you before the world began.

John 17:11
I will remain in the world no longer, but they are still in the world, and I am coming to you. Holy **Father**, protect them by the power of your name, the name you gave me, so that they may be one as we are one.

John 17:21
that all of them may be one, **Father**, just as you are in me and I am in you. May they also be in us so that the world may believe that you have sent me.

John 17:24
"**Father**, I want those you have given me to be with me where I am, and to see my glory, the glory you have given me because you loved me before the creation of the world.

John 17:25
"Righteous **Father**, though the world does not know you, I know you, and they know that you have sent me.

John 18:11
Jesus commanded Peter, "Put your sword away! Shall I not drink the cup the **Father** has given me?"

John 20:17
Jesus said, "Do not hold on to me, for I have not yet ascended to the **Father**. Go instead to my brothers and tell them, 'I am ascending to my **Father** and your **Father**, to my God and your God.'"

John 20:21
Again Jesus said, "Peace be with you! As the **Father** has sent me, I am sending you."

Acts 1:4
On one occasion, while he was eating with them, he gave them this command: "Do not leave Jerusalem, but wait for the gift my **Father** promised, which you have heard me speak about.

Acts 1:7
He said to them: "It is not for you to know the times or dates the **Father** has set by his own authority.

Acts 2:33
Exalted to the right hand of God, he has received from the **Father** the promised Holy Spirit and has poured out what you now see and hear.

Romans 6:4
We were therefore buried with him through baptism into death in order that, just as Christ was raised from the dead through the glory of the **Father**, we too may live a new life.

Romans 8:15
The Spirit you received does not make you slaves, so that you live in fear again; rather, the Spirit you received brought about your adoption to sonship. And by him we cry, "Abba, **Father**."

Romans 15:6
so that with one mind and one voice you may glorify the God and **Father** of our Lord Jesus Christ.

1 Corinthians 1:3
Grace and peace to you from God our **Father** and the Lord Jesus Christ.

1 Corinthians 8:6
yet for us there is but one God, the **Father**, from whom all things came and for whom we live; and there is but one Lord, Jesus Christ, through whom all things came and through whom we live.

1 Corinthians 15:24
Then the end will come, when he hands over the kingdom to God the **Father** after he has destroyed all dominion, authority and power.

2 Corinthians 1:2
Grace and peace to you from God our **Father** and the Lord Jesus Christ.

2 Corinthians 1:3
Praise be to the God and **Father** of our Lord Jesus Christ, the **Father** of compassion and the God of all comfort,

2 Corinthians 6:18
And, "I will be a **Father** to you, and you will be my sons and daughters, says the Lord Almighty."

2 Corinthians 11:31
The God and **Father** of the Lord Jesus, who is to be praised forever, knows that I am not lying.

Galatians 1:1
Paul, an apostle—sent not from men nor by a man, but by Jesus Christ and God the **Father**, who raised him from the dead—

Galatians 1:3
Grace and peace to you from God our **Father** and the Lord Jesus Christ,

Galatians 1:4
who gave himself for our sins to rescue us from the present evil age, according to the will of our God and **Father**,

Galatians 4:6
Because you are his sons, God sent the Spirit of his Son into our hearts, the Spirit who calls out, "Abba, **Father**."

Ephesians 1:2
Grace and peace to you from God our **Father** and the Lord Jesus Christ.

Ephesians 1:3
Praise be to the God and **Father** of our Lord Jesus Christ, who has blessed us in the heavenly realms with every spiritual blessing in Christ.

God Our Father

Ephesians 1:17
I keep asking that the God of our Lord Jesus Christ, the glorious **Father**, may give you the Spirit of wisdom and revelation, so that you may know him better.

Ephesians 2:18
For through him we both have access to the **Father** by one Spirit.

Ephesians 3:14
For this reason I kneel before the **Father**,

Ephesians 4:6
one God and **Father** of all, who is over all and through all and in all.

Ephesians 5:20
always giving thanks to God the **Father** for everything, in the name of our Lord Jesus Christ.

Ephesians 6:23
Peace to the brothers and sisters, and love with faith from God the **Father** and the Lord Jesus Christ.

Philippians 1:2
Grace and peace to you from God our **Father** and the Lord Jesus Christ.

Philippians 2:11
and every tongue acknowledge that Jesus Christ is Lord, to the glory of God the **Father**.

Philippians 4:20
To our God and **Father** be glory for ever and ever. Amen.

Colossians 1:2
To God's holy people in Colossae, the faithful brothers and sisters in Christ: Grace and peace to you from God our **Father**.

Colossians 1:3
We always thank God, the **Father** of our Lord Jesus Christ, when we pray for you,

Colossians 1:12
and giving joyful thanks to the **Father**, who has qualified you to share in the inheritance of his holy people in the kingdom of light.

Colossians 3:17
And whatever you do, whether in word or deed, do it all in the name of the Lord Jesus, giving thanks to God the **Father** through him.

1 Thessalonians 1:1
Paul, Silas and Timothy, To the church of the Thessalonians in God the **Father** and the Lord Jesus Christ: Grace and peace to you.

1 Thessalonians 1:3
We remember before our God and **Father** your work produced by faith, your labor prompted by love, and your endurance inspired by hope in our Lord Jesus Christ.

1 Thessalonians 3:11
Now may our God and **Father** himself and our Lord Jesus clear the way for us to come to you.

1 Thessalonians 3:13
May he strengthen your hearts so that you will be blameless and holy in the presence of our God and **Father** when our Lord Jesus comes with all his holy ones.

2 Thessalonians 1:1
Paul, Silas and Timothy, To the church of the Thessalonians in God our **Father** and the Lord Jesus Christ:

2 Thessalonians 1:2
Grace and peace to you from God the **Father** and the Lord Jesus Christ.

2 Thessalonians 2:16
May our Lord Jesus Christ himself and God our **Father**, who loved us and by his grace gave us eternal encouragement and good hope,

1 Timothy 1:2
To Timothy my true son in the faith: Grace, mercy and peace from God the **Father** and Christ Jesus our Lord.

2 Timothy 1:2
To Timothy, my dear son: Grace, mercy and peace from God the **Father** and Christ Jesus our Lord.

Titus 1:4
To Titus, my true son in our common faith: Grace and peace from God the **Father** and Christ Jesus our Savior.

Philemon 1:3
Grace and peace to you from God our **Father** and the Lord Jesus Christ.

Hebrews 1:5
For to which of the angels did God ever say, "You are my Son; today I have become your **Father**"? Or again, "I will be his **Father**, and he will be my Son"?

Hebrews 5:5
In the same way, Christ did not take on himself the glory of becoming a high priest. But God said to him, "You are my Son; today I have become your **Father**."

Hebrews 12:9
Moreover, we have all had human fathers who disciplined us and we respected them for it. How much more should we submit to the **Father** of spirits and live!

James 1:17
Every good and perfect gift is from above, coming down from the **Father** of the heavenly lights, who does not change like shifting shadows.

James 1:27
Religion that God our **Father** accepts as pure and faultless is this: to look after orphans and widows in their distress and to keep oneself from being polluted by the world.

James 3:9
With the tongue we praise our Lord and **Father**, and with it we curse human beings, who have been made in God's likeness.

1 Peter 1:2
who have been chosen according to the foreknowledge of God the **Father**, through the sanctifying work of the Spirit, to be obedient to Jesus Christ and sprinkled with his blood: Grace and peace be yours in abundance.

1 Peter 1:3
Praise be to the God and **Father** of our Lord Jesus Christ! In his great mercy he has given us new birth into a living hope through the resurrection of Jesus Christ from the dead,

1 Peter 1:17
Since you call on a **Father** who judges each person's work impartially, live out your time as foreigners here in reverent fear.

2 Peter 1:17
He received honor and glory from God the **Father** when the voice came to him from the Majestic Glory, saying, "This is my Son, whom I love; with him I am well pleased."

1 John 1:2
The life appeared; we have seen it and testify to it, and we proclaim to you the eternal life, which was with the **Father** and has appeared to us.

1 John 1:3
We proclaim to you what we have seen and heard, so that you also may have fellowship with us. And our fellowship is with the **Father** and with his Son, Jesus Christ.

1 John 2:1
My dear children, I write this to you so that you will not sin. But if anybody does sin, we have an advocate with the **Father**—Jesus Christ, the Righteous One.

God Our Father

1 John 2:14
I write to you, dear children, because you know the **Father**. I write to you, fathers, because you know him who is from the beginning. I write to you, young men, because you are strong, and the word of God lives in you, and you have overcome the evil one.

1 John 2:15
Do not love the world or anything in the world. If anyone loves the world, love for the **Father** is not in them.

1 John 2:16
For everything in the world—the lust of the flesh, the lust of the eyes, and the pride of life—comes not from the **Father** but from the world.

1 John 2:22
Who is the liar? It is whoever denies that Jesus is the Christ. Such a person is the antichrist—denying the **Father** and the Son.

1 John 2:23
No one who denies the Son has the **Father**; whoever acknowledges the Son has the **Father** also.

1 John 2:24
As for you, see that what you have heard from the beginning remains in you. If it does, you also will remain in the Son and in the **Father**.

1 John 3:1
See what great love the **Father** has lavished on us, that we should be called children of God! And that is what we are! The reason the world does not know us is that it did not know him.

1 John 4:14
And we have seen and testify that the **Father** has sent his Son to be the Savior of the world.

2 John 1:3
Grace, mercy and peace from God the **Father** and from Jesus Christ, the **Father's** Son, will be with us in truth and love.

2 John 1:4
It has given me great joy to find some of your children walking in the truth, just as the **Father** commanded us.

2 John 1:9
Anyone who runs ahead and does not continue in the teaching of Christ does not have God; whoever continues in the teaching has both the **Father** and the Son.

Jude 1:1
Jude, a servant of Jesus Christ and a brother of James, To those who have been called, who are loved in God the **Father** and kept for Jesus Christ:

Revelation 1:6
and has made us to be a kingdom and priests to serve his God and **Father**—to him be glory and power for ever and ever! Amen.

Revelation 2:27
that one 'will rule them with an iron scepter and will dash them to pieces like pottery' —just as I have received authority from my **Father**.

Revelation 3:5
The one who is victorious will, like them, be dressed in white. I will never blot out the name of that person from the book of life, but will acknowledge that name before my **Father** and his angels.

Revelation 3:21
To the one who is victorious, I will give the right to sit with me on my throne, just as I was victorious and sat down with my **Father** on his throne.

Revelation 14:1
Then I looked, and there before me was the Lamb, standing on Mount Zion, and with him 144,000 who had his name and his **Father's** name written on their foreheads.

God is Forgiving
Able to Forgive

Forgiving:
One who releases another from something owed; Clearing or removing a debt.

*For I will **forgive** their wickedness and will remember their sins no more.*

- Hebrews 8:12

God is Forgiving

1. DEFINE FORGIVENESS USING YOUR OWN WORDS, SYNONYMS, OR DESCRIPTIONS:

_____

_____

_____

2. JEREMIAH 31:34, "FOR I WILL FORGIVE THEIR WICKENESS AND WILL REMEMBER THEIR SINS NO MORE." WHAT AN AMAZING STATEMENT! WHAT DOES IT MEAN TO YOU?

_____

_____

_____

3. IT SEEMS OUR FORGIVENESS IS CONNECTED TO HOW WE FORGIVE OTHERS (Matthew 6:14-15; Mark 11:25). WHY DO YOU THINK THAT IS?

_____

_____

_____

4. JESUS TOLD HIS DISCIPLES, "I WANT YOU TO KNOW THAT THE SON OF MAN HAS AUTHORITY ON EARTH TO FORGIVE SINS." (Mark 2:10) WHY DID HE WANT TO EXPLAIN THAT AND WHAT GIVES HIM THIS AUTHORITY?

_____

_____

_____

_____

_____

5. DO YOU HAVE ANY OBSERVATIONS ABOUT THIS CHARACTER TRAIT OF GOD OR WHY GOD WANTS US TO KNOW THAT HE IS ABLE TO FORGIVE?

_____

_____

_____

_____

_____

_____

Let us go to Calvary to learn how we may be forgiven.
And then let us linger there to learn how to forgive.
                                        - Charles Spurgeon

God has cast our confessed sins into the depths of the sea,
and He's even put a "no fishing" sign over the spot.
                                        - Dwight Moody

NOTES:

God is Forgiving

Exodus 34:7
maintaining love to thousands, and **forgiving** wickedness, rebellion and sin. Yet he does not leave the guilty unpunished;

Exodus 34:9
"Lord," he said, "if I have found favor in your eyes, then let the Lord go with us. Although this is a stiff-necked people, **forgive** our wickedness and our sin, and take us as your inheritance."

Leviticus 6:7
In this way the priest will make atonement for them before the LORD, and they will be **forgiven** for any of the things they did that made them guilty."

Numbers 14:18
'The LORD is slow to anger, abounding in love and **forgiving** sin and rebellion. Yet he does not leave the guilty unpunished;

Numbers 14:19-20
In accordance with your great love, **forgive** the sin of these people, just as you have pardoned them from the time they left Egypt until now." The LORD replied, "I have **forgiven** them, as you asked.

1 Kings 8:39
then hear from heaven, your dwelling place. **Forgive** and act; deal with everyone according to all they do, since you know their hearts

2 Chronicles 6:39
then from heaven, your dwelling place, hear their prayer and their pleas, and uphold their cause. And **forgive** your people, who have sinned against you.

2 Chronicles 7:14
if my people, who are called by my name, will humble themselves and pray and seek my face and turn from their wicked ways, then I will hear from heaven, and I will **forgive** their sin and will heal their land.

Nehemiah 9:17
But you are a **forgiving** God, gracious and compassionate, slow to anger and abounding in love.

Psalm 25:11
For the sake of your name, LORD, **forgive** my iniquity, though it is great.

Psalm 32:1
Blessed is the one whose transgressions are **forgiven**, whose sins are covered.

Psalm 32:5
I said, "I will confess my transgressions to the LORD." And you **forgave** the guilt of my sin.

Psalm 65:3
When we were overwhelmed by sins, you **forgave** our transgressions.

Psalm 78:38
Yet he was merciful; he **forgave** their iniquities and did not destroy them. Time after time he restrained his anger and did not stir up his full wrath.

Psalm 79:9
Help us, God our Savior, for the glory of your name; deliver us and **forgive** our sins for your name's sake.

Psalm 85:2
You **forgave** the iniquity of your people and covered all their sins.

Psalm 86:5
You, Lord, are **forgiving** and good, abounding in love to all who call to you.

Psalm 99:8
LORD our God, you answered them; you were to Israel a **forgiving** God, though you punished their misdeeds.

Psalm 103:3
who **forgives** all your sins and heals all your diseases,

Psalm 130:4
But with you there is **forgiveness**, so that we can, with reverence, serve you.

Jeremiah 31:34
No longer will they teach their neighbor, or say to one another, 'Know the LORD,' because they will all know me, from the least of them to the greatest," declares the LORD. "For I will **forgive** their wickedness and will remember their sins no more."

Jeremiah 33:8
I will cleanse them from all the sin they have committed against me and will **forgive** all their sins of rebellion against me.

Jeremiah 36:3
they will each turn from their wicked ways; then I will **forgive** their wickedness and their sin."

Jeremiah 50:20
In those days, at that time," declares the LORD, "search will be made for Israel's guilt, but there will be none, and for the sins of Judah, but none will be found, for I will **forgive** the remnant I spare.

Daniel 9:9
The Lord our God is merciful and **forgiving**, even though we have rebelled against him;

Micah 7:18
Who is a God like you, who pardons sin and **forgives** the transgression of the remnant of his inheritance? You do not stay angry forever but delight to show mercy.

Matthew 6:12
And **forgive** us our debts, as we also have forgiven our debtors.

Matthew 6:14-15
For if you forgive other people when they sin against you, your heavenly Father will also **forgive** you. But if you do not forgive others their sins, your Father will not forgive your sins.

Matthew 9:2
When Jesus saw their faith, he said to the man, "Take heart, son; your sins are **forgiven**."

Matthew 9:6
But I want you to know that the Son of Man has authority on earth to **forgive** sins."

Matthew 26:28
This is my blood of the covenant, which is poured out for many for the **forgiveness** of sins.

Mark 2:5
When Jesus saw their faith, he said to the paralyzed man, "Son, your sins are **forgiven**."

Mark 2:10
But I want you to know that the Son of Man has authority on earth to **forgive** sins."

Mark 11:25
And when you stand praying, if you hold anything against anyone, forgive them, so that your Father in heaven may **forgive** you your sins."

Luke 1:77
to give his people the knowledge of salvation through the **forgiveness** of their sins,

Luke 3:3
He went into all the country around the Jordan, preaching a baptism of repentance for the **forgiveness** of sins.

God is Forgiving

Luke 5:20
When Jesus saw their faith, he said, "Friend, your sins are **forgiven**."

Luke 5:24
But I want you to know that the Son of Man has authority on earth to **forgive** sins."

Luke 7:48
Then Jesus said to her, "Your sins are **forgiven**."

Luke 7:49
The other guests began to say among themselves, "Who is this who even **forgives** sins?"

Luke 23:34
Jesus said, "Father, **forgive** them, for they do not know what they are doing."

Acts 5:31
God exalted him to his own right hand as Prince and Savior that he might bring Israel to repentance and **forgive** their sins.

Acts 10:43
All the prophets testify about him that everyone who believes in him receives **forgiveness** of sins through his name."

Acts 13:38
"Therefore, my friends, I want you to know that through Jesus the **forgiveness** of sins is proclaimed to you.

Ephesians 1:7
In him we have redemption through his blood, the **forgiveness** of sins, in accordance with the riches of God's grace

Ephesians 4:32
Be kind and compassionate to one another, forgiving each other, just as in Christ God **forgave** you.

Colossians 1:14
in whom we have redemption, the **forgiveness** of sins.

Colossians 2:13
When you were dead in your sins and in the uncircumcision of your flesh, God made you alive with Christ. He **forgave** us all our sins,

Colossians 3:13
Forgive as the Lord **forgave** you.

Hebrews 8:12
For I will **forgive** their wickedness and will remember their sins no more."

1 John 1:9
If we confess our sins, he is faithful and just and will **forgive** us our sins and purify us from all unrighteousness.

1 John 2:12
because your sins have been **forgiven** on account of his name.

God Our Fortress
Our Stronghold

Fortress:
A place that is fortified and safe from attack;
A place having tactical advantage against an enemy.

*I will say of the Lord, "He is my refuge and my **fortress**, my God, in whom I trust."*

- Psalm 91:2

God Our Fortress

1. DEFINE FORTRESS USING YOUR OWN WORDS, SYNONYMS, OR DESCRIPTIONS:

_____

_____

_____

2. ALMOST ALL REFERENCES TO GOD BEING A FORTRESS OR STRONGHOLD ARE WRITTEN BY DAVID. WHAT WAS GOING ON IN DAVID'S LIFE THAT HE NEEDED GOD'S PROTECTION? (See: 1 Samuel, chapters 17-31).

_____

_____

_____

3. DO YOU HAVE ANY OBSERVATIONS ABOUT THIS CHARACTER TRAIT OF GOD OR WHY GOD WANTS US TO KNOW THAT HE OUR FORTRESS OR STRONGHOLD?

_____

_____

_____

_____

_____

Security is not the absence of danger, but the presence of God no matter what the danger.

NOTES:

God Our Fortress

2 Samuel 22:2
He said: "The LORD is my rock, my **fortress** and my deliverer;

2 Samuel 22:3
my God is my rock, in whom I take refuge, my shield and the horn of my salvation. He is my **stronghold**, my refuge and my savior— from violent people you save me.

Psalm 9:9
The LORD is a refuge for the oppressed, a **stronghold** in times of trouble.

Psalm 18:2
The LORD is my rock, my **fortress** and my deliverer; my God is my rock, in whom I take refuge, my shield and the horn of my salvation, my **stronghold**.

Psalm 27:1
Of David. The LORD is my light and my salvation— whom shall I fear? The LORD is the **stronghold** of my life— of whom shall I be afraid?

Psalm 28:8
The LORD is the strength of his people, a **fortress** of salvation for his anointed one.

Psalm 31:2
Turn your ear to me, come quickly to my rescue; be my rock of refuge, a **strong fortress** to save me.

Psalm 31:3
Since you are my rock and my **fortress**, for the sake of your name lead and guide me.

Psalm 37:39
The salvation of the righteous comes from the LORD; he is their **stronghold** in time of trouble.

Psalm 46:7
The LORD Almighty is with us; the God of Jacob is our **fortress**.

Psalm 46:11
The LORD Almighty is with us; the God of Jacob is our **fortress**.

Psalm 48:3
God is in her citadels; he has shown himself to be her **fortress**.

Psalm 52:7
"Here now is the man who did not make God his **stronghold** but trusted in his great wealth and grew strong by destroying others!"

Psalm 59:1
Deliver me from my enemies, O God; be my **fortress** against those who are attacking me.

Psalm 59:9
You are my strength, I watch for you; you, God, are my **fortress**,

Psalm 59:16
But I will sing of your strength, in the morning I will sing of your love; for you are my **fortress**, my refuge in times of trouble.

Psalm 59:17
You are my strength, I sing praise to you; you, God, are my **fortress**, my God on whom I can rely.

Psalm 62:2
Truly he is my rock and my salvation; he is my **fortress**, I will never be shaken.

Psalm 62:6
Truly he is my rock and my salvation; he is my **fortress**, I will not be shaken.

Psalm 71:3
Be my rock of refuge, to which I can always go; give the command to save me, for you are my rock and my **fortress**.

Psalm 91:2
I will say of the LORD, "He is my refuge and my **fortress**, my God, in whom I trust."

Psalm 94:22
But the LORD has become my **fortress**, and my God the rock in whom I take refuge.

Psalm 144:2
He is my loving God and my **fortress**, my **stronghold** and my deliverer, my shield, in whom I take refuge, who subdues peoples under me.

Proverbs 14:26
Whoever fears the LORD has a secure **fortress**, and for their children it will be a refuge.

Isaiah 17:10
You have forgotten God your Savior; you have not remembered the Rock, your **fortress**.

God Our Friend

Friend:
A person with whom there is mutual affection and respect.

*The Lord would speak to Moses face to face, as one speaks to a **friend**.*

- Exodus 33:11

God Our Friend

1. DEFINE FRIEND USING YOUR OWN WORDS, SYNONYMS, OR DESCRIPTIONS:

_____

_____

_____

2. JAMES 4:4 SAYS WE CAN'T BE BOTH A FRIEND TO THE WORLD AND TO GOD. WHAT DOES THAT MEAN? (See also: 1 John 2:15-16)

_____

_____

_____

3. DO YOU HAVE ANY OBSERVATIONS ABOUT THIS CHARACTER TRAIT OF GOD OR WHY GOD WANTS US TO KNOW THAT HE IS OUR FRIEND?

_____

_____

_____

_____

_____

_____

Oh, the comfort, the inexpressible comfort of feeling safe with a person, having neither to weigh thoughts, nor measure words, but pouring them all out, just as they are, chaff and grain together, certain that a faithful hand will take and sift them, keep what is worth keeping, and with a breath of kindness blow the rest away.

- Dinah Mulock Craik

How Thou canst think so well of us, and be the God Thou art,
Is darkness to my intellect, but sunshine to my heart.

NOTES:

God Our Friend

Exodus 33:11
The LORD would speak to Moses face to face, as one speaks to a **friend**.

Proverbs 18:24
One who has unreliable friends soon comes to ruin, but there is a **friend** who sticks closer than a brother.

Isaiah 41:8
"But you, Israel, my servant, Jacob, whom I have chosen, you descendants of Abraham my **friend**,

Matthew 11:19
The Son of Man came eating and drinking, and they say, 'Here is a glutton and a drunkard, a **friend** of tax collectors and sinners.'

Matthew 26:50
[*Jesus' betrayal by Judas*] Jesus replied, "Do what you came for, **friend**." Then the men stepped forward, seized Jesus and arrested him.

Luke 5:20
When Jesus saw their faith, he said, "**Friend,** your sins are forgiven."

Luke 12:4
"I tell you, my **friends**, do not be afraid of those who kill the body and after that can do no more.

John 11:11
After he had said this, he went on to tell them, "Our **friend** Lazarus has fallen asleep; but I am going there to wake him up."

John 15:13
Greater love has no one than this: to lay down one's life for one's **friends**.

John 15:14
You are my **friends** if you do what I command.

John 15:15
I no longer call you servants, because a servant does not know his master's business. Instead, I have called you **friends**, for everything that I learned from my Father I have made known to you.

John 21:5
He called out to them, "**Friends,** haven't you any fish?" "No," they answered.

James 2:23
And the scripture was fulfilled that says, "Abraham believed God, and it was credited to him as righteousness," and he was called God's **friend**.

God is Gentle

Gentle:
A person who does not have harsh or rough characteristics.

*Take my yoke upon you and learn from me, for I am **gentle** and humble in heart, and you will find rest for your souls.*

- *Matthew 11:29*

God is Gentle

1. DEFINE GENTLE USING YOUR OWN WORDS, SYNONYMS, OR DESCRIPTIONS:

_____

_____

_____

2. IMAGINE GOD AS A SHEPHERD, GENTLY LEADING HIS FLOCK AND CARRYING THE LAMBS CLOSE TO HIS HEART AS DESCRIBED IN ISAIAH 40:11.

_____

_____

_____

3. DO YOU HAVE ANY OBSERVATIONS ABOUT THIS CHARACTER TRAIT OF GOD OR WHY GOD WANTS US TO KNOW THAT HE IS GENTLE?

_____

_____

_____

_____

_____

_____

The darker the night, the brighter the stars,
The deeper the grief, the closer is God!
- Fyodor Dostoyevsky

NOTES:

God is Gentle

Isaiah 40:11
He tends his flock like a shepherd: He gathers the lambs in his arms and carries them close to his heart; he **gently** leads those that have young.

Matthew 11:29
Take my yoke upon you and learn from me, for I am **gentle** and humble in heart, and you will find rest for your souls.

Matthew 21:5
"Say to Daughter Zion, 'See, your king comes to you, **gentle** and riding on a donkey, and on a colt, the foal of a donkey.'"

2 Corinthians 10:1
By the humility and **gentleness** of Christ, I appeal to you

Hebrews 5:2
He is able to deal **gently** with those who are ignorant and are going astray, since he himself is subject to weakness.

God is Glorious
Possessing Glory
Deserving to be Glorified

Glorious:
Fame and honor won by great deeds; Praise;
Adoration; Worship; Possessing beauty and
magnificance; Deserving of praise and honor.

*The city does not need the sun or the moon to shine
on it, for the **glory** of God gives it light, and the Lamb
is its lamp.*

- Revelation 21:23

God is Glorious

1. DEFINE GLORIOUS USING YOUR OWN WORDS, SYNONYMS, OR DESCRIPTIONS:

_____

_____

_____

2. ISAIAH 42:8 "I AM THE LORD; THAT IS MY NAME! I WILL NOT YIELD MY GLORY TO ANOTHER OR MY PRAISE TO IDOLS." WHY IS IMPORTANT THAT GOD BE "PROTECTIVE" OF HIS GLORY?

_____

_____

_____

3. THE BIBLE TALKS ABOUT PEOPLE SEEING GOD'S GLORY AND IT FILLING A TEMPLE OR SHINING BRIGHTLY. WHAT DO YOU THINK GOD'S GLORY LOOKS LIKE? AND WHAT WILL IT BE LIKE TO FINALLY SEE GOD'S GLORY?

_____

_____

_____

4. DO YOU HAVE ANY OBSERVATIONS ABOUT THIS CHARACTER TRAIT OF GOD OR WHY GOD WANTS US TO KNOW THAT HE IS GLORIOUS AND DESERVING TO BE GLORIFIED?

_____

_____

_____

_____

_____

_____

_____

A man can no more diminish God's glory by refusing to worship Him than a lunatic can put out the sun by scribbling the word "darkness" on the walls of his cell.

- C. S. Lewis

NOTES:

God is Glorious

Exodus 14:4
And I will harden Pharaoh's heart, and he will pursue them. But I will gain **glory** for myself through Pharaoh and all his army, and the Egyptians will know that I am the LORD." So the Israelites did this.

Exodus 14:17
I will harden the hearts of the Egyptians so that they will go in after them. And I will gain **glory** through Pharaoh and all his army, through his chariots and his horsemen.

Exodus 14:18
The Egyptians will know that I am the LORD when I gain **glory** through Pharaoh, his chariots and his horsemen."

Exodus 15:11
Who among the gods is like you, LORD? Who is like you— majestic in holiness, awesome in **glory**, working wonders?

Exodus 16:7
and in the morning you will see the **glory** of the LORD,

Exodus 16:10
While Aaron was speaking to the whole Israelite community, they looked toward the desert, and there was the **glory** of the LORD appearing in the cloud.

Exodus 24:16
and the **glory** of the LORD settled on Mount Sinai. For six days the cloud covered the mountain, and on the seventh day the LORD called to Moses from within the cloud.

Exodus 24:17
To the Israelites the **glory** of the LORD looked like a consuming fire on top of the mountain.

Exodus 29:43
there also I will meet with the Israelites, and the place will be consecrated by my **glory**.

Exodus 33:18
Then Moses said, "Now show me your **glory**."

Exodus 33:22
When my **glory** passes by, I will put you in a cleft in the rock and cover you with my hand until I have passed by.

Exodus 40:34
Then the cloud covered the tent of meeting, and the **glory** of the LORD filled the tabernacle.

Exodus 40:35
Moses could not enter the tent of meeting because the cloud had settled on it, and the **glory** of the LORD filled the tabernacle.

Leviticus 9:23
When they came out, they blessed the people; and the **glory** of the LORD appeared to all the people.

Numbers 14:10
But the whole assembly talked about stoning them. Then the **glory** of the LORD appeared at the tent of meeting to all the Israelites.

Numbers 14:21
Nevertheless, as surely as I live and as surely as the **glory** of the LORD fills the whole earth,

Numbers 14:22
not one of those who saw my **glory** and the signs I performed in Egypt and in the wilderness but who disobeyed me and tested me ten times—

Numbers 16:19
the **glory** of the LORD appeared to the entire assembly.

Numbers 16:42
But when the assembly gathered in opposition to Moses and Aaron and turned toward the tent of meeting, suddenly the cloud covered it and the **glory** of the LORD appeared.

Numbers 20:6
Moses and Aaron went from the assembly to the entrance to the tent of meeting and fell facedown, and the **glory** of the LORD appeared to them.

Deuteronomy 5:24
And you said, "The LORD our God has shown us his **glory** and his majesty, and we have heard his voice from the fire.

Deuteronomy 28:58
If you do not carefully follow all the words of this law, which are written in this book, and do not revere this **glorious** and awesome name—the LORD your God—

Deuteronomy 33:29
Blessed are you, Israel! Who is like you, a people saved by the LORD? He is your shield and helper and your **glorious** sword.

Joshua 7:19
Then Joshua said to Achan, "My son, give **glory** to the LORD, the God of Israel, and honor him.

1 Samuel 6:5
and give **glory** to Israel's god. Perhaps he will lift his hand from you and your gods and your land.

1 Samuel 15:29
He who is the **Glory** of Israel does not lie or change his mind; for he is not a human being, that he should change his mind."

1 Chronicles 16:10
Glory in his holy name; let the hearts of those who seek the LORD rejoice.

1 Chronicles 16:24
Declare his **glory** among the nations, his marvelous deeds among all peoples.

1 Chronicles 16:28
Ascribe to the LORD, all you families of nations, ascribe to the LORD **glory** and strength.

1 Chronicles 16:29
Ascribe to the LORD the **glory** due his name; bring an offering and come before him. Worship the LORD in the splendor of his holiness.

1 Chronicles 16:35
Cry out, "Save us, God our Savior; gather us and deliver us from the nations, that we may give thanks to your holy name, and **glory** in your praise."

1 Chronicles 29:11
Yours, LORD, is the greatness and the power and the **glory** and the majesty and the splendor, for everything in heaven and earth is yours. Yours, LORD, is the kingdom; you are exalted as head over all.

1 Chronicles 29:13
Now, our God, we give you thanks, and praise your **glorious** name.

2 Chronicles 5:14
and the priests could not perform their service because of the cloud, for the **glory** of the LORD filled the temple of God.

2 Chronicles 7:1
[*The Dedication of the Temple*] When Solomon finished praying, fire came down from heaven and consumed the burnt offering and the sacrifices, and the **glory** of the LORD filled the temple.

2 Chronicles 7:2
The priests could not enter the temple of the LORD because the **glory** of the LORD filled it.

God is Glorious

2 Chronicles 7:3
When all the Israelites saw the fire coming down and the **glory** of the LORD above the temple, they knelt on the pavement with their faces to the ground, and they worshiped and gave thanks to the LORD, saying, "He is good; his love endures forever."

Nehemiah 9:5
"Stand up and praise the LORD your God, who is from everlasting to everlasting. " "Blessed be your **glorious** name, and may it be exalted above all blessing and praise.

Psalm 3:3
But you, LORD, are a shield around me, my **glory,** the One who lifts my head high.

Psalm 8:1
LORD, our Lord, how majestic is your name in all the earth! You have set your **glory** in the heavens.

Psalm 19:1
The heavens declare the **glory** of God; the skies proclaim the work of his hands.

Psalm 24:7
Lift up your heads, you gates; be lifted up, you ancient doors, that the King of **glory** may come in.

Psalm 24:8
Who is this King of **glory**? The LORD strong and mighty, the LORD mighty in battle.

Psalm 24:9
Lift up your heads, you gates; lift them up, you ancient doors, that the King of **glory** may come in.

Psalm 24:10
Who is he, this King of **glory**? The LORD Almighty— he is the King of **glory**.

Psalm 26:8
LORD, I love the house where you live, the place where your **glory** dwells.

Psalm 29:1
Ascribe to the LORD, you heavenly beings, ascribe to the LORD **glory** and strength.

Psalm 29:2
Ascribe to the LORD the **glory** due his name; worship the LORD in the splendor of his holiness.

Psalm 29:3
The voice of the LORD is over the waters; the God of **glory** thunders, the LORD thunders over the mighty waters.

Psalm 29:9
The voice of the LORD twists the oaks and strips the forests bare. And in his temple all cry, "**Glory**!"

Psalm 34:3
Glorify the LORD with me; let us exalt his name together.

Psalm 57:5
Be exalted, O God, above the heavens; let your **glory** be over all the earth.

Psalm 57:11
Be exalted, O God, above the heavens; let your **glory** be over all the earth.

Psalm 63:2
I have seen you in the sanctuary and beheld your power and your **glory**.

Psalm 63:3
Because your love is better than life, my lips will **glorify** you.

Psalm 63:11
But the king will rejoice in God; all who swear by God will **glory** in him, while the mouths of liars will be silenced.

Psalm 64:10
The righteous will rejoice in the LORD and take refuge in him; all the upright in heart will **glory** in him!

Psalm 66:2
Sing the **glory** of his name; make his praise **glorious**.

Psalm 69:30
I will praise God's name in song and **glorify** him with thanksgiving.

Psalm 72:19
Praise be to his **glorious** name forever; may the whole earth be filled with his **glory**.

Psalm 73:24
You guide me with your counsel, and afterward you will take me into **glory**.

Psalm 79:9
Help us, God our Savior, for the **glory** of your name; deliver us and forgive our sins for your name's sake.

Psalm 85:9
Surely his salvation is near those who fear him, that his **glory** may dwell in our land.

Psalm 86:9
All the nations you have made will come and worship before you, Lord; they will bring **glory** to your name.

Psalm 86:12
I will praise you, Lord my God, with all my heart; I will **glorify** your name forever.

Psalm 89:17
For you are their **glory** and strength, and by your favor you exalt our horn.

Psalm 96:3
Declare his **glory** among the nations, his marvelous deeds among all peoples.

Psalm 96:6
Splendor and majesty are before him; strength and **glory** are in his sanctuary.

Psalm 96:7
Ascribe to the LORD, all you families of nations, ascribe to the LORD **glory** and strength.

Psalm 96:8
Ascribe to the LORD the **glory** due his name; bring an offering and come into his courts.

Psalm 97:6
The heavens proclaim his righteousness, and all peoples see his **glory**.

Psalm 102:15
The nations will fear the name of the LORD, all the kings of the earth will revere your **glory**.

Psalm 102:16
For the LORD will rebuild Zion and appear in his **glory**.

Psalm 104:31
May the **glory** of the LORD endure forever; may the LORD rejoice in his works—

Psalm 105:3
Glory in his holy name; let the hearts of those who seek the LORD rejoice.

God is Glorious

Psalm 106:20
They exchanged their **glorious** God for an image of a bull,

Psalm 106:47
Save us, LORD our God, and gather us from the nations, that we may give thanks to your holy name and **glory** in your praise.

Psalm 108:5
Be exalted, O God, above the heavens; let your **glory** be over all the earth.

Psalm 111:3
Glorious and majestic are his deeds, and his righteousness endures forever.

Psalm 113:4
The LORD is exalted over all the nations, his **glory** above the heavens.

Psalm 115:1
Not to us, LORD, not to us but to your name be the **glory**, because of your love and faithfulness.

Psalm 138:5
May they sing of the ways of the LORD, for the **glory** of the LORD is great.

Psalm 145:5
They speak of the **glorious** splendor of your majesty— and I will meditate on your wonderful works.

Psalm 145:11
They tell of the **glory** of your kingdom and speak of your might,

Psalm 145:12
so that all people may know of your mighty acts and the **glorious** splendor of your kingdom.

Isaiah 3:8
Jerusalem staggers, Judah is falling; their words and deeds are against the LORD, defying his **glorious** presence.

Isaiah 4:2
In that day the Branch of the LORD will be beautiful and **glorious,**

Isaiah 4:5
Then the LORD will create over all of Mount Zion and over those who assemble there a cloud of smoke by day and a glow of flaming fire by night; over everything the **glory** will be a canopy.

Isaiah 6:3
And they were calling to one another: "Holy, holy, holy is the LORD Almighty; the whole earth is full of his **glory**."

Isaiah 11:10
In that day the Root of Jesse will stand as a banner for the peoples; the nations will rally to him, and his resting place will be **glorious**.

Isaiah 12:5
Sing to the LORD, for he has done **glorious** things; let this be known to all the world.

Isaiah 24:15
Therefore in the east give **glory** to the LORD; exalt the name of the LORD, the God of Israel, in the islands of the sea.

Isaiah 24:16
From the ends of the earth we hear singing: "**Glory** to the Righteous One."

Isaiah 24:23
The moon will be dismayed, the sun ashamed; for the LORD Almighty will reign on Mount Zion and in Jerusalem, and before its elders—with great **glory**.

Isaiah 26:15
You have gained **glory** for yourself; you have extended all the borders of the land.

Isaiah 28:5
In that day the LORD Almighty will be a **glorious** crown, a beautiful wreath for the remnant of his people.

Isaiah 35:2
they will see the **glory** of the LORD, the splendor of our God.

Isaiah 40:5
And the **glory** of the LORD will be revealed, and all people will see it together.

Isaiah 41:16
But you will rejoice in the LORD and **glory** in the Holy One of Israel.

Isaiah 42:8
"I am the LORD; that is my name! I will not yield my **glory** to another or my praise to idols.

Isaiah 42:12
Let them give **glory** to the LORD and proclaim his praise in the islands.

Isaiah 42:21
It pleased the LORD for the sake of his righteousness to make his law great and **glorious**.

Isaiah 43:7
everyone who is called by my name, whom I created for my **glory**, whom I formed and made."

Isaiah 48:11
I will not yield my **glory** to another.

Isaiah 58:8
Then your light will break forth like the dawn, and your healing will quickly appear; then your righteousness will go before you, and the **glory** of the LORD will be your rear guard.

Isaiah 59:19
From the west, people will fear the name of the LORD, and from the rising of the sun, they will revere his **glory**.

Isaiah 60:1
"Arise, shine, for your light has come, and the **glory** of the LORD rises upon you.

Isaiah 60:2
See, darkness covers the earth and thick darkness is over the peoples, but the LORD rises upon you and his **glory** appears over you.

Isaiah 60:19
The sun will no more be your light by day, nor will the brightness of the moon shine on you, for the LORD will be your everlasting light, and your God will be your **glory**.

Isaiah 63:12
who sent his **glorious** arm of power to be at Moses' right hand, who divided the waters before them, to gain for himself everlasting renown,

Isaiah 63:14
they were given rest by the Spirit of the LORD. This is how you guided your people to make for yourself a **glorious** name.

Isaiah 63:15
Look down from heaven and see, from your lofty throne, holy and **glorious**.

Isaiah 66:5
'Let the LORD be **glorified**, that we may see your joy!'

Isaiah 66:18
"And I, because of what they have planned and done, am about to come and gather the people of all nations and languages, and they will come and see my **glory**.

Isaiah 66:19
to the distant islands that have not heard of my fame or seen my **glory**. They will proclaim my **glory** among the nations.

Jeremiah 2:11
Has a nation ever changed its gods? (Yet they are not gods at all.) But my people have exchanged their **glorious** God for worthless idols.

God is Glorious

Jeremiah 13:16
Give **glory** to the LORD your God before he brings the darkness,

Jeremiah 17:12
A **glorious** throne, exalted from the beginning, is the place of our sanctuary.

Ezekiel 1:28
Like the appearance of a rainbow in the clouds on a rainy day, so was the radiance around him. This was the appearance of the likeness of the **glory** of the LORD. When I saw it, I fell facedown, and I heard the voice of one speaking.

Ezekiel 3:12
Then the Spirit lifted me up, and I heard behind me a loud rumbling sound as the **glory** of the LORD rose from the place where it was standing.

Ezekiel 3:23
And the **glory** of the LORD was standing there, like the **glory** I had seen by the Kebar River, and I fell facedown.

Ezekiel 8:4
And there before me was the **glory** of the God of Israel, as in the vision I had seen in the plain.

Ezekiel 9:3
Now the **glory** of the God of Israel went up from above the cherubim,

Ezekiel 10:4
Then the **glory** of the LORD rose from above the cherubim and moved to the threshold of the temple. The cloud filled the temple, and the court was full of the radiance of the **glory** of the LORD.

Ezekiel 10:18
Then the **glory** of the LORD departed from over the threshold of the temple and stopped above the cherubim.

Ezekiel 10:19
They stopped at the entrance of the east gate of the LORD's house, and the **glory** of the God of Israel was above them.

Ezekiel 11:22
Then the cherubim, with the wheels beside them, spread their wings, and the **glory** of the God of Israel was above them.

Ezekiel 11:23
The **glory** of the LORD went up from within the city and stopped above the mountain east of it.

Ezekiel 28:22
and among you I will display my **glory**. You will know that I am the LORD

Ezekiel 39:13
All the people of the land will bury them, and the day I display my **glory** will be a memorable day for them, declares the Sovereign LORD.

Ezekiel 39:21
"I will display my **glory** among the nations,

Ezekiel 43:2
and I saw the **glory** of the God of Israel coming from the east. His voice was like the roar of rushing waters, and the land was radiant with his **glory**.

Ezekiel 43:4
The **glory** of the LORD entered the temple through the gate facing east.

Ezekiel 43:5
Then the Spirit lifted me up and brought me into the inner court, and the **glory** of the LORD filled the temple.

Ezekiel 44:4
I looked and saw the **glory** of the LORD filling the temple of the LORD, and I fell facedown.

Daniel 2:37
Your Majesty, you are the king of kings. The God of heaven has given you dominion and power and might and **glory**;

Daniel 4:34
At the end of that time, I, Nebuchadnezzar, raised my eyes toward heaven, and my sanity was restored. Then I praised the Most High; I honored and **glorified** him who lives forever. His dominion is an eternal dominion; his kingdom endures from generation to generation.

Daniel 4:37
Now I, Nebuchadnezzar, praise and exalt and **glorify** the King of heaven, because everything he does is right and all his ways are just. And those who walk in pride he is able to humble.

Daniel 7:14
He was given authority, **glory** and sovereign power; all nations and peoples of every language worshiped him. His dominion is an everlasting dominion that will not pass away, and his kingdom is one that will never be destroyed.

Hosea 4:7
The more priests there were, the more they sinned against me; they exchanged their **glorious** God for something disgraceful.

Habakkuk 2:14
For the earth will be filled with the knowledge of the **glory** of the LORD as the waters cover the sea.

Habakkuk 3:3
His **glory** covered the heavens and his praise filled the earth.

Haggai 2:7
I will shake all nations, and what is desired by all nations will come, and I will fill this house with **glory**,' says the LORD Almighty.

Zechariah 2:5
And I myself will be a wall of fire around it,' declares the LORD, 'and I will be its **glory** within.'

Zechariah 2:8
For this is what the LORD Almighty says: "After the **Glorious** One has sent me against the nations that have plundered you—for whoever touches you touches the apple of his eye—

Matthew 16:27
For the Son of Man is going to come in his Father's **glory** with his angels,

Matthew 19:28
Jesus said to them, "Truly I tell you, at the renewal of all things, when the Son of Man sits on his **glorious** throne, you who have followed me will also sit on twelve thrones, judging the twelve tribes of Israel.

Matthew 24:30
"Then will appear the sign of the Son of Man in heaven. And then all the peoples of the earth will mourn when they see the Son of Man coming on the clouds of heaven, with power and great **glory**.

Matthew 25:31
"When the Son of Man comes in his **glory**, and all the angels with him, he will sit on his glorious throne.

Mark 8:38
If anyone is ashamed of me and my words in this adulterous and sinful generation, the Son of Man will be ashamed of them when he comes in his Father's **glory** with the holy angels."

Mark 13:26
"At that time people will see the Son of Man coming in clouds with great power and **glory**.

Luke 2:9
An angel of the Lord appeared to them, and the **glory** of the Lord shone around them, and they were terrified.

Luke 2:14
"**Glory** to God in the highest heaven, and on earth peace to those on whom his favor rests."

God is Glorious

Luke 2:20
The shepherds returned, **glorifying** and praising God for all the things they had heard and seen, which were just as they had been told.

Luke 2:32
a light for revelation to the Gentiles, and the **glory** of your people Israel."

John 7:39
By this he meant the Spirit, whom those who believed in him were later to receive. Up to that time the Spirit had not been given, since Jesus had not yet been **glorified**.

John 8:54
Jesus replied, "If I **glorify** myself, my **glory** means nothing. My Father, whom you claim as your God, is the one who **glorifies** me.

Luke 9:26
Whoever is ashamed of me and my words, the Son of Man will be ashamed of them when he comes in his **glory** and in the **glory** of the Father and of the holy angels.

Luke 9:32
Peter and his companions were very sleepy, but when they became fully awake, they saw his **glory** and the two men standing with him.

Luke 19:38
"Blessed is the king who comes in the name of the Lord!" "Peace in heaven and **glory** in the highest!"

Luke 21:27
At that time they will see the Son of Man coming in a cloud with power and great **glory**.

John 1:14
The Word became flesh and made his dwelling among us. We have seen his **glory,** the **glory** of the one and only Son, who came from the Father, full of grace and truth.

John 2:11
What Jesus did here in Cana of Galilee was the first of the signs through which he revealed his **glory**; and his disciples believed in him.

John 7:39
Up to that time the Spirit had not been given, since Jesus had not yet been **glorified**.

John 8:54
Jesus replied, "If I **glorify** myself, my **glory** means nothing. My Father, whom you claim as your God, is the one who **glorifies** me.

John 11:4
When he heard this, Jesus said, "This sickness will not end in death. No, it is for God's **glory** so that God's Son may be **glorified** through it."

John 11:40
Then Jesus said, "Did I not tell you that if you believe, you will see the **glory** of God?"

John 12:16
At first his disciples did not understand all this. Only after Jesus was **glorified** did they realize that these things had been written about him and that these things had been done to him.

John 12:23
Jesus replied, "The hour has come for the Son of Man to be **glorified**.

John 12:28
Father, **glorify** your name!" Then a voice came from heaven, "I have **glorified** it, and will **glorify** it again."

God is Glorious

John 12:41
Isaiah said this because he saw Jesus' **glory** and spoke about him.

John 13:31
Jesus said, "Now the Son of Man is **glorified** and God is **glorified** in him.

John 13:32
If God is **glorified** in him, God will **glorify** the Son in himself, and will **glorify** him at once.

John 14:13
And I will do whatever you ask in my name, so that the Father may be **glorified** in the Son.

John 16:14
He will **glorify** me because it is from me that he will receive what he will make known to you.

John 17:1
After Jesus said this, he looked toward heaven and prayed: "Father, the hour has come. **Glorify** your Son, that your Son may **glorify** you.

John 17:4
I have brought you **glory** on earth by finishing the work you gave me to do.

John 17:5
And now, Father, **glorify** me in your presence with the glory I had with you before the world began.

John 17:24
"Father, I want those you have given me to be with me where I am, and to see my **glory**, the **glory** you have given me because you loved me before the creation of the world.

Acts 2:20
The sun will be turned to darkness and the moon to blood before the coming of the great and **glorious** day of the Lord.

Acts 3:13
The God of Abraham, Isaac and Jacob, the God of our fathers, has **glorified** his servant Jesus.

Acts 7:2
The God of **glory** appeared to our father Abraham

Acts 7:55
But Stephen, full of the Holy Spirit, looked up to heaven and saw the **glory** of God, and Jesus standing at the right hand of God.

Romans 1:21
For although they knew God, they neither **glorified** him as God nor gave thanks to him, but their thinking became futile and their foolish hearts were darkened.

Romans 3:23
for all have sinned and fall short of the **glory** of God,

Romans 4:20
Yet he did not waver through unbelief regarding the promise of God, but was strengthened in his faith and gave **glory** to God,

Romans 5:2
through whom we have gained access by faith into this grace in which we now stand. And we boast in the hope of the **glory** of God.

Romans 6:4
just as Christ was raised from the dead through the **glory** of the Father, we too may live a new life.

Romans 9:23
What if he did this to make the riches of his **glory** known to the objects of his mercy, whom he prepared in advance for **glory**—

God is Glorious

Romans 11:36
To him be the **glory** forever!

Romans 15:6
so that with one mind and one voice you may **glorify** the God and Father of our Lord Jesus Christ.

Romans 15:9
and, moreover, that the Gentiles might **glorify** God for his mercy.

Romans 16:27
to the only wise God be **glory** forever through Jesus Christ!

1 Corinthians 2:8
None of the rulers of this age understood it, for if they had, they would not have crucified the Lord of **glory**.

2 Corinthians 3:8
will not the ministry of the Spirit be even more **glorious**?

2 Corinthians 3:10
For what was glorious has no glory now in comparison with the surpassing **glory**.

2 Corinthians 3:11
And if what was transitory came with glory, how much greater is the **glory** of that which lasts!

2 Corinthians 3:18
And we all, who with unveiled faces contemplate the Lord's **glory**, are being transformed into his image with ever-increasing **glory**, which comes from the Lord, who is the Spirit.

2 Corinthians 4:4
The god of this age has blinded the minds of unbelievers, so that they cannot see the light of the gospel that displays the **glory** of Christ, who is the image of God.

2 Corinthians 4:6
For God, who said, "Let light shine out of darkness," made his light shine in our hearts to give us the light of the knowledge of God's **glory** displayed in the face of Christ.

Galatians 1:5
to whom be **glory** for ever and ever.

Ephesians 1:6
to the praise of his **glorious** grace, which he has freely given us in the One he loves.

Ephesians 1:12
in order that we, who were the first to put our hope in Christ, might be for the praise of his **glory**.

Ephesians 1:17
I keep asking that the God of our Lord Jesus Christ, the **glorious** Father, may give you the Spirit of wisdom and revelation, so that you may know him better.

Ephesians 1:18
I pray that the eyes of your heart may be enlightened in order that you may know the hope to which he has called you, the riches of his **glorious** inheritance in his holy people,

Ephesians 3:16
I pray that out of his **glorious** riches he may strengthen you with power through his Spirit in your inner being,

Ephesians 3:21
to him be **glory** in the church and in Christ Jesus throughout all generations, for ever and ever!

Philippians 3:21
who, by the power that enables him to bring everything under his control, will transform our lowly bodies so that they will be like his **glorious** body.

Philippians 4:20
To our God and Father be **glory** for ever and ever.

Colossians 1:11
being strengthened with all power according to his **glorious** might so that you may have great endurance and patience,

1 Thessalonians 2:12
encouraging, comforting and urging you to live lives worthy of God, who calls you into his kingdom and **glory**.

2 Thessalonians 1:9
They will be punished with everlasting destruction and shut out from the presence of the Lord and from the **glory** of his might

2 Thessalonians 1:10
on the day he comes to be **glorified** in his holy people and to be marveled at among all those who have believed.

2 Thessalonians 2:14
He called you to this through our gospel, that you might share in the **glory** of our Lord Jesus Christ.

1 Timothy 1:11
that conforms to the gospel concerning the **glory** of the blessed God,

1 Timothy 1:17
Now to the King eternal, immortal, invisible, the only God, be honor and **glory** for ever and ever.

1 Timothy 3:16
He appeared in the flesh, was vindicated by the Spirit, was seen by angels, was preached among the nations, was believed on in the world, was taken up in **glory**.

2 Timothy 4:18
To him be **glory** for ever and ever.

Titus 2:13
while we wait for the blessed hope—the appearing of the **glory** of our great God and Savior, Jesus Christ,

Hebrews 1:3
The Son is the radiance of God's **glory** and the exact representation of his being, sustaining all things by his powerful word.

Hebrews 2:9
But we do see Jesus, who was made lower than the angels for a little while, now crowned with **glory** and honor because he suffered death, so that by the grace of God he might taste death for everyone.

Hebrews 13:21
through Jesus Christ, to whom be **glory** for ever and ever.

James 2:1
My brothers and sisters, believers in our **glorious** Lord Jesus Christ must not show favoritism.

1 Peter 1:21
Through him you believe in God, who raised him from the dead and **glorified** him,

1 Peter 4:11
so that in all things God may be praised through Jesus Christ. To him be the **glory** and the power for ever and ever.

1 Peter 4:13
But rejoice inasmuch as you participate in the sufferings of Christ, so that you may be overjoyed when his **glory** is revealed.

1 Peter 5:10
And the God of all grace, who called you to his eternal **glory** in Christ,

2 Peter 1:3
His divine power has given us everything we need for a godly life through our knowledge of him who called us by his own **glory** and goodness.

God is Glorious

2 Peter 1:17
He received honor and **glory** from God the Father when the voice came to him from the Majestic **Glory**, saying, "This is my Son, whom I love; with him I am well pleased."

2 Peter 3:18
But grow in the grace and knowledge of our Lord and Savior Jesus Christ. To him be **glory** both now and forever!

Jude 1:24
To him who is able to keep you from stumbling and to present you before his **glorious** presence without fault and with great joy—

Jude 1:25
to the only God our Savior be **glory**, majesty, power and authority, through Jesus Christ our Lord, before all ages, now and forevermore!

Revelation 1:6
to serve his God and Father—to him be **glory** and power for ever and ever!

Revelation 4:11
"You are worthy, our Lord and God, to receive **glory** and honor and power, for you created all things, and by your will they were created and have their being."

Revelation 5:12
In a loud voice they were saying: "Worthy is the Lamb, who was slain, to receive power and wealth and wisdom and strength and honor and **glory** and praise!"

Revelation 5:13
Then I heard every creature in heaven and on earth and under the earth and on the sea, and all that is in them, saying: "To him who sits on the throne and to the Lamb be praise and honor and **glory** and power, for ever and ever!"

Revelation 7:12
saying: "Amen! Praise and **glory** and wisdom and thanks and honor and power and strength be to our God for ever and ever. Amen!"

Revelation 11:13
and the survivors were terrified and gave **glory** to the God of heaven.

Revelation 14:7
He said in a loud voice, "Fear God and give him **glory**, because the hour of his judgment has come. Worship him who made the heavens, the earth, the sea and the springs of water."

Revelation 15:4
Who will not fear you, Lord, and bring **glory** to your name? For you alone are holy. All nations will come and worship before you, for your righteous acts have been revealed."

Revelation 15:8
And the temple was filled with smoke from the **glory** of God and from his power, and no one could enter the temple until the seven plagues of the seven angels were completed.

Revelation 16:9
They were seared by the intense heat and they cursed the name of God, who had control over these plagues, but they refused to repent and **glorify** him.

Revelation 19:1
After this I heard what sounded like the roar of a great multitude in heaven shouting: "Hallelujah! Salvation and **glory** and power belong to our God,

Revelation 19:7
Let us rejoice and be glad and give him **glory**!

Revelation 21:11
It shone with the **glory** of God, and its brilliance was like that of a very precious jewel, like a jasper, clear as crystal.

Revelation 21:23
The city does not need the sun or the moon to shine on it, for the **glory** of God gives it light, and the Lamb is its lamp.

God is Good
Possessing Goodness
Giver of Good Things

Good:
One who is morally correct, virtuous and kindly; Having right or desireable properties.

*The Lord is **good** to all; he has compassion on all he has made.*

- Psalm 145:9

God is Good

1. DEFINE GOOD USING YOUR OWN WORDS, SYNONYMS, OR DESCRIPTIONS:

_____

_____

_____

2. WE OFTEN THINK THAT BECAUSE GOD IS GOOD, NO EVIL SHOULD EXIST IN THE WORLD. WHAT CAN WE LEARN FROM JOB WHO STATED IN JOB 2:10, "SHALL WE ACCEPT GOOD FROM GOD, AND NOT TROUBLE?" OR FROM JOSEPH IN GENESIS 50:20, "YOU INTENDED TO HARM ME, BUT GOD INTENDED IT FOR GOOD TO ACCOMPLISH WHAT IS NOW BEING DONE, THE SAVING OF MANY LIVES."?

_____

_____

_____

3. GOD IS GOOD AND GIVES US GOOD THINGS DAILY. MAKE A LIST OF THE GOODNESS OF GOD IN YOUR LIFE.

_____

_____

_____

_____

_____

4. DO YOU HAVE ANY OBSERVATIONS ABOUT THIS CHARACTER TRAIT OF GOD OR WHY GOD WANTS US TO KNOW THAT HE IS GOOD?

_____

_____

_____

_____

_____

_I must believe that God is good and that He cares
for me. How do I know? Calvary!_

- Forrest Nash

The fact that God is good does not ban bad things from our lives.

NOTES:

God is Good

Genesis 50:20
You intended to harm me, but God intended it for **good** to accomplish what is now being done, the saving of many lives.

Exodus 18:9
Jethro was delighted to hear about all the **good** things the LORD had done for Israel in rescuing them from the hand of the Egyptians.

Exodus 33:19
And the LORD said, "I will cause all my **goodness** to pass in front of you, and I will proclaim my name, the LORD, in your presence.

Numbers 10:29
Now Moses said to Hobab son of Reuel the Midianite, Moses' father-in-law, "We are setting out for the place about which the LORD said, 'I will give it to you.' Come with us and we will treat you well, for the LORD has promised **good** things to Israel."

Numbers 10:32
If you come with us, we will share with you whatever **good** things the LORD gives us."

Deuteronomy 26:11
Then you and the Levites and the foreigners residing among you shall rejoice in all the **good** things the LORD your God has given to you and your household.

Joshua 21:45
Not one of all the LORD's **good** promises to Israel failed; every one was fulfilled.

Joshua 23:14
"Now I am about to go the way of all the earth. You know with all your heart and soul that not one of all the **good** promises the LORD your God gave you has failed. Every promise has been fulfilled; not one has failed.

Judges 17:13
And Micah said, "Now I know that the LORD will be **good** to me, since this Levite has become my priest."

1 Samuel 25:30
When the LORD has fulfilled for my lord every **good** thing he promised concerning him and has appointed him ruler over Israel,

2 Samuel 7:28
Sovereign LORD, you are God! Your covenant is trustworthy, and you have promised these **good** things to your servant.

2 Samuel 10:12
Be strong, and let us fight bravely for our people and the cities of our God. The LORD will do what is **good** in his sight."

1 Kings 8:56
"Praise be to the LORD, who has given rest to his people Israel just as he promised. Not one word has failed of all the **good** promises he gave through his servant Moses.

1 Kings 8:66
On the following day he sent the people away. They blessed the king and then went home, joyful and glad in heart for all the **good** things the LORD had done for his servant David and his people Israel.

1 Chronicles 16:34
Give thanks to the LORD, for he is **good**; his love endures forever.

1 Chronicles 17:26
You, LORD, are God! You have promised these **good** things to your servant.

1 Chronicles 19:13
Be strong, and let us fight bravely for our people and the cities of our God. The LORD will do what is **good** in his sight."

2 Chronicles 5:13
The trumpeters and musicians joined in unison to give praise and thanks to the LORD. Accompanied by trumpets, cymbals and other instruments, the singers raised their voices in praise to the LORD and sang: "He is **good**; his love endures forever." Then the temple of the LORD was filled with the cloud,

2 Chronicles 6:41
"Now arise, LORD God, and come to your resting place, you and the ark of your might. May your priests, LORD God, be clothed with salvation, may your faithful people rejoice in your **goodness**."

2 Chronicles 7:3
When all the Israelites saw the fire coming down and the glory of the LORD above the temple, they knelt on the pavement with their faces to the ground, and they worshiped and gave thanks to the LORD, saying, "He is **good**; his love endures forever."

2 Chronicles 7:10
On the twenty-third day of the seventh month he sent the people to their homes, joyful and glad in heart for the **good** things the LORD had done for David and Solomon and for his people Israel.

2 Chronicles 30:18
But Hezekiah prayed for them, saying, "May the LORD, who is **good**, pardon everyone

Ezra 3:11
With praise and thanksgiving they sang to the LORD: "He is **good**; his love toward Israel endures forever."

Nehemiah 9:20
You gave your **good** Spirit to instruct them. You did not withhold your manna from their mouths, and you gave them water for their thirst.

Nehemiah 9:25
They captured fortified cities and fertile land; they took possession of houses filled with all kinds of good things, wells already dug, vineyards, olive groves and fruit trees in abundance. They ate to the full and were well-nourished; they reveled in your great **goodness**.

Nehemiah 9:35
Even while they were in their kingdom, enjoying your great **goodness** to them in the spacious and fertile land you gave them, they did not serve you or turn from their evil ways.

Job 2:10
He replied, "You are talking like a foolish woman. Shall we accept **good** from God, and not trouble?" In all this, Job did not sin in what he said.

Psalm 13:6
I will sing the LORD's praise, for he has been **good** to me.

Psalm 23:6
Surely your **goodness** and love will follow me all the days of my life, and I will dwell in the house of the LORD forever.

Psalm 25:7
Do not remember the sins of my youth and my rebellious ways; according to your love remember me, for you, LORD, are **good**.

Psalm 25:8
Good and upright is the LORD; therefore he instructs sinners in his ways.

Psalm 27:13
I remain confident of this: I will see the **goodness** of the LORD in the land of the living.

Psalm 34:8
Taste and see that the LORD is **good**; blessed is the one who takes refuge in him.

God is Good

Psalm 34:10
The lions may grow weak and hungry, but those who seek the LORD lack no **good** thing.

Psalm 52:9
For what you have done I will always praise you in the presence of your faithful people. And I will hope in your name, for your name is **good**.

Psalm 73:1
Surely God is **good** to Israel, to those who are pure in heart.

Psalm 85:12
The LORD will indeed give what is **good**, and our land will yield its harvest.

Psalm 86:5
You, Lord, are forgiving and **good**, abounding in love to all who call to you.

Psalm 86:17
Give me a sign of your **goodness**, that my enemies may see it and be put to shame, for you, LORD, have helped me and comforted me.

Psalm 100:5
For the LORD is **good** and his love endures forever; his faithfulness continues through all generations.

Psalm 103:5
who satisfies your desires with **good** things so that your youth is renewed like the eagle's.

Psalm 104:28
When you give it to them, they gather it up; when you open your hand, they are satisfied with **good** things.

Psalm 106:1
Praise the LORD. Give thanks to the LORD, for he is **good**; his love endures forever.

Psalm 107:1
Give thanks to the LORD, for he is **good**; his love endures forever.

Psalm 107:9
for he satisfies the thirsty and fills the hungry with **good** things.

Psalm 116:7
Return to your rest, my soul, for the LORD has been **good** to you.

Psalm 116:12
What shall I return to the LORD for all his **goodness** to me?

Psalm 118:1
Give thanks to the LORD, for he is **good**; his love endures forever.

Psalm 118:29
Give thanks to the LORD, for he is **good**; his love endures forever.

Psalm 119:39
Take away the disgrace I dread, for your laws are **good**.

Psalm 119:65
Do **good** to your servant according to your word, LORD.

Psalm 119:68
You are **good**, and what you do is **good**; teach me your decrees.

Psalm 135:3
Praise the LORD, for the LORD is **good**; sing praise to his name, for that is pleasant.

Psalm 136:1
Give thanks to the LORD, for he is **good**. His love endures forever.

Psalm 142:7
Set me free from my prison, that I may praise your name. Then the righteous will gather about me because of your **goodness** to me.

Psalm 143:10
Teach me to do your will, for you are my God; may your **good** Spirit lead me on level ground.

Psalm 145:7
They celebrate your abundant **goodness** and joyfully sing of your righteousness.

Psalm 145:9
The LORD is **good** to all; he has compassion on all he has made.

Isaiah 61:1
The Spirit of the Sovereign LORD is on me, because the LORD has anointed me to proclaim **good** news to the poor. He has sent me to bind up the brokenhearted, to proclaim freedom for the captives and release from darkness for the prisoners,

Isaiah 63:7
I will tell of the kindnesses of the LORD, the deeds for which he is to be praised, according to all the LORD has done for us—yes, the many **good** things he has done for Israel, according to his compassion and many kindnesses.

Jeremiah 15:11
The LORD said, "Surely I will deliver you for a **good** purpose; surely I will make your enemies plead with you in times of disaster and times of distress.

Jeremiah 18:10
and if it does evil in my sight and does not obey me, then I will reconsider the **good** I had intended to do for it.

Jeremiah 24:6
My eyes will watch over them for their **good**, and I will bring them back to this land. I will build them up and not tear them down; I will plant them and not uproot them.

Jeremiah 29:10
This is what the LORD says: "When seventy years are completed for Babylon, I will come to you and fulfill my **good** promise to bring you back to this place.

Jeremiah 32:40
I will make an everlasting covenant with them: I will never stop doing **good** to them, and I will inspire them to fear me, so that they will never turn away from me.

Jeremiah 32:41
I will rejoice in doing them **good** and will assuredly plant them in this land with all my heart and soul.

Jeremiah 33:9
Then this city will bring me renown, joy, praise and honor before all nations on earth that hear of all the **good** things I do for it; and they will be in awe and will tremble at the abundant prosperity and peace I provide for it.'

Jeremiah 33:11
the sounds of joy and gladness, the voices of bride and bridegroom, and the voices of those who bring thank offerings to the house of the LORD, saying, "Give thanks to the LORD Almighty, for the LORD is **good**; his love endures forever." For I will restore the fortunes of the land as they were before,' says the LORD.

Jeremiah 33:14
"'The days are coming,' declares the LORD, 'when I will fulfill the **good** promise I made to the people of Israel and Judah.

Lamentations 3:25
The LORD is **good** to those whose hope is in him, to the one who seeks him;

God is Good

Lamentations 3:38
Is it not from the mouth of the Most High that both calamities and **good** things come?

Micah 6:8
He has shown you, O mortal, what is **good**. And what does the LORD require of you? To act justly and to love mercy and to walk humbly with your God.

Nahum 1:7
The LORD is **good**, a refuge in times of trouble. He cares for those who trust in him,

Zechariah 8:15
"so now I have determined to do **good** again to Jerusalem and Judah. Do not be afraid.

Matthew 7:11
If you, then, though you are evil, know how to give good gifts to your children, how much more will your Father in heaven give **good** gifts to those who ask him!

Matthew 9:35
Jesus went through all the towns and villages, teaching in their synagogues, proclaiming the **good** news of the kingdom and healing every disease and sickness.

Matthew 12:12
How much more valuable is a person than a sheep! Therefore it is lawful to do **good** on the Sabbath."

Matthew 19:17
"Why do you ask me about what is good?" Jesus replied. "There is only One who is **good**. If you want to enter life, keep the commandments."

Mark 1:14
After John was put in prison, Jesus went into Galilee, proclaiming the **good** news of God.

Mark 1:15
"The time has come," he said. "The kingdom of God has come near. Repent and believe the **good** news!"

Mark 3:4
Then Jesus asked them, "Which is lawful on the Sabbath: to do **good** or to do evil, to save life or to kill?" But they remained silent.

Mark 10:17
As Jesus started on his way, a man ran up to him and fell on his knees before him. "**Good** teacher," he asked, "what must I do to inherit eternal life?"

Mark 10:18
"Why do you call me **good**?" Jesus answered. "No one is **good**—except God alone.

Luke 1:53
He has filled the hungry with **good** things but has sent the rich away empty.

Luke 4:18
"The Spirit of the Lord is on me, because he has anointed me to proclaim **good** news to the poor. He has sent me to proclaim freedom for the prisoners and recovery of sight for the blind, to set the oppressed free,

Luke 4:43
But he said, "I must proclaim the **good** news of the kingdom of God to the other towns also, because that is why I was sent."

Luke 18:18
A certain ruler asked him, "**Good** teacher, what must I do to inherit eternal life?"

Luke 18:19
"Why do you call me **good**?" Jesus answered. "No one is **good**—except God alone.

Luke 20:1
One day as Jesus was teaching the people in the temple courts and proclaiming the **good** news, the chief priests and the teachers of the law, together with the elders, came up to him.

John 10:11
"I am the **good** shepherd. The **good** shepherd lays down his life for the sheep.

John 10:14
"I am the **good** shepherd; I know my sheep and my sheep know me—

John 10:32
but Jesus said to them, "I have shown you many **good** works from the Father.

Acts 13:32
"We tell you the **good** news: What God promised our ancestors

Romans 8:28
And we know that in all things God works for the **good** of those who love him, who have been called according to his purpose.

Romans 12:2
Do not conform to the pattern of this world, but be transformed by the renewing of your mind. Then you will be able to test and approve what God's will is—his **good**, pleasing and perfect will.

Galatians 5:22
But the fruit of the Spirit is love, joy, peace, forbearance, kindness, **goodness**, faithfulness,

Ephesians 1:9
he made known to us the mystery of his will according to his **good** pleasure, which he purposed in Christ,

Philippians 1:6
being confident of this, that he who began a **good** work in you will carry it on to completion until the day of Christ Jesus.

Philippians 2:13
for it is God who works in you to will and to act in order to fulfill his **good** purpose.

1 Timothy 4:4
For everything God created is **good**, and nothing is to be rejected if it is received with thanksgiving,

Hebrews 6:5
who have tasted the **goodness** of the word of God and the powers of the coming age

Hebrews 9:11
But when Christ came as high priest of the **good** things that are now already here, he went through the greater and more perfect tabernacle that is not made with human hands, that is to say, is not a part of this creation.

Hebrews 10:1
[*Christ's Sacrifice Once for All*] The law is only a shadow of the **good** things that are coming—not the realities themselves. For this reason it can never, by the same sacrifices repeated endlessly year after year, make perfect those who draw near to worship.

Hebrews 12:10
They disciplined us for a little while as they thought best; but God disciplines us for our **good**, in order that we may share in his holiness.

James 1:17
Every **good** and perfect gift is from above, coming down from the Father of the heavenly lights, who does not change like shifting shadows.

God is Good

James 3:17
But the wisdom that comes from heaven is first of all pure; then peace-loving, considerate, submissive, full of mercy and **good** fruit, impartial and sincere.

1 Peter 2:3
now that you have tasted that the Lord is **good**.

2 Peter 1:3
His divine power has given us everything we need for a godly life through our knowledge of him who called us by his own glory and **goodness**.

God is Gracious

Gracious:
Divine grace and mercy; Being kind and pleasant, especially to subordinates.

*The Lord is **gracious** and compassionate, slow to anger and rich in love.*

- Psalm 145:8

God is Gracious

1. DEFINE GRACIOUS USING YOUR OWN WORDS, SYNONYMS, OR DESCRIPTIONS:

_____

_____

_____

2. FIND THE MANY SCRIPTURES WHERE GOD'S GRACIOUSNESS AND COMPASSION ARE MENTIONED TOGETHER. WHAT IS THE SIGNIFICANCE OF THIS?

_____

_____

_____

3. DO YOU HAVE ANY OBSERVATIONS ABOUT THIS CHARACTER TRAIT OF GOD OR WHY GOD WANTS US TO KNOW THAT HE IS GRACIOUS?

_____

_____

_____

_____

_____

There will always be the seeming contradition--that while God's saving grace is always and forever free, it is never, never cheap.

- Herman Gockel

NOTES:

God is Gracious

Genesis 21:1
[*The Birth of Isaac*] Now the LORD was **gracious** to Sarah as he had said, and the LORD did for Sarah what he had promised.

Genesis 33:5
Then Esau looked up and saw the women and children. "Who are these with you?" he asked. Jacob answered, "They are the children God has **graciously** given your servant."

Genesis 33:11
Please accept the present that was brought to you, for God has been **gracious** to me and I have all I need." And because Jacob insisted, Esau accepted it.

Exodus 34:6
And he passed in front of Moses, proclaiming, "The LORD, the LORD, the compassionate and **gracious** God, slow to anger, abounding in love and faithfulness,

1 Samuel 2:21
And the LORD was **gracious** to Hannah; she gave birth to three sons and two daughters. Meanwhile, the boy Samuel grew up in the presence of the LORD.

2 Samuel 12:22
He answered, "While the child was still alive, I fasted and wept. I thought, 'Who knows? The LORD may be **gracious** to me and let the child live.'

2 Kings 13:23
But the LORD was **gracious** to them and had compassion and showed concern for them because of his covenant with Abraham, Isaac and Jacob. To this day he has been unwilling to destroy them or banish them from his presence.

2 Chronicles 30:9
If you return to the LORD, then your fellow Israelites and your children will be shown compassion by their captors and will return to this land, for the LORD your God is **gracious** and compassionate. He will not turn his face from you if you return to him."

Ezra 7:9
He had begun his journey from Babylon on the first day of the first month, and he arrived in Jerusalem on the first day of the fifth month, for the **gracious** hand of his God was on him.

Ezra 8:18
Because the **gracious** hand of our God was on us,

Ezra 8:22
I was ashamed to ask the king for soldiers and horsemen to protect us from enemies on the road, because we had told the king, "The **gracious** hand of our God is on everyone who looks to him, but his great anger is against all who forsake him."

Ezra 9:8
"But now, for a brief moment, the LORD our God has been **gracious** in leaving us a remnant and giving us a firm place in his sanctuary, and so our God gives light to our eyes and a little relief in our bondage.

Nehemiah 2:8
And because the **gracious** hand of my God was on me, the king granted my requests.

Nehemiah 2:18
I also told them about the **gracious** hand of my God on me and what the king had said to me. They replied, "Let us start rebuilding." So they began this good work.

Nehemiah 9:17
They refused to listen and failed to remember the miracles you performed among them. They became stiff-necked and in their rebellion appointed a leader in order to return to their slavery. But you are a forgiving God, **gracious** and compassionate, slow to anger and abounding in love. Therefore you did not desert them,

God is Gracious

Nehemiah 9:31
But in your great mercy you did not put an end to them or abandon them, for you are a **gracious** and merciful God.

Psalm 25:16
Turn to me and be **gracious** to me, for I am lonely and afflicted.

Psalm 67:1
May God be **gracious** to us and bless us and make his face shine on us—

Psalm 86:15
But you, Lord, are a compassionate and **gracious** God, slow to anger, abounding in love and faithfulness.

Psalm 103:8
The LORD is compassionate and **gracious**, slow to anger, abounding in love.

Psalm 111:4
He has caused his wonders to be remembered; the LORD is **gracious** and compassionate.

Psalm 116:5
The LORD is **gracious** and righteous; our God is full of compassion.

Psalm 119:29
Keep me from deceitful ways; be **gracious** to me and teach me your law.

Psalm 119:58
I have sought your face with all my heart; be **gracious** to me according to your promise.

Psalm 145:8
The LORD is **gracious** and compassionate, slow to anger and rich in love.

Isaiah 30:18
Yet the LORD longs to be **gracious** to you; therefore he will rise up to show you compassion. For the LORD is a God of justice. Blessed are all who wait for him!

Isaiah 30:19
People of Zion, who live in Jerusalem, you will weep no more. How **gracious** he will be when you cry for help! As soon as he hears, he will answer you.

Isaiah 33:2
LORD, be **gracious** to us; we long for you. Be our strength every morning, our salvation in time of distress.

Joel 2:13
Rend your heart and not your garments. Return to the LORD your God, for he is **gracious** and compassionate, slow to anger and abounding in love, and he relents from sending calamity.

Jonah 4:2
He prayed to the LORD, "Isn't this what I said, LORD, when I was still at home? That is what I tried to forestall by fleeing to Tarshish. I knew that you are a **gracious** and compassionate God, slow to anger and abounding in love, a God who relents from sending calamity.

Malachi 1:9
"Now plead with God to be **gracious** to us. With such offerings from your hands, will he accept you?"—says the LORD Almighty.

Luke 4:22
All spoke well of him and were amazed at the **gracious** words that came from his lips. "Isn't this Joseph's son?" they asked.

God is Gracious

Acts 27:24
and said, 'Do not be afraid, Paul. You must stand trial before Caesar; and God has **graciously** given you the lives of all who sail with you.'

Romans 8:32
He who did not spare his own Son, but gave him up for us all—how will he not also, along with him, **graciously** give us all things?

God is Great
Able to Do Great Things
Possessing Great Qualities and Characteristics

Great:
Above average in size, amount or intensity; of remarkable ability or character; Someone or something of huge importance.

*Yours, Lord, is the **greatness** and the power and the glory and the majesty and the splendor, for everything in heaven and earth is yours. Yours, Lord, is the kingdom; you are exalted as head over all.*

- *I Chronicles 29:11*

God is Great

1. DEFINE GREAT USING YOUR OWN WORDS, SYNONYMS, OR DESCRIPTIONS:

_____

_____

_____

3. IN THE FOLLOWING VERSES, WE ARE TOLD NOT TO BE AFRAID BECAUSE GOD IS GREATER THAN ANY OTHER GOD: Deuteronomy 7:21; 2 Chronicles 32:7; Nehemiah 4:14 and I John 4:4. THEN IN THESE VERSES WE ARE TOLD TO BE ASSURED GOD IS GREATER THAN AND ABOVE ALL OTHERS, INCLUDING OTHER GODS: Exodus 18:11; 1 Chronicles 16:25; 1 Chronicles 29:11; 2 Chronicles 2:5; Psalm 47:2; Psalm 95:3; Psalm 96:4; Psalm 135:5; Jeremiah 10:6 and Malachi 1:14. WHY IS THIS SUCH AN IMPORTANT THEME?

_____

_____

_____

4. SEVERAL TIMES GOD SAYS HE SHOWS HIS GREAT POWER WITH HIS OUTSTRETCHED/STRONG/MIGHTY HAND OR ARM. WHAT IS THE SIGNIFICANCE OF HIS HAND OR ARM HERE?

_____

_____

_____

5. DO YOU HAVE ANY OBSERVATIONS ABOUT THIS CHARACTER TRAIT OF GOD OR WHY GOD WANTS US TO KNOW THAT HE IS GREAT AND ABLE TO DO GREAT THINGS?

_____

_____

_____

_____

_____

For those who believe, no proof is necessary.
For those who don't believe, no proof is possible.
- Stuart Chase

NOTES:

God is Great

Exodus 15:7
"In the **greatness** of your majesty you threw down those who opposed you.

Exodus 18:11
Now I know that the LORD is **greater** than all other gods,

Numbers 14:19
In accordance with your **great** love, forgive the sin of these people, just as you have pardoned them from the time they left Egypt until now."

Deuteronomy 3:24
"Sovereign LORD, you have begun to show to your servant your **greatness** and your strong hand. For what god is there in heaven or on earth who can do the deeds and mighty works you do?

Deuteronomy 4:34
Has any god ever tried to take for himself one nation out of another nation, by testings, by signs and wonders, by war, by a mighty hand and an outstretched arm, or by **great** and awesome deeds, like all the things the LORD your God did for you in Egypt before your very eyes?

Deuteronomy 4:36
From heaven he made you hear his voice to discipline you. On earth he showed you his **great** fire, and you heard his words from out of the fire.

Deuteronomy 4:37
Because he loved your ancestors and chose their descendants after them, he brought you out of Egypt by his Presence and his **great** strength,

Deuteronomy 5:25
This **great** fire will consume us, and we will die if we hear the voice of the LORD our God any longer.

Deuteronomy 6:22
Before our eyes the LORD sent signs and wonders—**great** and terrible—on Egypt and Pharaoh and his whole household.

Deuteronomy 7:19
You saw with your own eyes the **great** trials, the signs and wonders, the mighty hand and outstretched arm, with which the LORD your God brought you out.

Deuteronomy 7:21
Do not be terrified by them, for the LORD your God, who is among you, is a **great** and awesome God.

Deuteronomy 9:26
I prayed to the LORD and said, "Sovereign LORD, do not destroy your people, your own inheritance that you redeemed by your **great** power and brought out of Egypt with a mighty hand.

Deuteronomy 9:29
But they are your people, your inheritance that you brought out by your **great** power and your outstretched arm."

Deuteronomy 10:17
For the LORD your God is God of gods and Lord of lords, the **great** God, mighty and awesome, who shows no partiality and accepts no bribes.

Deuteronomy 10:21
He is the one you praise; he is your God, who performed for you those **great** and awesome wonders you saw with your own eyes.

Deuteronomy 11:7
But it was your own eyes that saw all these **great** things the LORD has done.

Deuteronomy 26:8
So the LORD brought us out of Egypt with a mighty hand and an outstretched arm, with **great** terror and with signs and wonders.

Deuteronomy 29:3
With your own eyes you saw those great trials, those signs and **great** wonders.

Deuteronomy 29:28
In furious anger and in **great** wrath the LORD uprooted them from their land and thrust them into another land, as it is now."

Deuteronomy 32:3
I will proclaim the name of the LORD. Oh, praise the **greatness** of our God!

Joshua 24:17
It was the LORD our God himself who brought us and our parents up out of Egypt, from that land of slavery, and performed those **great** signs before our eyes.

Judges 2:7
The people served the LORD throughout the lifetime of Joshua and of the elders who outlived him and who had seen all the **great** things the LORD had done for Israel.

1 Samuel 12:16
"Now then, stand still and see this **great** thing the LORD is about to do before your eyes!

1 Samuel 12:22
For the sake of his **great** name the LORD will not reject his people, because the LORD was pleased to make you his own.

1 Samuel 12:24
But be sure to fear the LORD and serve him faithfully with all your heart; consider what **great** things he has done for you.

2 Samuel 7:22
"How **great** you are, Sovereign LORD! There is no one like you, and there is no God but you,

2 Samuel 7:23
And who is like your people Israel—the one nation on earth that God went out to redeem as a people for himself, and to make a name for himself, and to perform **great** and awesome wonders by driving out nations and their gods from before your people, whom you redeemed from Egypt?

2 Samuel 7:26
so that your name will be **great** forever. Then people will say, 'The LORD Almighty is God over Israel!'

2 Samuel 22:51
"He gives his king **great** victories; he shows unfailing kindness to his anointed, to David and his descendants forever."

2 Samuel 23:12
and the LORD brought about a **great** victory.

2 Samuel 24:14
"I am in deep distress. Let us fall into the hands of the LORD, for his mercy is **great**;

1 Kings 3:6
"You have shown great kindness to your servant, my father David, because he was faithful to you and righteous and upright in heart. You have continued this **great** kindness to him and have given him a son to sit on his throne this very day.

1 Kings 4:29
God gave Solomon wisdom and very **great** insight, and a breadth of understanding as measureless as the sand on the seashore.

1 Kings 8:42
for they will hear of your **great** name and your mighty hand and your outstretched arm—when they come and pray toward this temple,

1 Chronicles 11:14
and the LORD brought about a **great** victory.

God is Great

1 Chronicles 16:25
For **great** is the LORD and most worthy of praise; he is to be feared above all gods.

1 Chronicles 17:19
For the sake of your servant and according to your will, you have done this **great** thing and made known all these great promises.

1 Chronicles 17:21
And who is like your people Israel—the one nation on earth whose God went out to redeem a people for himself, and to make a name for yourself, and to perform **great** and awesome wonders by driving out nations from before your people, whom you redeemed from Egypt?

1 Chronicles 17:24
so that it will be established and that your name will be **great** forever. Then people will say, 'The LORD Almighty, the God over Israel, is Israel's God!'

1 Chronicles 21:13
David said to Gad, "I am in deep distress. Let me fall into the hands of the LORD, for his mercy is very **great**;

1 Chronicles 29:11
Yours, LORD, is the **greatness** and the power and the glory and the majesty and the splendor, for everything in heaven and earth is yours. Yours, LORD, is the kingdom; you are exalted as head over all.

2 Chronicles 1:8
Solomon answered God, "You have shown **great** kindness to David my father and have made me king in his place.

2 Chronicles 2:5
"The temple I am going to build will be great, because our God is **greater** than all other gods.

2 Chronicles 6:32
"As for the foreigner who does not belong to your people Israel but has come from a distant land because of your **great** name and your mighty hand and your outstretched arm—when they come and pray toward this temple,

2 Chronicles 6:42
LORD God, do not reject your anointed one. Remember the **great** love promised to David your servant."

2 Chronicles 32:7
"Be strong and courageous. Do not be afraid or discouraged because of the king of Assyria and the vast army with him, for there is a **greater** power with us than with him.

Ezra 5:8
The king should know that we went to the district of Judah, to the temple of the **great** God.

Ezra 8:22
"The gracious hand of our God is on everyone who looks to him, but his **great** anger is against all who forsake him."

Nehemiah 1:5
Then I said: "LORD, the God of heaven, the **great** and awesome God, who keeps his covenant of love with those who love him and keep his commandments,

Nehemiah 1:10
"They are your servants and your people, whom you redeemed by your **great** strength and your mighty hand.

Nehemiah 4:14
After I looked things over, I stood up and said to the nobles, the officials and the rest of the people, "Don't be afraid of them. Remember the Lord, who is **great** and awesome,

Nehemiah 8:6
Ezra praised the LORD, the **great** God; and all the people lifted their hands and responded, "Amen! Amen!" Then they bowed down and worshiped the LORD with their faces to the ground.

Nehemiah 9:19
"Because of your **great** compassion you did not abandon them in the wilderness. By day the pillar of cloud did not fail to guide them on their path, nor the pillar of fire by night to shine on the way they were to take.

Nehemiah 9:25
They ate to the full and were well-nourished; they reveled in your **great** goodness.

Nehemiah 9:27
But when they were oppressed they cried out to you. From heaven you heard them, and in your **great** compassion you gave them deliverers, who rescued them from the hand of their enemies.

Nehemiah 9:31
But in your **great** mercy you did not put an end to them or abandon them, for you are a gracious and merciful God.

Nehemiah 9:32
"Now therefore, our God, the **great** God, mighty and awesome, who keeps his covenant of love,

Nehemiah 9:35
Even while they were in their kingdom, enjoying your **great** goodness to them in the spacious and fertile land you gave them, they did not serve you or turn from their evil ways.

Nehemiah 13:22
Remember me for this also, my God, and show mercy to me according to your **great** love.

Job 12:23
He makes nations **great,** and destroys them; he enlarges nations, and disperses them.

Job 36:26
How **great** is God—beyond our understanding! The number of his years is past finding out.

Job 37:5
God's voice thunders in marvelous ways; he does **great** things beyond our understanding.

Job 37:23
The Almighty is beyond our reach and exalted in power; in his justice and **great** righteousness,

Psalm 5:7
But I, by your **great** love, can come into your house; in reverence I bow down toward your holy temple.

Psalm 17:7
Show me the wonders of your **great** love, you who save by your right hand those who take refuge in you from their foes.

Psalm 18:14
He shot his arrows and scattered the enemy, with **great** bolts of lightning he routed them.

Psalm 18:50
He gives his king **great** victories; he shows unfailing love to his anointed, to David and to his descendants forever.

Psalm 25:6
Remember, LORD, your **great** mercy and love, for they are from of old.

Psalm 40:16
But may all who seek you rejoice and be glad in you; may those who long for your saving help always say, "The LORD is **great!**"

Psalm 47:2
For the LORD Most High is awesome, the **great** King over all the earth.

Psalm 47:9
The nobles of the nations assemble as the people of the God of Abraham, for the kings of the earth belong to God; he is **greatly** exalted.

God is Great

Psalm 48:1
Great is the LORD, and most worthy of praise, in the city of our God, his holy mountain.

Psalm 48:2
Beautiful in its loftiness, the joy of the whole earth, like the heights of Zaphon is Mount Zion, the city of the **Great** King.

Psalm 51:1
Have mercy on me, O God, according to your unfailing love; according to your **great** compassion blot out my transgressions.

Psalm 57:10
For **great** is your love, reaching to the heavens; your faithfulness reaches to the skies.

Psalm 66:3
Say to God, "How awesome are your deeds! So **great** is your power that your enemies cringe before you.

Psalm 69:13
But I pray to you, LORD, in the time of your favor; in your **great** love, O God, answer me with your sure salvation.

Psalm 69:16
Answer me, LORD, out of the goodness of your love; in your **great** mercy turn to me.

Psalm 70:4
But may all who seek you rejoice and be glad in you; may those who long for your saving help always say, "The LORD is **great**!"

Psalm 71:19
Your righteousness, God, reaches to the heavens, you who have done **great** things. Who is like you, God?

Psalm 76:1
God is renowned in Judah; in Israel his name is **great**.

Psalm 77:13
Your ways, God, are holy. What god is as **great** as our God?

Psalm 86:10
For you are **great** and do marvelous deeds; you alone are God.

Psalm 86:13
For **great** is your love toward me; you have delivered me from the depths,

Psalm 89:1
I will sing of the LORD's **great** love forever; with my mouth I will make your faithfulness known through all generations.

Psalm 90:11
If only we knew the power of your anger! Your wrath is as **great** as the fear that is your due.

Psalm 92:5
How **great** are your works, LORD, how profound your thoughts!

Psalm 95:3
For the LORD is the **great** God, the **great** King above all gods.

Psalm 96:4
For **great** is the LORD and most worthy of praise; he is to be feared above all gods.

Psalm 99:2
Great is the LORD in Zion; he is exalted over all the nations.

Psalm 99:3
Let them praise your **great** and awesome name— he is holy.

Psalm 102:10
because of your **great** wrath, for you have taken me up and thrown me aside.

Psalm 103:11
For as high as the heavens are above the earth, so **great** is his love for those who fear him;

Psalm 104:1
Praise the LORD, my soul. LORD my God, you are very **great**; you are clothed with splendor and majesty.

Psalm 106:21
They forgot the God who saved them, who had done **great** things in Egypt,

Psalm 106:45
for their sake he remembered his covenant and out of his **great** love he relented.

Psalm 108:4
For **great** is your love, higher than the heavens; your faithfulness reaches to the skies.

Psalm 111:2
Great are the works of the LORD; they are pondered by all who delight in them.

Psalm 117:2
For **great** is his love toward us, and the faithfulness of the LORD endures forever.

Psalm 119:156
Your compassion, LORD, is **great**; preserve my life according to your laws.

Psalm 126:2
Then it was said among the nations, "The LORD has done **great** things for them."

Psalm 126:3
The LORD has done **great** things for us, and we are filled with joy.

Psalm 135:5
I know that the LORD is **great**, that our Lord is **greater** than all gods.

Psalm 136:4
to him who alone does **great** wonders, His love endures forever.

Psalm 136:7
who made the **great** lights— His love endures forever.

Psalm 138:5
May they sing of the ways of the LORD, for the glory of the LORD is **great**.

Psalm 145:3
Great is the LORD and most worthy of praise; his **greatness** no one can fathom.

Psalm 145:6
They tell of the power of your awesome works— and I will proclaim your **great** deeds.

Psalm 147:5
Great is our Lord and mighty in power; his understanding has no limit.

Psalm 150:2
Praise him for his acts of power; praise him for his surpassing **greatness**.

Isaiah 9:2
The people walking in darkness have seen a **great** light; on those living in the land of deep darkness a light has dawned.

God is Great

Isaiah 9:7
Of the **greatness** of his government and peace there will be no end. He will reign on David's throne and over his kingdom, establishing and upholding it with justice and righteousness from that time on and forever.

Isaiah 10:33
See, the Lord, the LORD Almighty, will lop off the boughs with **great** power.

Isaiah 12:6
Shout aloud and sing for joy, people of Zion, for **great** is the Holy One of Israel among you."

Isaiah 24:23
The moon will be dismayed, the sun ashamed; for the LORD Almighty will reign on Mount Zion and in Jerusalem, and before its elders—with **great** glory.

Isaiah 27:1
In that day, the LORD will punish with his sword— his fierce, **great** and powerful sword—

Isaiah 29:6
the LORD Almighty will come with thunder and earthquake and **great** noise, with windstorm and tempest and flames of a devouring fire.

Isaiah 40:26
Lift up your eyes and look to the heavens: Who created all these? He who brings out the starry host one by one and calls forth each of them by name. Because of his **great** power and mighty strength, not one of them is missing.

Isaiah 42:21
It pleased the LORD for the sake of his righteousness to make his law **great** and glorious.

Isaiah 63:1
Who is this coming from Edom, from Bozrah, with his garments stained crimson? Who is this, robed in splendor, striding forward in the **greatness** of his strength? "It is I, proclaiming victory, mighty to save."

Jeremiah 10:6
No one is like you, LORD; you are **great**, and your name is mighty in power.

Jeremiah 21:5
I myself will fight against you with an outstretched hand and a mighty arm in furious anger and in **great** wrath.

Jeremiah 27:5
With my **great** power and outstretched arm I made the earth and its people and the animals that are on it, and I give it to anyone I please.

Jeremiah 31:20
Is not Ephraim my dear son, the child in whom I delight? Though I often speak against him, I still remember him. Therefore my heart yearns for him; I have **great** compassion for him," declares the LORD.

Jeremiah 32:17
"Ah, Sovereign LORD, you have made the heavens and the earth by your **great** power and outstretched arm. Nothing is too hard for you.

Jeremiah 32:18
You show love to thousands but bring the punishment for the parents' sins into the laps of their children after them. **Great** and mighty God, whose name is the LORD Almighty,

Jeremiah 32:19
great are your purposes and mighty are your deeds. Your eyes are open to the ways of all mankind; you reward each person according to their conduct and as their deeds deserve.

Jeremiah 32:21
You brought your people Israel out of Egypt with signs and wonders, by a mighty hand and an outstretched arm and with **great** terror.

Jeremiah 32:37
I will surely gather them from all the lands where I banish them in my furious anger and **great** wrath; I will bring them back to this place and let them live in safety.

Jeremiah 33:3
'Call to me and I will answer you and tell you **great** and unsearchable things you do not know.'

Jeremiah 36:7
Perhaps they will bring their petition before the LORD and will each turn from their wicked ways, for the anger and wrath pronounced against this people by the LORD are **great**."

Jeremiah 44:2
"This is what the LORD Almighty, the God of Israel, says: You saw the **great** disaster I brought on Jerusalem and on all the towns of Judah. Today they lie deserted and in ruins

Jeremiah 44:26
But hear the word of the LORD, all you Jews living in Egypt: 'I swear by my **great** name,' says the LORD, 'that no one from Judah living anywhere in Egypt will ever again invoke my name or swear, "As surely as the Sovereign LORD lives."

Lamentations 3:22
Because of the LORD's **great** love we are not consumed, for his compassions never fail.

Lamentations 3:23
They are new every morning; **great** is your faithfulness.

Lamentations 3:32
Though he brings grief, he will show compassion, so **great** is his unfailing love.

Ezekiel 25:17
I will carry out **great** vengeance on them and punish them in my wrath. Then they will know that I am the LORD, when I take vengeance on them.'"

Ezekiel 36:23
I will show the holiness of my **great** name, which has been profaned among the nations, the name you have profaned among them. Then the nations will know that I am the LORD, declares the Sovereign LORD, when I am proved holy through you before their eyes.

Ezekiel 38:23
And so I will show my **greatness** and my holiness, and I will make myself known in the sight of many nations. Then they will know that I am the LORD.'

Daniel 2:45
"The **great** God has shown the king what will take place in the future. The dream is true and its interpretation is trustworthy."

Daniel 4:3
How **great** are his signs, how mighty his wonders! His kingdom is an eternal kingdom; his dominion endures from generation to generation.

Daniel 9:4
I prayed to the LORD my God and confessed: "Lord, the **great** and awesome God, who keeps his covenant of love with those who love him and keep his commandments,

Daniel 9:18
We do not make requests of you because we are righteous, but because of your **great** mercy.

Joel 2:11
The LORD thunders at the head of his army; his forces are beyond number, and mighty is the army that obeys his command. The day of the LORD is **great**; it is dreadful. Who can endure it?

Joel 2:21
Do not be afraid, land of Judah; be glad and rejoice. Surely the LORD has done **great** things!

God is Great

Joel 2:31
The sun will be turned to darkness and the moon to blood before the coming of the **great** and dreadful day of the LORD.

Jonah 1:4
Then the LORD sent a **great** wind on the sea, and such a violent storm arose that the ship threatened to break up.

Micah 5:4
He will stand and shepherd his flock in the strength of the LORD, in the majesty of the name of the LORD his God. And they will live securely, for then his **greatness** will reach to the ends of the earth.

Nahum 1:3
The LORD is slow to anger but **great** in power;

Zephaniah 1:14
The **great** day of the LORD is near— near and coming quickly.

Zephaniah 3:17
The LORD your God is with you, the Mighty Warrior who saves. He will take **great** delight in you; in his love he will no longer rebuke you, but will rejoice over you with singing."

Malachi 1:5
You will see it with your own eyes and say, 'Great is the LORD—even beyond the borders of Israel!'

Malachi 1:11
My name will be great among the nations, from where the sun rises to where it sets. In every place incense and pure offerings will be brought to me, because my name will be **great** among the nations," says the LORD Almighty.

Malachi 1:14
For I am a **great** king," says the LORD Almighty, "and my name is to be feared among the nations.

Malachi 4:5
"See, I will send the prophet Elijah to you before that **great** and dreadful day of the LORD comes.

Matthew 4:16
the people living in darkness have seen a **great** light; on those living in the land of the shadow of death a light has dawned."

Matthew 5:35
or by the earth, for it is his footstool; or by Jerusalem, for it is the city of the **Great** King.

Matthew 12:6
I tell you that something **greater** than the temple is here.

Matthew 12:41
The men of Nineveh will stand up at the judgment with this generation and condemn it; for they repented at the preaching of Jonah, and now something **greater** than Jonah is here.

Matthew 12:42
The Queen of the South will rise at the judgment with this generation and condemn it; for she came from the ends of the earth to listen to Solomon's wisdom, and now something **greater** than Solomon is here.

Matthew 24:30
"Then will appear the sign of the Son of Man in heaven. And then all the peoples of the earth will mourn when they see the Son of Man coming on the clouds of heaven, with power and **great** glory.

Mark 13:26
"At that time people will see the Son of Man coming in clouds with **great** power and glory.

Luke 1:32
He will be **great** and will be called the Son of the Most High. The Lord God will give him the throne of his father David,

Luke 1:49
for the Mighty One has done **great** things for me— holy is his name.

Luke 1:58
Her neighbors and relatives heard that the Lord had shown her **great** mercy, and they shared her joy.

Luke 9:43
And they were all amazed at the **greatness** of God.

Luke 11:31
The Queen of the South will rise at the judgment with the people of this generation and condemn them, for she came from the ends of the earth to listen to Solomon's wisdom; and now something **greater** than Solomon is here.

Luke 11:32
The men of Nineveh will stand up at the judgment with this generation and condemn it, for they repented at the preaching of Jonah; and now something **greater** than Jonah is here.

Luke 21:27
At that time they will see the Son of Man coming in a cloud with power and **great** glory.

John 5:20
For the Father loves the Son and shows him all he does. Yes, and he will show him even **greater** works than these, so that you will be amazed.

John 10:29
My Father, who has given them to me, is **greater** than all; no one can snatch them out of my Father's hand.

John 14:28
"You heard me say, 'I am going away and I am coming back to you.' If you loved me, you would be glad that I am going to the Father, for the Father is **greater** than I.

Acts 2:20
The sun will be turned to darkness and the moon to blood before the coming of the **great** and glorious day of the Lord.

Ephesians 1:19
and his incomparably **great** power for us who believe.

Ephesians 2:4
But because of his **great** love for us, God, who is rich in mercy,

Titus 2:13
while we wait for the blessed hope—the appearing of the glory of our **great** God and Savior, Jesus Christ,

Hebrews 2:3
how shall we escape if we ignore so **great** a salvation? This salvation, which was first announced by the Lord,

Hebrews 3:3
Jesus has been found worthy of **greater** honor than Moses, just as the builder of a house has greater honor than the house itself.

Hebrews 4:14
Therefore, since we have a **great** high priest who has ascended into heaven, Jesus the Son of God, let us hold firmly to the faith we profess.

Hebrews 6:13
When God made his promise to Abraham, since there was no one **greater** for him to swear by, he swore by himself,

Hebrews 10:21
and since we have a **great** priest over the house of God,

Hebrews 13:20
Now may the God of peace, who through the blood of the eternal covenant brought back from the dead our Lord Jesus, that **great** Shepherd of the sheep,

God is Great

1 Peter 1:3
Praise be to the God and Father of our Lord Jesus Christ! In his **great** mercy he has given us new birth into a living hope through the resurrection of Jesus Christ from the dead,

2 Peter 1:4
Through these he has given us his very **great** and precious promises, so that through them you may participate in the divine nature, having escaped the corruption in the world caused by evil desires.

1 John 3:1
See what **great** love the Father has lavished on us, that we should be called children of God!

1 John 3:20
If our hearts condemn us, we know that God is **greater** than our hearts, and he knows everything.

1 John 4:4
You, dear children, are from God and have overcome them, because the one who is in you is **greater** than the one who is in the world.

1 John 5:9
We accept human testimony, but God's testimony is **greater** because it is the testimony of God, which he has given about his Son.

Revelation 11:17
saying: "We give thanks to you, Lord God Almighty, the One who is and who was, because you have taken your **great** power and have begun to reign.

Revelation 15:1
I saw in heaven another **great** and marvelous sign:

Revelation 15:3
and sang the song of God's servant Moses and of the Lamb: "**Great** and marvelous are your deeds, Lord God Almighty. Just and true are your ways, King of the nations.

Revelation 19:17
And I saw an angel standing in the sun, who cried in a loud voice to all the birds flying in midair, "Come, gather together for the **great** supper of God,

God Our Guide

Guide:
Someone who shows others the way;
Leading or directing.

*I will lead the blind by ways they have not known, along unfamiliar paths I will **guide** them; I will turn the darkness into light before them and make the rough places smooth.*

- Isaiah 42:16

God Our Guide

1. DEFINE GUIDE USING YOUR OWN WORDS, SYNONYMS, OR DESCRIPTIONS:

_____

_____

_____

2. LIST CHARACTERISTICS OF A GUIDE (FOR EXAMPLE, A GUIDE LEADS BUT DOES NOT FORCE ONE'S DIRECTION).

_____

_____

_____

3. DO YOU HAVE ANY OBSERVATIONS ABOUT THIS CHARACTER TRAIT OF GOD OR WHY GOD WANTS US TO KNOW THAT HE IS OUR GUIDE?

_____

_____

_____

_____

_____

Our Father refreshes us on the journey with some pleasant inns,
but will not encourage us to mistake them for home.
- C. S. Lewis

NOTES:

God Our Guide

Exodus 13:21
By day the LORD went ahead of them in a pillar of cloud to **guide** them on their way and by night in a pillar of fire to give them light, so that they could travel by day or night.

Exodus 15:13
In your unfailing love you will lead the people you have redeemed. In your strength you will **guide** them to your holy dwelling.

Nehemiah 9:19
"Because of your great compassion you did not abandon them in the wilderness. By day the pillar of cloud did not fail to **guide** them on their path, nor the pillar of fire by night to shine on the way they were to take.

Psalm 23:3
He **guides** me along the right paths for his name's sake.

Psalm 25:5
Guide me in your truth and teach me, for you are God my Savior, and my hope is in you all day long.

Psalm 25:9
He **guides** the humble in what is right and teaches them his way.

Psalm 31:3
Since you are my rock and my fortress, for the sake of your name lead and **guide** me.

Psalm 48:14
For this God is our God for ever and ever; he will be our **guide** even to the end.

Psalm 67:4
May the nations be glad and sing for joy, for you rule the peoples with equity and **guide** the nations of the earth.

Psalm 73:24
You **guide** me with your counsel, and afterward you will take me into glory.

Psalm 78:14
He **guided** them with the cloud by day and with light from the fire all night.

Psalm 78:53
He **guided** them safely, so they were unafraid; but the sea engulfed their enemies.

Psalm 107:30
They were glad when it grew calm, and he **guided** them to their desired haven.

Psalm 139:10
even there your hand will **guide** me, your right hand will hold me fast.

Isaiah 42:16
I will lead the blind by ways they have not known, along unfamiliar paths I will **guide** them; I will turn the darkness into light before them and make the rough places smooth. These are the things I will do; I will not forsake them.

Isaiah 49:10
He who has compassion on them will **guide** them and lead them beside springs of water.

Isaiah 57:18
I have seen their ways, but I will heal them; I will **guide** them and restore comfort to Israel's mourners,

Isaiah 58:11
The LORD will **guide** you always; he will satisfy your needs in a sun-scorched land and will strengthen your frame.

Isaiah 63:14
This is how you **guided** your people to make for yourself a glorious name.

Luke 1:79
to shine on those living in darkness and in the shadow of death, to **guide** our feet into the path of peace."

John 16:13
But when he, the Spirit of truth, comes, he will **guide** you into all the truth.

God Our Healer
Able to Heal
Restoring Health

Healer:
One who cures what is sick, ill or broken.

*'But I will **restore you to health** and **heal** your wounds,' declares the Lord.*

- Jeremiah 30:17

God Our Healer

1. DEFINE HEALER USING YOUR OWN WORDS, SYNONYMS, OR DESCRIPTIONS:

_____
_____
_____

2. SOME OF JESUS' FIRST ACTIONS IN HIS MINISTRY WERE MIRACLES OF HEALING. WHY DO YOU THINK HE PRIORITIZED HEALING PEOPLE'S PHYSICAL CONDITION IN HIS MINISTRY?

_____
_____
_____

3. ISAIAH 53:5 SAYS, "BY HIS WOUNDS WE ARE _HEALED_" WHEN TALKING ABOUT JESUS' FUTURE DEATH BY BEATING AND CRUCIFIXION AND OUR CORRESPONDING FORGIVENESS OF SINS. WHERE ELSE DOES IT SEEM THAT HEALING AND FORGIVENESS ARE USED SYNONYMOUSLY?

_____
_____
_____

4. DO YOU HAVE ANY OBSERVATIONS ABOUT THIS CHARACTER TRAIT OF GOD OR WHY GOD WANTS US TO KNOW THAT HE IS OUR HEALER AND ABLE TO RESTORE OUR HEALTH?

_____
_____
_____
_____
_____

I feel the healing hands of God
Touch my heart and kiss my soul.
— Harley King

NOTES:

God Our Healer

Genesis 20:17
Then Abraham prayed to God, and God **healed** Abimelek,

Exodus 15:26
He said, "If you listen carefully to the LORD your God and do what is right in his eyes, if you pay attention to his commands and keep all his decrees, I will not bring on you any of the diseases I brought on the Egyptians, for I am the LORD, who **heals** you."

Numbers 12:13
So Moses cried out to the LORD, "Please, God, **heal** her!"

Deuteronomy 32:39
"See now that I myself am he! There is no god besides me. I put to death and I bring to life, I have wounded and I will **heal**, and no one can deliver out of my hand.

2 Kings 2:21
"This is what the LORD says: 'I have **healed** this water. Never again will it cause death or make the land unproductive.'"

2 Kings 20:5
"Go back and tell Hezekiah, the ruler of my people, 'This is what the LORD, the God of your father David, says: I have heard your prayer and seen your tears; I will **heal** you.

2 Chronicles 7:14
if my people, who are called by my name, will humble themselves and pray and seek my face and turn from their wicked ways, then I will hear from heaven, and I will forgive their sin and will **heal** their land.

2 Chronicles 30:20
And the LORD heard Hezekiah and **healed** the people.

Psalm 6:2
Have mercy on me, LORD, for I am faint; **heal** me, LORD, for my bones are in agony.

Psalm 30:2
LORD my God, I called to you for help, and you **healed** me.

Psalm 41:4
I said, "Have mercy on me, LORD; **heal** me,

Psalm 103:3
who forgives all your sins and **heals** all your diseases,

Psalm 107:20
He sent out his word and **healed** them; he rescued them from the grave.

Psalm 147:3
He **heals** the brokenhearted and binds up their wounds.

Isaiah 19:22
The LORD will strike Egypt with a plague; he will strike them and **heal** them. They will turn to the LORD, and he will respond to their pleas and **heal** them.

Isaiah 30:26
when the LORD binds up the bruises of his people and **heals** the wounds he inflicted.

Isaiah 38:16
Lord, by such things people live; and my spirit finds life in them too. You **restored me to health** and let me live.

Isaiah 53:5
But he was pierced for our transgressions, he was crushed for our iniquities; the punishment that brought us peace was on him, and by his wounds we are **healed**.

Isaiah 57:18
I have seen their ways, but I will **heal** them;

Isaiah 57:19
Peace, peace, to those far and near," says the LORD. "And I will **heal** them."

Jeremiah 17:14
Heal me, LORD, and I will be **healed**;

Jeremiah 30:17
But I will **restore you to health** and **heal** your wounds,' declares the LORD,

Jeremiah 33:6
"'Nevertheless, I will bring **health** and **healing** to it; I will **heal** my people and will let them enjoy abundant peace and security.

Hosea 6:1
"Come, let us return to the LORD. He has torn us to pieces but he will **heal** us; he has injured us but he will bind up our wounds.

Hosea 11:3
It was I who taught Ephraim to walk, taking them by the arms; but they did not realize it was I who **healed** them.

Hosea 14:4
"I will **heal** their waywardness and love them freely, for my anger has turned away from them.

Matthew 4:23
Jesus went throughout Galilee, teaching in their synagogues, proclaiming the good news of the kingdom, and **healing** every disease and sickness among the people.

Matthew 4:24
News about him spread all over Syria, and people brought to him all who were ill with various diseases, those suffering severe pain, the demon-possessed, those having seizures, and the paralyzed; and he **healed** them.

Matthew 8:13
Then Jesus said to the centurion, "Go! Let it be done just as you believed it would." And his servant was **healed** at that moment.

Matthew 8:16
When evening came, many who were demon-possessed were brought to him, and he drove out the spirits with a word and **healed** all the sick.

Matthew 9:22
Jesus turned and saw her. "Take heart, daughter," he said, "your faith has **healed** you." And the woman was **healed** at that moment.

Matthew 9:35
Jesus went through all the towns and villages, teaching in their synagogues, proclaiming the good news of the kingdom and **healing** every disease and sickness.

Matthew 10:1
Jesus called his twelve disciples to him and gave them authority to drive out impure spirits and to **heal** every disease and sickness.

Matthew 12:15
Jesus withdrew from that place. A large crowd followed him, and he **healed** all who were ill.

Matthew 12:22
Then they brought him a demon-possessed man who was blind and mute, and Jesus **healed** him, so that he could both talk and see.

God Our Healer

Matthew 13:15
For this people's heart has become calloused; they hardly hear with their ears, and they have closed their eyes. Otherwise they might see with their eyes, hear with their ears, understand with their hearts and turn, and I would **heal** them.'

Matthew 14:14
When Jesus landed and saw a large crowd, he had compassion on them and **healed** their sick.

Matthew 14:36
and begged him to let the sick just touch the edge of his cloak, and all who touched it were **healed**.

Matthew 15:28
Then Jesus said to her, "Woman, you have great faith! Your request is granted." And her daughter was **healed** at that moment.

Matthew 15:30
Great crowds came to him, bringing the lame, the blind, the crippled, the mute and many others, and laid them at his feet; and he **healed** them.

Matthew 17:18
Jesus rebuked the demon, and it came out of the boy, and he was **healed** at that moment.

Matthew 19:2
Large crowds followed him, and he **healed** them there.

Matthew 21:14
The blind and the lame came to him at the temple, and he **healed** them.

Mark 1:34
and Jesus **healed** many who had various diseases.

Mark 3:10
For he had **healed** many, so that those with diseases were pushing forward to touch him.

Mark 5:34
He said to her, "Daughter, your faith has **healed** you. Go in peace and be freed from your suffering."

Mark 6:5
He could not do any miracles there, except lay his hands on a few sick people and **heal** them.

Mark 6:13
They drove out many demons and anointed many sick people with oil and **healed** them.

Mark 6:56
And wherever he went—into villages, towns or countryside—they placed the sick in the marketplaces. They begged him to let them touch even the edge of his cloak, and all who touched it were **healed**.

Mark 10:52
"Go," said Jesus, "your faith has **healed** you."

Luke 4:40
At sunset, the people brought to Jesus all who had various kinds of sickness, and laying his hands on each one, he **healed** them.

Luke 5:17
And the power of the Lord was with Jesus to **heal** the sick.

Luke 6:19
and the people all tried to touch him, because power was coming from him and **healing** them all.

Luke 8:47
Then the woman, seeing that she could not go unnoticed, came trembling and fell at his feet. In the presence of all the people, she told why she had touched him and how she had been instantly **healed**.

Luke 8:48
Then he said to her, "Daughter, your faith has **healed** you. Go in peace."

Luke 8:50
Hearing this, Jesus said to Jairus, "Don't be afraid; just believe, and she will be **healed**."

Luke 9:2
and he sent them out to proclaim the kingdom of God and to **heal** the sick.

Luke 9:11
but the crowds learned about it and followed him. He welcomed them and spoke to them about the kingdom of God, and **healed** those who needed healing.

Luke 9:42
Even while the boy was coming, the demon threw him to the ground in a convulsion. But Jesus rebuked the impure spirit, **healed** the boy and gave him back to his father.

Luke 13:14
Indignant because Jesus had **healed** on the Sabbath,

Luke 13:32
He replied, "Go tell that fox, 'I will keep on driving out demons and **healing** people

Luke 14:4
But they remained silent. So taking hold of the man, he **healed** him and sent him on his way.

Luke 17:15
One of them, when he saw he was **healed**, came back, praising God in a loud voice.

Luke 18:42
Jesus said to him, "Receive your sight; your faith has **healed** you."

Luke 22:51
But Jesus answered, "No more of this!" And he touched the man's ear and **healed** him.

John 5:13
The man who was **healed** had no idea who it was, for Jesus had slipped away into the crowd that was there.

John 6:2
and a great crowd of people followed him because they saw the signs he had performed by **healing** the sick.

John 7:23
why are you angry with me for **healing** a man's whole body on the Sabbath?

John 12:40
"He has blinded their eyes and hardened their hearts, so they can neither see with their eyes, nor understand with their hearts, nor turn—and I would **heal** them."

Acts 3:16
By faith in the name of Jesus, this man whom you see and know was made strong. It is Jesus' name and the faith that comes through him that has completely **healed** him, as you can all see.

Acts 4:10
It is by the name of Jesus Christ of Nazareth, whom you crucified but whom God raised from the dead, that this man stands before you **healed**.

God Our Healer

Acts 4:30
Stretch out your hand to **heal** and perform signs and wonders through the name of your holy servant Jesus."

Acts 9:34
"Aeneas," Peter said to him, "Jesus Christ **heals** you. Get up and roll up your mat." Immediately Aeneas got up.

Acts 10:38
how God anointed Jesus of Nazareth with the Holy Spirit and power, and how he went around doing good and **healing** all who were under the power of the devil, because God was with him.

Acts 28:27
For this people's heart has become calloused; they hardly hear with their ears, and they have closed their eyes. Otherwise they might see with their eyes, hear with their ears, understand with their hearts and turn, and I would **heal** them.'

1 Corinthians 12:9
to another faith by the same Spirit, to another gifts of **healing** by that one Spirit,

1 Peter 2:24
"He himself bore our sins" in his body on the cross, so that we might die to sins and live for righteousness; "by his wounds you have been **healed**."

God Our Hiding Place

Hiding Place:
A secret, protected place away from any surrounding danger.

*You are my **hiding place**; you will protect me from trouble and surround me with songs of deliverance.*

- Psalm 32:7

God Our Hiding Place

1. DEFINE HIDING PLACE USING YOUR OWN WORDS, SYNONYMS, OR DESCRIPTIONS:

_____

_____

_____

2. IN WHAT WAYS DOES GOD PROTECT US FROM TROUBLE?

_____

_____

_____

3. DO YOU HAVE ANY OBSERVATIONS ABOUT THIS CHARACTER TRAIT OF GOD OR WHY HE WANTS US TO KNOW THAT HE IS OUR HIDING PLACE?

_____

_____

_____

_____

_____

_____

There is more safety with Christ in the tempest than without Christ in the calmest waters.

- Alexander Grosse

How often we look upon God as our last and feeblest resource. We go to Him because we have nowhere else to go. And then we learn that the storms of life have driven us, not upon rocks, but into the desired haven.

- George MacDonald

NOTES:

God Our Hiding Place

Psalm 32:7
You are my **hiding place**; you will protect me from trouble and surround me with songs of deliverance.

Isaiah 4:6
[*The LORD created a canopy of a cloud of smoke by day and a glow of flaming fire by night*] It will be a shelter and shade from the heat of the day, and a refuge and **hiding place** from the storm and rain.

God is Holy
Able to Make Holy
Possessing Holiness

Holy:
Of or associated with God and therefore regarded with reverence; Consecrated; Sacred.

*Who will not fear you, Lord, and bring glory to your name? For you alone are **holy**. All nations will come and worship before you, for your righteous acts have been revealed.*

- Revelation 15:4

God is Holy

1. DEFINE HOLY USING YOUR OWN WORDS, SYNONYMS, OR DESCRIPTIONS:

_____

_____

_____

2. THERE ARE NUMEROUS THINGS REFERRED TO AS HOLY IN THE BIBLE -- HOLY NAME, HOLY GROUND, HOLY MOUNTAIN, HOLY PEOPLE, HOLY TEMPLE, HOLY DAY, HOLY THRONE, AND EVEN HEAVEN GOD'S HOLY DWELLING. WHAT MAKES ALL THESE HOLY?

_____

_____

_____

3. DO YOU HAVE ANY OBSERVATIONS ABOUT THIS CHARACTER TRAIT OF GOD OR WHY GOD WANTS US TO KNOW THAT HE IS HOLY AND ABLE TO MAKE US HOLY?

_____

_____

_____

_____

_____

_____

All that is good, all that is right;
All that is truth, justice and light;
All that is pure, holy indeed,
All that is You, all that I need.
- Twila Paris

A person cannot have a greater concept of God than they are willing to conform their life to.
- Gordon Olson

NOTES:

God is Holy

Genesis 2:3
Then God blessed the seventh day and made it **holy**, because on it he rested from all the work of creating that he had done.

Exodus 3:5
"Do not come any closer," God said. "Take off your sandals, for the place where you are standing is **holy** ground."

Exodus 15:13
In your unfailing love you will lead the people you have redeemed. In your strength you will guide them to your **holy** dwelling.

Exodus 16:23
He said to them, "This is what the LORD commanded: 'Tomorrow is to be a day of sabbath rest, a **holy** sabbath to the LORD.

Exodus 20:11
For in six days the LORD made the heavens and the earth, the sea, and all that is in them, but he rested on the seventh day. Therefore the LORD blessed the Sabbath day and made it **holy**.

Exodus 28:36
[*God's instruction concerning His Holy Tabernacle in the wilderness*] "Make a plate of pure gold and engrave on it as on a seal: **HOLY** TO THE LORD.

Exodus 30:10
Once a year Aaron shall make atonement on its horns. This annual atonement must be made with the blood of the atoning sin offering for the generations to come. It is most **holy** to the LORD."

Exodus 31:13
"Say to the Israelites, 'You must observe my Sabbaths. This will be a sign between me and you for the generations to come, so you may know that I am the LORD, who makes you **holy**.

Leviticus 11:44
I am the LORD your God; consecrate yourselves and be **holy**, because I am **holy**.

Leviticus 11:45
I am the LORD, who brought you up out of Egypt to be your God; therefore be **holy**, because I am **holy**.

Leviticus 19:2
"Speak to the entire assembly of Israel and say to them: 'Be **holy** because I, the LORD your God, am **holy**.

Leviticus 20:3
I myself will set my face against him and will cut him off from his people; for by sacrificing his children to Molek, he has defiled my sanctuary and profaned my **holy** name.

Leviticus 20:7
"'Consecrate yourselves and be **holy**, because I am the LORD your God.

Leviticus 20:8
Keep my decrees and follow them. I am the LORD, who makes you **holy**.

Leviticus 20:26
You are to be **holy** to me because I, the LORD, am **holy**, and I have set you apart from the nations to be my own.

Leviticus 21:8
Regard them as **holy**, because they offer up the food of your God. Consider them **holy**, because I the LORD am **holy**—I who make you **holy**.

Leviticus 21:15
so that he will not defile his offspring among his people. I am the LORD, who makes him **holy**.'"

Leviticus 21:23
yet because of his defect, he must not go near the curtain or approach the altar, and so desecrate my sanctuary. I am the LORD, who makes them **holy**.'"

Leviticus 22:2
"Tell Aaron and his sons to treat with respect the sacred offerings the Israelites consecrate to me, so they will not profane my **holy** name. I am the LORD.

Leviticus 22:9
"'The priests are to perform my service in such a way that they do not become guilty and die for treating it with contempt. I am the LORD, who makes them **holy**.

Leviticus 22:16
by allowing them to eat the sacred offerings and so bring upon them guilt requiring payment. I am the LORD, who makes them **holy**.'"

Leviticus 22:32
Do not profane my holy name, for I must be acknowledged as holy by the Israelites. I am the LORD, who made you **holy**

Numbers 20:12
But the LORD said to Moses and Aaron, "Because you did not trust in me enough to honor me as **holy** in the sight of the Israelites, you will not bring this community into the land I give them."

Deuteronomy 7:6
For you are a people **holy** to the LORD your God. The LORD your God has chosen you out of all the peoples on the face of the earth to be his people, his treasured possession.

Deuteronomy 14:2
for you are a people **holy** to the LORD your God. Out of all the peoples on the face of the earth, the LORD has chosen you to be his treasured possession.

Joshua 5:15
The commander of the LORD's army replied, "Take off your sandals, for the place where you are standing is **holy**."

Joshua 24:19
Joshua said to the people, "You are not able to serve the LORD. He is a **holy** God; he is a jealous God. He will not forgive your rebellion and your sins.

1 Samuel 2:2
"There is no one **holy** like the LORD; there is no one besides you; there is no Rock like our God.

1 Samuel 6:20
And the people of Beth Shemesh asked, "Who can stand in the presence of the LORD, this **holy** God? To whom will the ark go up from here?"

2 Kings 19:22
Who is it you have ridiculed and blasphemed? Against whom have you raised your voice and lifted your eyes in pride? Against the **Holy** One of Israel!

1 Chronicles 16:10
Glory in his **holy** name; let the hearts of those who seek the LORD rejoice.

1 Chronicles 16:35
Cry out, "Save us, God our Savior; gather us and deliver us from the nations, that we may give thanks to your **holy** name, and glory in your praise."

1 Chronicles 29:16
LORD our God, all this abundance that we have provided for building you a temple for your **Holy** Name comes from your hand, and all of it belongs to you.

2 Chronicles 30:27
The priests and the Levites stood to bless the people, and God heard them, for their prayer reached heaven, his **holy** dwelling place.

God is Holy

Psalm 2:6
"I have installed my king on Zion, my **holy** mountain."

Psalm 3:4
I call out to the LORD, and he answers me from his **holy** mountain.

Psalm 5:7
But I, by your great love, can come into your house; in reverence I bow down toward your **holy** temple.

Psalm 11:4
The LORD is in his **holy** temple; the LORD is on his heavenly throne. He observes everyone on earth; his eyes examine them.

Psalm 22:3
Yet you are enthroned as the **Holy** One; you are the one Israel praises.

Psalm 24:3
Who may ascend the mountain of the LORD? Who may stand in his **holy** place?

Psalm 28:2
Hear my cry for mercy as I call to you for help, as I lift up my hands toward your Most **Holy** Place.

Psalm 30:4
Sing the praises of the LORD, you his faithful people; praise his **holy** name.

Psalm 33:21
In him our hearts rejoice, for we trust in his **holy** name.

Psalm 46:4
There is a river whose streams make glad the city of God, the **holy** place where the Most High dwells.

Psalm 47:8
God reigns over the nations; God is seated on his **holy** throne.

Psalm 48:1
Great is the LORD, and most worthy of praise, in the city of our God, his **holy** mountain.

Psalm 51:11
Do not cast me from your presence or take your **Holy Spirit** from me.

Psalm 68:5
A father to the fatherless, a defender of widows, is God in his **holy** dwelling.

Psalm 71:22
I will praise you with the harp for your faithfulness, my God; I will sing praise to you with the lyre, **Holy** One of Israel.

Psalm 77:13
Your ways, God, are **holy**. What god is as great as our God?

Psalm 78:41
Again and again they put God to the test; they vexed the **Holy** One of Israel.

Psalm 89:18
Indeed, our shield belongs to the LORD, our king to the **Holy** One of Israel.

Psalm 97:12
Rejoice in the LORD, you who are righteous, and praise his **holy** name.

Psalm 98:1
Sing to the LORD a new song, for he has done marvelous things; his right hand and his **holy** arm have worked salvation for him.

Psalm 99:3
Let them praise your great and awesome name— he is **holy**.

Psalm 99:5
Exalt the LORD our God and worship at his footstool; he is **holy**.

Psalm 99:9
Exalt the LORD our God and worship at his **holy** mountain, for the LORD our God is **holy**.

Psalm 103:1
Praise the LORD, my soul; all my inmost being, praise his **holy** name.

Psalm 105:3
Glory in his **holy** name; let the hearts of those who seek the LORD rejoice.

Psalm 105:42
For he remembered his **holy** promise given to his servant Abraham.

Psalm 106:47
Save us, LORD our God, and gather us from the nations, that we may give thanks to your **holy** name and glory in your praise.

Psalm 111:9
He provided redemption for his people; he ordained his covenant forever— **holy** and awesome is his name.

Psalm 138:2
I will bow down toward your **holy** temple and will praise your name for your unfailing love and your faithfulness, for you have so exalted your solemn decree that it surpasses your fame.

Psalm 145:21
My mouth will speak in praise of the LORD. Let every creature praise his **holy** name for ever and ever.

Proverbs 9:10
The fear of the LORD is the beginning of wisdom, and knowledge of the **Holy** One is understanding.

Proverbs 30:3
I have not learned wisdom, nor have I attained to the knowledge of the **Holy** One.

Isaiah 1:4
Woe to the sinful nation, a people whose guilt is great, a brood of evildoers, children given to corruption! They have forsaken the LORD; they have spurned the **Holy** One of Israel and turned their backs on him.

Isaiah 5:16
But the LORD Almighty will be exalted by his justice, and the **holy** God will be proved holy by his righteous acts.

Isaiah 5:24
Therefore, as tongues of fire lick up straw and as dry grass sinks down in the flames, so their roots will decay and their flowers blow away like dust; for they have rejected the law of the LORD Almighty and spurned the word of the **Holy** One of Israel.

Isaiah 6:3
And they were calling to one another: "**Holy, holy, holy** is the LORD Almighty; the whole earth is full of his glory."

Isaiah 8:13
The LORD Almighty is the one you are to regard as **holy**, he is the one you are to fear, he is the one you are to dread.

Isaiah 10:17
The Light of Israel will become a fire, their **Holy** One a flame; in a single day it will burn and consume his thorns and his briers.

Isaiah 10:20
[*The Remnant of Israel*] In that day the remnant of Israel, the survivors of Jacob, will no longer rely on him who struck them down but will truly rely on the LORD, the **Holy** One of Israel.

God is Holy

Isaiah 12:6
Shout aloud and sing for joy, people of Zion, for great is the **Holy** One of Israel among you."

Isaiah 17:7
In that day people will look to their Maker and turn their eyes to the **Holy** One of Israel.

Isaiah 29:19
Once more the humble will rejoice in the LORD; the needy will rejoice in the **Holy** One of Israel.

Isaiah 29:23
When they see among them their children, the work of my hands, they will keep my name **holy**; they will acknowledge the **holiness** of the **Holy** One of Jacob, and will stand in awe of the God of Israel.

Isaiah 30:12
Therefore this is what the **Holy** One of Israel says: "Because you have rejected this message, relied on oppression and depended on deceit,

Isaiah 30:15
This is what the Sovereign LORD, the **Hol**y One of Israel, says: "In repentance and rest is your salvation, in quietness and trust is your strength, but you would have none of it.

Isaiah 31:1
Woe to those who go down to Egypt for help, who rely on horses, who trust in the multitude of their chariots and in the great strength of their horsemen, but do not look to the **Holy** One of Israel, or seek help from the LORD.

Isaiah 37:23
Who is it you have ridiculed and blasphemed? Against whom have you raised your voice and lifted your eyes in pride? Against the **Holy** One of Israel!

Isaiah 40:25
"To whom will you compare me? Or who is my equal?" says the **Holy** One.

Isaiah 41:14
Do not be afraid, you worm Jacob, little Israel, do not fear, for I myself will help you," declares the LORD, your Redeemer, the **Holy** One of Israel.

Isaiah 41:16
You will winnow them, the wind will pick them up, and a gale will blow them away. But you will rejoice in the LORD and glory in the **Holy** One of Israel.

Isaiah 41:20
so that people may see and know, may consider and understand, that the hand of the LORD has done this, that the **Holy** One of Israel has created it.

Isaiah 43:3
For I am the LORD your God, the **Holy** One of Israel, your Savior; I give Egypt for your ransom, Cush and Seba in your stead.

Isaiah 43:14
This is what the LORD says— your Redeemer, the **Holy** One of Israel: "For your sake I will send to Babylon and bring down as fugitives all the Babylonians, in the ships in which they took pride.

Isaiah 43:15
I am the LORD, your **Holy** One, Israel's Creator, your King."

Isaiah 45:11
"This is what the LORD says— the **Holy** One of Israel, and its Maker: Concerning things to come, do you question me about my children, or give me orders about the work of my hands?

Isaiah 47:4
Our Redeemer—the LORD Almighty is his name— is the **Holy** One of Israel.

Isaiah 48:17
This is what the LORD says— your Redeemer, the **Holy** One of Israel: "I am the LORD your God, who teaches you what is best for you, who directs you in the way you should go.

Isaiah 49:7
This is what the LORD says— the Redeemer and **Holy** One of Israel— to him who was despised and abhorred by the nation, to the servant of rulers: "Kings will see you and stand up, princes will see and bow down, because of the LORD, who is faithful, the **Holy** One of Israel, who has chosen you."

Isaiah 52:10
The LORD will lay bare his **holy** arm in the sight of all the nations, and all the ends of the earth will see the salvation of our God.

Isaiah 54:5
For your Maker is your husband— the LORD Almighty is his name— the **Holy** One of Israel is your Redeemer; he is called the God of all the earth.

Isaiah 55:5
Surely you will summon nations you know not, and nations you do not know will come running to you, because of the LORD your God, the **Holy** One of Israel, for he has endowed you with splendor."

Isaiah 56:7
these I will bring to my **holy** mountain and give them joy in my house of prayer. Their burnt offerings and sacrifices will be accepted on my altar; for my house will be called a house of prayer for all nations."

Isaiah 57:15
For this is what the high and exalted One says— he who lives forever, whose name is **holy**: "I live in a high and **holy** place, but also with the one who is contrite and lowly in spirit, to revive the spirit of the lowly and to revive the heart of the contrite.

Isaiah 58:13
"If you keep your feet from breaking the Sabbath and from doing as you please on my **holy** day, if you call the Sabbath a delight and the LORD's **holy** day honorable, and if you honor it by not going your own way and not doing as you please or speaking idle words,

Isaiah 60:9
Surely the islands look to me; in the lead are the ships of Tarshish, bringing your children from afar, with their silver and gold, to the honor of the LORD your God, the **Holy** One of Israel, for he has endowed you with splendor.

Isaiah 60:14
The children of your oppressors will come bowing before you; all who despise you will bow down at your feet and will call you the City of the LORD, Zion of the **Holy** One of Israel.

Isaiah 63:10
Yet they rebelled and grieved his **Holy Spirit**. So he turned and became their enemy and he himself fought against them.

Isaiah 63:11
Then his people recalled the days of old, the days of Moses and his people— where is he who brought them through the sea, with the shepherd of his flock? Where is he who set his **Holy Spirit** among them,

Isaiah 63:15
Look down from heaven and see, from your lofty throne, **holy** and glorious. Where are your zeal and your might? Your tenderness and compassion are withheld from us.

Jeremiah 23:9
[*Concerning Lying Prophets*] Concerning the prophets: My heart is broken within me; all my bones tremble. I am like a drunken man, like a strong man overcome by wine, because of the LORD and his **holy** words.

Jeremiah 25:30
"Now prophesy all these words against them and say to them: "'The LORD will roar from on high; he will thunder from his **holy** dwelling and roar mightily against his land. He will shout like those who tread the grapes, shout against all who live on the earth.

God is Holy

Jeremiah 50:29
"Summon archers against Babylon, all those who draw the bow. Encamp all around her; let no one escape. Repay her for her deeds; do to her as she has done. For she has defied the LORD, the **Holy** One of Israel.

Jeremiah 51:5
For Israel and Judah have not been forsaken by their God, the LORD Almighty, though their land is full of guilt before the **Holy** One of Israel.

Ezekiel 20:12
Also I gave them my Sabbaths as a sign between us, so they would know that I the LORD made them **holy**.

Ezekiel 20:20
Keep my Sabbaths **holy**, that they may be a sign between us. Then you will know that I am the LORD your God."

Ezekiel 20:39
"'As for you, people of Israel, this is what the Sovereign LORD says: Go and serve your idols, every one of you! But afterward you will surely listen to me and no longer profane my **holy** name with your gifts and idols.

Ezekiel 20:41
I will accept you as fragrant incense when I bring you out from the nations and gather you from the countries where you have been scattered, and I will be proved **holy** through you in the sight of the nations.

Ezekiel 28:22
and say: 'This is what the Sovereign LORD says: "'I am against you, Sidon, and among you I will display my glory. You will know that I am the LORD, when I inflict punishment on you and within you am proved to be **holy**.

Ezekiel 28:25
"'This is what the Sovereign LORD says: When I gather the people of Israel from the nations where they have been scattered, I will be proved **holy** through them in the sight of the nations. Then they will live in their own land, which I gave to my servant Jacob.

Ezekiel 36:20
And wherever they went among the nations they profaned my **holy** name, for it was said of them, 'These are the LORD's people, and yet they had to leave his land.'

Ezekiel 36:21
I had concern for my **holy** name, which the people of Israel profaned among the nations where they had gone.

Ezekiel 36:22
"Therefore say to the Israelites, 'This is what the Sovereign LORD says: It is not for your sake, people of Israel, that I am going to do these things, but for the sake of my **holy** name, which you have profaned among the nations where you have gone.

Ezekiel 36:23
I will show the **holiness** of my great name, which has been profaned among the nations, the name you have profaned among them. Then the nations will know that I am the LORD, declares the Sovereign LORD, when I am proved **holy** through you before their eyes.

Ezekiel 38:16
You will advance against my people Israel like a cloud that covers the land. In days to come, Gog, I will bring you against my land, so that the nations may know me when I am proved **holy** through you before their eyes.

Ezekiel 39:7
"'I will make known my **holy** name among my people Israel. I will no longer let my **holy** name be profaned, and the nations will know that I the LORD am the **Holy** One in Israel.

Ezekiel 39:25
"Therefore this is what the Sovereign LORD says: I will now restore the fortunes of Jacob and will have compassion on all the people of Israel, and I will be zealous for my **holy** name.

Ezekiel 39:27
When I have brought them back from the nations and have gathered them from the countries of their enemies, I will be proved **holy** through them in the sight of many nations.

Ezekiel 43:7
He said: "Son of man, this is the place of my throne and the place for the soles of my feet. This is where I will live among the Israelites forever. The people of Israel will never again defile my **holy** name—neither they nor their kings—by their prostitution and the funeral offerings for their kings at their death.

Ezekiel 43:8
When they placed their threshold next to my threshold and their doorposts beside my doorposts, with only a wall between me and them, they defiled my **holy** name by their detestable practices. So I destroyed them in my anger.

Daniel 9:20
While I was speaking and praying, confessing my sin and the sin of my people Israel and making my request to the LORD my God for his **holy** hill—

Hosea 11:9
I will not carry out my fierce anger, nor will I devastate Ephraim again. For I am God, and not a man— the **Holy** One among you.

Hosea 11:12
Ephraim has surrounded me with lies, Israel with deceit. And Judah is unruly against God, even against the faithful **Holy** One.

Joel 3:17
"Then you will know that I, the LORD your God, dwell in Zion, my **holy** hill. Jerusalem will be **holy**; never again will foreigners invade her.

Amos 2:7
They trample on the heads of the poor as on the dust of the ground and deny justice to the oppressed. Father and son use the same girl and so profane my **holy** name.

Jonah 2:7
"When my life was ebbing away, I remembered you, LORD, and my prayer rose to you, to your **holy** temple.

Micah 1:2
Hear, you peoples, all of you, listen, earth and all who live in it, that the Sovereign LORD may bear witness against you, the Lord from his **holy** temple.

Habakkuk 1:12
LORD, are you not from everlasting? My God, my **Holy** One, you will never die. You, LORD, have appointed them to execute judgment; you, my Rock, have ordained them to punish.

Habakkuk 2:20
The LORD is in his **holy** temple; let all the earth be silent before him.

Habakkuk 3:3
God came from Teman, the **Holy** One from Mount Paran. His glory covered the heavens and his praise filled the earth.

Zechariah 2:13
Be still before the LORD, all mankind, because he has roused himself from his **holy** dwelling."

Zechariah 8:3
This is what the LORD says: "I will return to Zion and dwell in Jerusalem. Then Jerusalem will be called the Faithful City, and the mountain of the LORD Almighty will be called the **Holy** Mountain."

Zechariah 14:20
On that day **HOLY** TO THE LORD will be inscribed on the bells of the horses, and the cooking pots in the LORD's house will be like the sacred bowls in front of the altar.

Matthew 1:18
This is how the birth of Jesus the Messiah came about: His mother Mary was pledged to be married to Joseph, but before they came together, she was found to be pregnant through the **Holy Spirit**.

God is Holy

Matthew 1:20
But after he had considered this, an angel of the Lord appeared to him in a dream and said, "Joseph son of David, do not be afraid to take Mary home as your wife, because what is conceived in her is from the **Holy Spirit**.

Matthew 3:11
"I baptize you with water for repentance. But after me comes one who is more powerful than I, whose sandals I am not worthy to carry. He will baptize you with the **Holy Spirit** and fire.

Matthew 12:32
Anyone who speaks a word against the Son of Man will be forgiven, but anyone who speaks against the **Holy Spirit** will not be forgiven, either in this age or in the age to come.

Matthew 28:19
Therefore go and make disciples of all nations, baptizing them in the name of the Father and of the Son and of the **Holy Spirit**,

Mark 1:8
I baptize you with water, but he will baptize you with the **Holy Spirit**."

Mark 1:24
"What do you want with us, Jesus of Nazareth? Have you come to destroy us? I know who you are—the **Holy** One of God!"

Mark 3:29
but whoever blasphemes against the **Holy Spirit** will never be forgiven; they are guilty of an eternal sin."

Mark 12:36
David himself, speaking by the **Holy Spirit**, declared: "'The Lord said to my Lord: "Sit at my right hand until I put your enemies under your feet."'

Mark 13:11
Whenever you are arrested and brought to trial, do not worry beforehand about what to say. Just say whatever is given you at the time, for it is not you speaking, but the **Holy Spirit**.

Luke 1:15
for he will be great in the sight of the Lord. He is never to take wine or other fermented drink, and he will be filled with the **Holy Spirit** even before he is born.

Luke 1:35
The angel answered, "The **Holy Spirit** will come on you, and the power of the Most High will overshadow you. So the **holy** one to be born will be called the Son of God.

Luke 1:41
When Elizabeth heard Mary's greeting, the baby leaped in her womb, and Elizabeth was filled with the **Holy Spirit**.

Luke 1:49
for the Mighty One has done great things for me— **holy** is his name.

Luke 1:67
His father Zechariah was filled with the **Holy Spirit** and prophesied:

Luke 2:25
Now there was a man in Jerusalem called Simeon, who was righteous and devout. He was waiting for the consolation of Israel, and the **Holy Spirit** was on him.

Luke 2:26
It had been revealed to him by the **Holy Spirit** that he would not die before he had seen the Lord's Messiah.

Luke 3:16
John answered them all, "I baptize you with water. But one who is more powerful than I will come, the straps of whose sandals I am not worthy to untie. He will baptize you with the **Holy Spirit** and fire.

Luke 3:22
and the **Holy Spirit** descended on him in bodily form like a dove. And a voice came from heaven: "You are my Son, whom I love; with you I am well pleased."

Luke 4:1
[*Jesus Is Tested in the Wilderness*] Jesus, full of the **Holy Spirit**, left the Jordan and was led by the Spirit into the wilderness,

Luke 4:34
"Go away! What do you want with us, Jesus of Nazareth? Have you come to destroy us? I know who you are—the **Holy** One of God!"

Luke 10:21
At that time Jesus, full of joy through the **Holy Spirit**, said, "I praise you, Father, Lord of heaven and earth, because you have hidden these things from the wise and learned, and revealed them to little children. Yes, Father, for this is what you were pleased to do.

Luke 11:13
If you then, though you are evil, know how to give good gifts to your children, how much more will your Father in heaven give the **Holy Spirit** to those who ask him!"

Luke 12:10
And everyone who speaks a word against the Son of Man will be forgiven, but anyone who blasphemes against the **Holy Spirit** will not be forgiven.

Luke 12:12
for the **Holy Spirit** will teach you at that time what you should say."

John 1:33
And I myself did not know him, but the one who sent me to baptize with water told me, 'The man on whom you see the Spirit come down and remain is the one who will baptize with the **Holy Spirit**.'

John 6:69
We have come to believe and to know that you are the **Holy** One of God."

John 14:26
But the Advocate, the **Holy Spirit**, whom the Father will send in my name, will teach you all things and will remind you of everything I have said to you.

John 17:11
I will remain in the world no longer, but they are still in the world, and I am coming to you. **Holy** Father, protect them by the power of your name, the name you gave me, so that they may be one as we are one.

John 20:22
And with that he breathed on them and said, "Receive the **Holy Spirit**.

Acts 1:2
until the day he was taken up to heaven, after giving instructions through the **Holy Spirit** to the apostles he had chosen.

Acts 1:5
For John baptized with water, but in a few days you will be baptized with the **Holy Spirit**."

Acts 1:8
But you will receive power when the **Holy Spirit** comes on you; and you will be my witnesses in Jerusalem, and in all Judea and Samaria, and to the ends of the earth."

Acts 1:16
and said, "Brothers and sisters, the Scripture had to be fulfilled in which the **Holy Spirit** spoke long ago through David concerning Judas, who served as guide for those who arrested Jesus.

God is Holy

Acts 2:4
All of them were filled with the **Holy Spirit** and began to speak in other tongues as the Spirit enabled them.

Acts 2:33
Exalted to the right hand of God, he has received from the Father the promised **Holy Spirit** and has poured out what you now see and hear.

Acts 2:38
Peter replied, "Repent and be baptized, every one of you, in the name of Jesus Christ for the forgiveness of your sins. And you will receive the gift of the **Holy Spirit**.

Acts 3:14
You disowned the **Holy** and Righteous One and asked that a murderer be released to you

Acts 4:8
Then Peter, filled with the **Holy Spirit**, said to them:

Acts 4:25
You spoke by the **Holy Spirit** through the mouth of your servant, our father David: "'Why do the nations rage and the peoples plot in vain?

Acts 4:27
Indeed Herod and Pontius Pilate met together with the Gentiles and the people of Israel in this city to conspire against your **holy** servant Jesus, whom you anointed.

Acts 4:30
Stretch out your hand to heal and perform signs and wonders through the name of your **holy** servant Jesus."

Acts 4:31
After they prayed, the place where they were meeting was shaken. And they were all filled with the **Holy Spirit** and spoke the word of God boldly.

Acts 5:3
Then Peter said, "Ananias, how is it that Satan has so filled your heart that you have lied to the **Holy Spirit** and have kept for yourself some of the money you received for the land?

Acts 5:32
We are witnesses of these things, and so is the **Holy Spirit**, whom God has given to those who obey him."

Acts 6:5
This proposal pleased the whole group. They chose Stephen, a man full of faith and of the **Holy Spirit**;

Acts 7:51
"You stiff-necked people! Your hearts and ears are still uncircumcised. You are just like your ancestors: You always resist the **Holy Spirit**!

Acts 7:55
But Stephen, full of the **Holy Spirit**, looked up to heaven and saw the glory of God, and Jesus standing at the right hand of God.

Acts 8:15
When they arrived, they prayed for the new believers there that they might receive the **Holy Spirit**,

Acts 8:16
because the **Holy Spirit** had not yet come on any of them; they had simply been baptized in the name of the Lord Jesus.

Acts 8:17
Then Peter and John placed their hands on them, and they received the **Holy Spirit**.

Acts 8:19
and said, "Give me also this ability so that everyone on whom I lay my hands may receive the **Holy Spirit**."

Acts 9:17
Then Ananias went to the house and entered it. Placing his hands on Saul, he said, "Brother Saul, the Lord—Jesus, who appeared to you on the road as you were coming here—has sent me so that you may see again and be filled with the **Holy Spirit**."

Acts 9:31
Then the church throughout Judea, Galilee and Samaria enjoyed a time of peace and was strengthened. Living in the fear of the Lord and encouraged by the **Holy Spirit**, it increased in numbers.

Acts 10:38
how God anointed Jesus of Nazareth with the **Holy Spirit** and power, and how he went around doing good and healing all who were under the power of the devil, because God was with him.

Acts 10:44
While Peter was still speaking these words, the **Holy Spirit** came on all who heard the message.

Acts 10:45
The circumcised believers who had come with Peter were astonished that the gift of the **Holy Spirit** had been poured out even on Gentiles.

Acts 10:47
"Surely no one can stand in the way of their being baptized with water. They have received the **Holy Spirit** just as we have."

Acts 11:15
"As I began to speak, the **Holy Spirit** came on them as he had come on us at the beginning.

Acts 11:16
Then I remembered what the Lord had said: 'John baptized with water, but you will be baptized with the **Holy Spirit**.'

Acts 11:24
He was a good man, full of the **Holy Spirit** and faith, and a great number of people were brought to the Lord.

Acts 13:2
While they were worshiping the Lord and fasting, the **Holy Spirit** said, "Set apart for me Barnabas and Saul for the work to which I have called them."

Acts 13:4
The two of them, sent on their way by the **Holy Spirit**, went down to Seleucia and sailed from there to Cyprus.

Acts 13:9
Then Saul, who was also called Paul, filled with the **Holy Spirit**, looked straight at Elymas and said,

Acts 15:8
God, who knows the heart, showed that he accepted them by giving the **Holy Spirit** to them, just as he did to us.

Acts 15:28
It seemed good to the **Holy Spirit** and to us not to burden you with anything beyond the following requirements:

Acts 16:6
Paul and his companions traveled throughout the region of Phrygia and Galatia, having been kept by the **Holy Spirit** from preaching the word in the province of Asia.

Acts 19:2
and asked them, "Did you receive the **Holy Spirit** when you believed?" They answered, "No, we have not even heard that there is a **Holy Spirit**."

Acts 19:6
When Paul placed his hands on them, the **Holy Spirit** came on them, and they spoke in tongues and prophesied.

God is Holy

Acts 20:23
I only know that in every city the **Holy Spirit** warns me that prison and hardships are facing me.

Acts 20:28
Keep watch over yourselves and all the flock of which the **Holy Spirit** has made you overseers. Be shepherds of the church of God, which he bought with his own blood.

Acts 21:11
Coming over to us, he took Paul's belt, tied his own hands and feet with it and said, "The **Holy Spirit** says, 'In this way the Jewish leaders in Jerusalem will bind the owner of this belt and will hand him over to the Gentiles.'"

Acts 28:25
They disagreed among themselves and began to leave after Paul had made this final statement: "The **Holy Spirit** spoke the truth to your ancestors when he said through Isaiah the prophet:

Romans 5:5
And hope does not put us to shame, because God's love has been poured out into our hearts through the **Holy Spirit**, who has been given to us.

Romans 9:1
I speak the truth in Christ—I am not lying, my conscience confirms it through the **Holy Spirit**—

Romans 14:17
For the kingdom of God is not a matter of eating and drinking, but of righteousness, peace and joy in the **Holy Spirit**,

Romans 15:13
May the God of hope fill you with all joy and peace as you trust in him, so that you may overflow with hope by the power of the **Holy Spirit**.

Romans 15:16
to be a minister of Christ Jesus to the Gentiles. He gave me the priestly duty of proclaiming the gospel of God, so that the Gentiles might become an offering acceptable to God, sanctified by the **Holy Spirit**.

1 Corinthians 6:19
Do you not know that your bodies are temples of the **Holy Spirit**, who is in you, whom you have received from God? You are not your own;

1 Corinthians 12:3
Therefore I want you to know that no one who is speaking by the Spirit of God says, "Jesus be cursed," and no one can say, "Jesus is Lord," except by the **Holy Spirit**.

2 Corinthians 6:6
in purity, understanding, patience and kindness; in the **Holy Spirit** and in sincere love;

2 Corinthians 13:14
May the grace of the Lord Jesus Christ, and the love of God, and the fellowship of the **Holy Spirit** be with you all.

Ephesians 1:13
And you also were included in Christ when you heard the message of truth, the gospel of your salvation. When you believed, you were marked in him with a seal, the promised **Holy Spirit**,

Ephesians 4:30
And do not grieve the **Holy Spirit** of God, with whom you were sealed for the day of redemption.

1 Thessalonians 1:5
because our gospel came to you not simply with words but also with power, with the **Holy Spirit** and deep conviction.

1 Thessalonians 1:6
You became imitators of us and of the Lord, for you welcomed the message in the midst of severe suffering with the joy given by the **Holy Spirit**.

God is Holy

1 Thessalonians 4:8
Therefore, anyone who rejects this instruction does not reject a human being but God, the very God who gives you his **Holy Spirit**.

2 Timothy 1:14
Guard the good deposit that was entrusted to you—guard it with the help of the **Holy Spirit** who lives in us.

2 Timothy 3:15
and how from infancy you have known the **Holy** Scriptures, which are able to make you wise for salvation through faith in Christ Jesus.

Titus 3:5
he saved us, not because of righteous things we had done, but because of his mercy. He saved us through the washing of rebirth and renewal by the **Holy Spirit**,

Hebrews 2:4
God also testified to it by signs, wonders and various miracles, and by gifts of the **Holy Spirit** distributed according to his will.

Hebrews 3:7
So, as the **Holy Spirit** says: "Today, if you hear his voice,

Hebrews 6:4
It is impossible for those who have once been enlightened, who have tasted the heavenly gift, who have shared in the **Holy Spirit**,

Hebrews 7:26
Such a high priest truly meets our need—one who is **holy**, blameless, pure, set apart from sinners, exalted above the heavens.

Hebrews 9:8
The **Holy Spirit** was showing by this that the way into the Most **Holy** Place had not yet been disclosed as long as the first tabernacle was still functioning.

Hebrews 10:10
And by that will, we have been made **holy** through the sacrifice of the body of Jesus Christ once for all.

Hebrews 10:15
The **Holy Spirit** also testifies to us about this.

Hebrews 13:12
And so Jesus also suffered outside the city gate to make the people **holy** through his own blood.

1 Peter 1:12
It was revealed to them that they were not serving themselves but you, when they spoke of the things that have now been told you by those who have preached the gospel to you by the **Holy Spirit** sent from heaven. Even angels long to look into these things.

1 Peter 1:15
But just as he who called you is **holy**, so be **holy** in all you do;

1 Peter 1:16
for it is written: "Be **holy**, because I am **holy**."

2 Peter 1:21
For prophecy never had its origin in the human will, but prophets, though human, spoke from God as they were carried along by the **Holy Spirit**.

1 John 2:20
But you have an anointing from the **Holy** One, and all of you know the truth.

Jude 1:20
But you, dear friends, by building yourselves up in your most **holy** faith and praying in the **Holy Spirit**,

God is Holy

Revelation 3:7
"To the angel of the church in Philadelphia write: These are the words of him who is **holy** and true, who holds the key of David. What he opens no one can shut, and what he shuts no one can open.

Revelation 4:8
Each of the four living creatures had six wings and was covered with eyes all around, even under its wings. Day and night they never stop saying: "'**Holy, holy, holy** is the Lord God Almighty,' who was, and is, and is to come."

Revelation 6:10
They called out in a loud voice, "How long, Sovereign Lord, **holy** and true, until you judge the inhabitants of the earth and avenge our blood?"

Revelation 15:4
Who will not fear you, Lord, and bring glory to your name? For you alone are **holy**. All nations will come and worship before you, for your righteous acts have been revealed."

Revelation 16:5
Then I heard the angel in charge of the waters say: "You are just in these judgments, O **Holy** One, you who are and who were;

Revelation 21:2
I saw the **Holy** City, the new Jerusalem, coming down out of heaven from God, prepared as a bride beautifully dressed for her husband.

Revelation 21:10
And he carried me away in the Spirit to a mountain great and high, and showed me the **Holy** City, Jerusalem, coming down out of heaven from God.

God is Impartial
Showing No Partiality

Impartial:
Not showing favoritism or having an unfair bias toward one person or group.

*Judge carefully, for with the Lord our God there is **no injustice or partiality** or bribery.*

- I Chronicles 19:7

God is Impartial

1. DEFINE IMPARTIAL USING YOUR OWN WORDS, SYNONYMS, OR DESCRIPTIONS:

_____

_____

_____

2. HOW IMPORTANT IS IT THAT GOD NOT HAVE UNFAIR BIAS OR FAVORTISM?

_____

_____

_____

3. DO YOU HAVE ANY OBSERVATIONS ABOUT THIS CHARACTER TRAIT OF GOD OR WHY GOD WANTS US TO KNOW THAT HE IS IMPARTIAL OR SHOWS NO PARTIALITY?

_____

_____

_____

_____

_____

_____

In my view of such harmony in the cosmos which I, with my limited human mind, am able to recognize, there are yet people who say there is no God. But what makes me really angry is that they quote me for support of such views.

- Albert Einstein

NOTES:

God is Impartial

Deuteronomy 10:17
For the LORD your God is God of gods and Lord of lords, the great God, mighty and awesome, who **shows no partiality** and accepts no bribes.

2 Chronicles 19:7
Now let the fear of the LORD be on you. Judge carefully, for with the LORD our God there is **no injustice or partiality** or bribery."

God is Jealous
Having Jealousy

Jealous:
An unwillingness to share the affection or attention of one loved; An emotional reaction to being disregarded or disrespected by the object of one's affection.

*Do not worship any other god, for the Lord, whose name is **Jealous**, is a **jealous** God.*

- Exodus 34:14

God is Jealous

1. DEFINE JEALOUS USING YOUR OWN WORDS, SYNONYMS, OR DESCRIPTIONS:

_____

_____

_____

2. WE USUALLY THINK OF "JEALOUS" IN NEGATIVE TERMS. WHY IS THIS A POSITIVE CHARACTER TRAIT FOR GOD?

_____

_____

_____

3. DEUTERONOMY 32:21 SAYS, "THEY MADE ME JEALOUS BY WHAT IS NO GOD AND ANGERED ME WITH THEIR WORTHLESS IDOLS." DO IDOLS HAVE TO BE STATUES AND FIGURES OR CAN THEY ALSO BE ANY THING -- OR EVEN PEOPLE -- WHO TAKE OUR LOVE AND ATTENTION AWAY FROM GOD?

_____

_____

_____

4. DO YOU HAVE ANY OBSERVATIONS ABOUT THIS CHARACTER TRAIT OF GOD OR WHY GOD WANTS US TO KNOW THAT HE IS JEALOUS?

_____

_____

_____

_____

_____

The greatest enemy of hunger for God is not poison but apple pie. It is not the banquet of the wicked that dulls our appetite for heaven, but endless nibbling at the table of the world.
- John Piper

The man who doesn't read his Bible is no better off than the man who doesn't have a Bible.

NOTES:

God is Jealous

Exodus 20:5
You shall not bow down to them or worship them; for I, the LORD your God, am a **jealous** God, punishing the children for the sin of the parents to the third and fourth generation of those who hate me,

Exodus 34:14
Do not worship any other god, for the LORD, whose name is **Jealous**, is a **jealous** God.

Deuteronomy 4:24
For the LORD your God is a consuming fire, a **jealous** God.

Deuteronomy 5:9
You shall not bow down to them or worship them; for I, the LORD your God, am a **jealous** God, punishing the children for the sin of the parents to the third and fourth generation of those who hate me,

Deuteronomy 6:15
for the LORD your God, who is among you, is a **jealous** God and his anger will burn against you, and he will destroy you from the face of the land.

Deuteronomy 32:16
They made him **jealous** with their foreign gods and angered him with their detestable idols.

Deuteronomy 32:21
They made me **jealous** by what is no god and angered me with their worthless idols.

Joshua 24:19
Joshua said to the people, "You are not able to serve the LORD. He is a holy God; he is a **jealous** God.

1 Kings 14:22
Judah did evil in the eyes of the LORD. By the sins they committed they stirred up his **jealous** anger more than those who were before them had done.

Psalm 78:58
They angered him with their high places; they aroused his **jealousy** with their idols.

Psalm 79:5
How long, LORD? Will you be angry forever? How long will your **jealousy** burn like fire?

Ezekiel 8:3
He stretched out what looked like a hand and took me by the hair of my head. The Spirit lifted me up between earth and heaven and in visions of God he took me to Jerusalem, to the entrance of the north gate of the inner court, where the idol that provokes to **jealousy** stood.

Ezekiel 16:38
I will sentence you to the punishment of women who commit adultery and who shed blood; I will bring on you the blood vengeance of my wrath and **jealous** anger.

Ezekiel 16:42
Then my wrath against you will subside and my **jealous** anger will turn away from you; I will be calm and no longer angry.

Ezekiel 23:25
I will direct my **jealous** anger against you, and they will deal with you in fury.

Ezekiel 36:6
Therefore prophesy concerning the land of Israel and say to the mountains and hills, to the ravines and valleys: 'This is what the Sovereign LORD says: I speak in my **jealous** wrath because you have suffered the scorn of the nations.

Joel 2:18
Then the LORD was **jealous** for his land and took pity on his people.

Joel 2:18
Then the LORD was **jealous** for his land and took pity on his people.

Nahum 1:2
The LORD is a **jealous** and avenging God; the LORD takes vengeance and is filled with wrath. The LORD takes vengeance on his foes and vents his wrath against his enemies.

Zephaniah 1:18
Neither their silver nor their gold will be able to save them on the day of the LORD's wrath." In the fire of his **jealousy** the whole earth will be consumed, for he will make a sudden end of all who live on the earth.

Zephaniah 3:8
Therefore wait for me," declares the LORD, "for the day I will stand up to testify. I have decided to assemble the nations, to gather the kingdoms and to pour out my wrath on them— all my fierce anger. The whole world will be consumed by the fire of my **jealous** anger.

Zechariah 1:14
Then the angel who was speaking to me said, "Proclaim this word: This is what the LORD Almighty says: 'I am very **jealous** for Jerusalem and Zion,

Zechariah 8:2
This is what the LORD Almighty says: "I am very **jealous** for Zion; I am burning with **jealousy** for her."

James 4:5
Or do you think Scripture says without reason that he **jealously** longs for the spirit he has caused to dwell in us?

God Our Judge
Showing Judgement
Giving Judgement

Judge:
One with discernment and good sense who has the authority to decide or make an opinion in a matter.

*The Lord takes his place in court; he rises to **judge** the people.*

- Isaiah 3:13

God Our Judge

1. DEFINE JUDGE USING YOUR OWN WORDS, SYNONYMS, OR DESCRIPTIONS:

_____

_____

_____

2. THE BIBLE INDICATES THAT GOD WILL JUDGE US ACCORDING TO OUR DECISIONS AND ACTIONS. CAN YOU FIND THE VERSES WHERE IT STATES THIS?

_____

_____

_____

_____

_____

3. DO YOU HAVE ANY OBSERVATIONS ABOUT THIS CHARACTER TRAIT OF GOD OR WHY HE WANTS US TO KNOW THAT HE IS OUR JUDGE AND GIVES JUDGEMENT?

_____

_____

_____

_____

_____

The fact that when we are "in Christ" there is no condemnation for our sins does not mean there is no examination of our works.

- Samuel Leith

NOTES:

God Our Judge

Genesis 16:5
Then Sarai said to Abram, "You are responsible for the wrong I am suffering. I put my slave in your arms, and now that she knows she is pregnant, she despises me. May the LORD **judge** between you and me."

Genesis 18:25
Far be it from you to do such a thing—to kill the righteous with the wicked, treating the righteous and the wicked alike. Far be it from you! Will not the **Judge** of all the earth do right?"

Genesis 31:53
May the God of Abraham and the God of Nahor, the God of their father, **judge** between us."

Judges 11:27
I have not wronged you, but you are doing me wrong by waging war against me. Let the LORD, the **Judge**, decide the dispute this day between the Israelites and the Ammonites."

1 Samuel 2:10
those who oppose the LORD will be broken. The Most High will thunder from heaven; the LORD will **judge** the ends of the earth.

1 Samuel 24:12
May the LORD **judge** between you and me. And may the LORD avenge the wrongs you have done to me, but my hand will not touch you.

1 Samuel 24:15
May the LORD be our **judge** and decide between us. May he consider my cause and uphold it; may he vindicate me by delivering me from your hand."

1 Kings 8:32
then hear from heaven and act. **Judge** between your servants, condemning the guilty by bringing down on their heads what they have done, and vindicating the innocent by treating them in accordance with their innocence.

1 Chronicles 12:17
David went out to meet them and said to them, "If you have come to me in peace to help me, I am ready for you to join me. But if you have come to betray me to my enemies when my hands are free from violence, may the God of our ancestors see it and **judge** you."

1 Chronicles 16:33
Let the trees of the forest sing, let them sing for joy before the LORD, for he comes to **judge** the earth.

2 Chronicles 6:23
Judge between your servants, condemning the guilty and bringing down on their heads what they have done, and vindicating the innocent by treating them in accordance with their innocence.

2 Chronicles 20:12
Our God, will you not **judge** them? For we have no power to face this vast army that is attacking us. We do not know what to do, but our eyes are on you."

Job 9:15
Though I were innocent, I could not answer him; I could only plead with my **Judge** for mercy.

Job 21:22
"Can anyone teach knowledge to God, since he **judges** even the highest?

Psalm 7:8
Let the LORD **judge** the peoples. Vindicate me, LORD, according to my righteousness, according to my integrity, O Most High.

Psalm 7:11
God is a righteous **judge**, a God who displays his wrath every day.

Psalm 9:4
For you have upheld my right and my cause, sitting enthroned as the righteous **judge**.

Psalm 9:8
He rules the world in righteousness and **judges** the peoples with equity.

Psalm 9:19
Arise, LORD, do not let mortals triumph; let the nations be **judged** in your presence.

Psalm 50:4
He summons the heavens above, and the earth, that he may **judge** his people:

Psalm 51:4
Against you, you only, have I sinned and done what is evil in your sight; so you are right in your verdict and justified when you **judge**.

Psalm 58:11
Then people will say, "Surely the righteous still are rewarded; surely there is a God who **judges** the earth."

Psalm 75:2
You say, "I choose the appointed time; it is I who **judge** with equity.

Psalm 75:7
It is God who **judges**: He brings one down, he exalts another.

Psalm 76:9
when you, God, rose up to **judge**, to save all the afflicted of the land.

Psalm 82:8
Rise up, O God, **judge** the earth, for all the nations are your inheritance.

Psalm 94:2
Rise up, **Judge** of the earth; pay back to the proud what they deserve.

Psalm 96:10
Say among the nations, "The LORD reigns." The world is firmly established, it cannot be moved; he will **judge** the peoples with equity.

Psalm 96:13
Let all creation rejoice before the LORD, for he comes, he comes to **judge** the earth. He will **judge** the world in righteousness and the peoples in his faithfulness.

Psalm 98:9
let them sing before the LORD, for he comes to **judge** the earth. He will **judge** the world in righteousness and the peoples with equity.

Psalm 110:6
He will **judge** the nations, heaping up the dead and crushing the rulers of the whole earth.

Ecclesiastes 3:17
I said to myself, "God will bring into judgment both the righteous and the wicked, for there will be a time for every activity, a time to **judge** every deed."

Isaiah 2:4
He will **judge** between the nations and will settle disputes for many peoples. They will beat their swords into plowshares and their spears into pruning hooks. Nation will not take up sword against nation, nor will they train for war anymore.

Isaiah 3:13
The LORD takes his place in court; he rises to **judge** the people.

God Our Judge

Isaiah 11:3
and he will delight in the fear of the LORD. He will not **judge** by what he sees with his eyes, or decide by what he hears with his ears;

Isaiah 11:4
but with righteousness he will **judge** the needy, with justice he will give decisions for the poor of the earth. He will strike the earth with the rod of his mouth; with the breath of his lips he will slay the wicked.

Isaiah 33:22
For the LORD is our **judge**, the LORD is our lawgiver, the LORD is our king; it is he who will save us.

Jeremiah 11:20
But you, LORD Almighty, who **judge** righteously and test the heart and mind, let me see your vengeance on them, for to you I have committed my cause.

Ezekiel 7:3
The end is now upon you, and I will unleash my anger against you. I will **judge** you according to your conduct and repay you for all your detestable practices.

Ezekiel 7:8
I am about to pour out my wrath on you and spend my anger against you. I will **judge** you according to your conduct and repay you for all your detestable practices.

Ezekiel 7:27
The king will mourn, the prince will be clothed with despair, and the hands of the people of the land will tremble. I will deal with them according to their conduct, and by their own standards I will **judge** them. "'Then they will know that I am the LORD.'"

Ezekiel 18:30
"Therefore, you Israelites, I will **judge** each of you according to your own ways, declares the Sovereign LORD. Repent! Turn away from all your offenses; then sin will not be your downfall.

Ezekiel 20:36
As I **judged** your ancestors in the wilderness of the land of Egypt, so I will **judge** you, declares the Sovereign LORD.

Ezekiel 21:30
"'Let the sword return to its sheath. In the place where you were created, in the land of your ancestry, I will **judge** you.

Ezekiel 24:14
"'I the LORD have spoken. The time has come for me to act. I will not hold back; I will not have pity, nor will I relent. You will be **judged** according to your conduct and your actions, declares the Sovereign LORD.'"

Ezekiel 33:20
Yet you Israelites say, 'The way of the Lord is not just.' But I will **judge** each of you according to your own ways."

Ezekiel 34:17
"'As for you, my flock, this is what the Sovereign LORD says: I will **judge** between one sheep and another, and between rams and goats.

Ezekiel 34:20
"'Therefore this is what the Sovereign LORD says to them: See, I myself will **judge** between the fat sheep and the lean sheep.

Ezekiel 34:22
I will save my flock, and they will no longer be plundered. I will **judge** between one sheep and another.

Ezekiel 35:11
therefore as surely as I live, declares the Sovereign LORD, I will treat you in accordance with the anger and jealousy you showed in your hatred of them and I will make myself known among them when I **judge** you.

Ezekiel 36:19
I dispersed them among the nations, and they were scattered through the countries; I **judged** them according to their conduct and their actions.

Joel 3:12
"Let the nations be roused; let them advance into the Valley of Jehoshaphat, for there I will sit to **judge** all the nations on every side.

Micah 4:3
He will **judge** between many peoples and will settle disputes for strong nations far and wide. They will beat their swords into plowshares and their spears into pruning hooks. Nation will not take up sword against nation, nor will they train for war anymore.

Matthew 7:1
"Do not judge, or you too will be **judged**.

Matthew 7:2
For in the same way you judge others, you will be **judged**, and with the measure you use, it will be measured to you.

Luke 6:37
"Do not judge, and you will not be **judged**. Do not condemn, and you will not be condemned. Forgive, and you will be forgiven.

John 5:22
Moreover, the Father judges no one, but has entrusted all **judgment** to the Son,

John 5:24
"Very truly I tell you, whoever hears my word and believes him who sent me has eternal life and will not be **judged** but has crossed over from death to life.

John 5:27
And he has given him authority to **judge** because he is the Son of Man.

John 5:30
By myself I can do nothing; I **judge** only as I hear, and my **judgment** is just, for I seek not to please myself but him who sent me.

John 8:16
But if I do **judge**, my decisions are true, because I am not alone. I stand with the Father, who sent me.

John 8:50
I am not seeking glory for myself; but there is one who seeks it, and he is the **judge**.

John 12:47
"If anyone hears my words but does not keep them, I do not **judge** that person. For I did not come to **judge** the world, but to save the world.

John 12:48
There is a **judge** for the one who rejects me and does not accept my words; the very words I have spoken will condemn them at the last day.

Acts 17:31
For he has set a day when he will **judge** the world with justice by the man he has appointed. He has given proof of this to everyone by raising him from the dead."

Romans 2:16
This will take place on the day when God **judges** people's secrets through Jesus Christ, as my gospel declares.

Romans 3:6
Certainly not! If that were so, how could God **judge** the world?

1 Corinthians 4:4
My conscience is clear, but that does not make me innocent. It is the Lord who **judges** me.

God Our Judge

1 Corinthians 5:13
God will **judge** those outside. "Expel the wicked person from among you."

1 Corinthians 11:32
Nevertheless, when we are **judged** in this way by the Lord, we are being disciplined so that we will not be finally condemned with the world.

2 Timothy 4:1
In the presence of God and of Christ Jesus, who will **judge** the living and the dead, and in view of his appearing and his kingdom,

2 Timothy 4:8
Now there is in store for me the crown of righteousness, which the Lord, the righteous **Judge**, will award to me on that day—and not only to me, but also to all who have longed for his appearing.

Hebrews 4:12
For the word of God is alive and active. Sharper than any double-edged sword, it penetrates even to dividing soul and spirit, joints and marrow; it **judges** the thoughts and attitudes of the heart.

Hebrews 10:30
For we know him who said, "It is mine to avenge; I will repay," and again, "The Lord will **judge** his people."

Hebrews 12:23
You have come to God, the **Judge** of all, to the spirits of the righteous made perfect,

Hebrews 13:4
Marriage should be honored by all, and the marriage bed kept pure, for God will **judge** the adulterer and all the sexually immoral.

James 4:12
There is only one Lawgiver and **Judge**, the one who is able to save and destroy.

James 5:9
Don't grumble against one another, brothers and sisters, or you will be **judged**. The **Judge** is standing at the door!

1 Peter 1:17
Since you call on a Father who **judges** each person's work impartially, live out your time as foreigners here in reverent fear.

1 Peter 2:23
When they hurled their insults at him, he did not retaliate; when he suffered, he made no threats. Instead, he entrusted himself to him who **judges** justly.

1 Peter 4:5
But they will have to give account to him who is ready to **judge** the living and the dead.

Jude 1:15
to **judge** everyone, and to convict all of them of all the ungodly acts they have committed in their ungodliness, and of all the defiant words ungodly sinners have spoken against him."

Revelation 6:10
They called out in a loud voice, "How long, Sovereign Lord, holy and true, until you **judge** the inhabitants of the earth and avenge our blood?"

Revelation 18:8
She will be consumed by fire, for mighty is the Lord God who **judges** her.

Revelation 18:20
For God has **judged** her with the judgment she imposed on you."

Revelation 19:11
With justice he **judges** and wages war.

Revelation 20:12
And I saw the dead, great and small, standing before the throne, and books were opened. Another book was opened, which is the book of life. The dead were **judged** according to what they had done as recorded in the books.

Revelation 20:13
The sea gave up the dead that were in it, and death and Hades gave up the dead that were in them, and each person was **judged** according to what they had done.

God is Just
Giving Justice
Able to Justify

Just:
To give proper and fair treatment; To give what is deserved.

*He is the Rock, his works are perfect, and all his ways are **just**. A faithful God who does no wrong, upright and **just** is he.*

- Deuteronomy 32:4

God is Just

1. DEFINE JUST USING YOUR OWN WORDS, SYNONYMS, OR DESCRIPTIONS:

_____

_____

_____

2. GOD'S RIGHTEOUSNESS AND JUSTICE (OR RIGHT AND JUST) SEEM TO GO HAND-IN-HAND, SUCH AS WHERE IT SAYS, "GOD LOVES RIGHTEOUSNESS AND JUSTICE" AND "YOU HAVE DONE WHAT IS JUST AND RIGHT." FIND THESE VERSES, AND OTHERS, WHERE THESE TWO TRAITS EXIST TOGETHER.

_____

_____

_____

_____

_____

3. GOD IS JUST AND ABLE TO JUSTIFY US (TO MAKE JUST OR RIGHT) THROUGH FAITH IN JESUS. FIND THE VERSES THAT STATE THIS.

_____

_____

_____

4. DO YOU HAVE ANY OBSERVATIONS ABOUT THIS CHARACTER TRAIT OF GOD OR WHY GOD WANTS US TO KNOW THAT HE IS JUST, GIVES JUSTICE AND IS ABLE TO JUSTIFY?

_____

_____

_____

_____

_____

My argument against God was that the universe seemed so cruel and unjust. But how had I got this idea of just and unjust? A man does not call a line crooked unless he has some idea of a straight line. What was I comparing this universe with when I called it unjust?

- C. S. Lewis

NOTES:

God is Just

Deuteronomy 32:4
He is the Rock, his works are perfect, and all his ways are **just**. A faithful God who does no wrong, upright and **just** is he.

2 Chronicles 12:6
The leaders of Israel and the king humbled themselves and said, "The LORD is **just**."

2 Chronicles 19:7
Now let the fear of the LORD be on you. Judge carefully, for with the LORD our God there is **no injustice** or partiality or bribery."

Nehemiah 9:13
"You came down on Mount Sinai; you spoke to them from heaven. You gave them regulations and laws that are **just** and right, and decrees and commands that are good.

Psalm 7:6
Arise, LORD, in your anger; rise up against the rage of my enemies. Awake, my God; decree **justice**.

Psalm 9:16
The LORD is known by his acts of **justice**;

Psalm 11:7
For the LORD is righteous, he loves **justice**; the upright will see his face.

Psalm 33:5
The LORD loves righteousness and **justice**; the earth is full of his unfailing love.

Psalm 36:6
Your righteousness is like the highest mountains, your **justice** like the great deep. You, LORD, preserve both people and animals.

Psalm 45:4
In your majesty ride forth victoriously in the cause of truth, humility and **justice**; let your right hand achieve awesome deeds.

Psalm 45:6
Your throne, O God, will last for ever and ever; a scepter of **justice** will be the scepter of your kingdom.

Psalm 50:6
And the heavens proclaim his righteousness, for he is a God of **justice**.

Psalm 51:4
Against you, you only, have I sinned and done what is evil in your sight; so you are right in your verdict and **justified** when you judge.

Psalm 89:14
Righteousness and **justice** are the foundation of your throne; love and faithfulness go before you.

Psalm 97:2
Clouds and thick darkness surround him; righteousness and **justice** are the foundation of his throne.

Psalm 99:4
The King is mighty, he loves **justice**— you have established equity; in Jacob you have done what is **just** and right.

Psalm 101:1
I will sing of your love and **justice**; to you, LORD, I will sing praise.

Psalm 103:6
The LORD works righteousness and **justice** for all the oppressed.

Psalm 140:12
I know that the LORD secures **justice** for the poor and upholds the cause of the needy.

Isaiah 1:27
Zion will be delivered with **justice**, her penitent ones with righteousness.

Isaiah 5:16
But the LORD Almighty will be exalted by his **justice**, and the holy God will be proved holy by his righteous acts.

Isaiah 11:4
but with righteousness he will judge the needy, with **justice** he will give decisions for the poor of the earth. He will strike the earth with the rod of his mouth; with the breath of his lips he will slay the wicked.

Isaiah 28:6
He will be a spirit of **justice** to the one who sits in judgment,

Isaiah 28:17
I will make **justice** the measuring line and righteousness the plumb line; hail will sweep away your refuge, the lie, and water will overflow your hiding place.

Isaiah 30:18
For the LORD is a God of **justice**. Blessed are all who wait for him!

Isaiah 32:1
See, a king will reign in righteousness and rulers will rule with **justice**.

Isaiah 32:16
The LORD's **justice** will dwell in the desert, his righteousness live in the fertile field.

Isaiah 33:5
The LORD is exalted, for he dwells on high; he will fill Zion with his **justice** and righteousness.

Isaiah 42:3
A bruised reed he will not break, and a smoldering wick he will not snuff out. In faithfulness he will bring forth **justice**;

Isaiah 42:4
he will not falter or be discouraged till he establishes **justice** on earth.

Isaiah 51:4
"Listen to me, my people; hear me, my nation: Instruction will go out from me; my **justice** will become a light to the nations.

Isaiah 51:5
My righteousness draws near speedily, my salvation is on the way, and my arm will bring **justice** to the nations.

Isaiah 53:11
by his knowledge my righteous servant will **justify** many, and he will bear their iniquities.

Isaiah 61:8
"For I, the LORD, love **justice**; I hate robbery and wrongdoing.

Jeremiah 9:24
but let the one who boasts boast about this: that they have the understanding to know me, that I am the LORD, who exercises kindness, **justice** and righteousness on earth, for in these I delight," declares the LORD.

Jeremiah 23:5
"The days are coming," declares the LORD, "when I will raise up for David a righteous Branch, a King who will reign wisely and do what is **just** and right in the land.

God is Just

Jeremiah 33:15
"'In those days and at that time I will make a righteous Branch sprout from David's line; he will do what is **just** and right in the land.

Ezekiel 34:16
I will shepherd the flock with **justice**.

Hosea 2:19
I will betroth you to me forever; I will betroth you in righteousness and **justice**, in love and compassion.

Zephaniah 3:5
The LORD within her is righteous; he does no wrong. Morning by morning he dispenses his **justice**, and every new day he does not fail, yet the unrighteous know no shame.

Matthew 12:18
"Here is my servant whom I have chosen, the one I love, in whom I delight; I will put my Spirit on him, and he will proclaim **justice** to the nations.

Matthew 12:20
A bruised reed he will not break, and a smoldering wick he will not snuff out, till he has brought **justice** through to victory.

Luke 18:7
And will not God bring about **justice** for his chosen ones, who cry out to him day and night? Will he keep putting them off?

Luke 18:8
I tell you, he will see that they get **justice**, and quickly. However, when the Son of Man comes, will he find faith on the earth?"

hn 5:30
By myself I can do nothing; I judge only as I hear, and my judgment is **just**, for I seek not to please myself but him who sent me.

Acts 13:39
Through him everyone who believes is set free from every sin, a **justification** you were not able to obtain under the law of Moses.

Acts 17:31
For he has set a day when he will judge the world with **justice** by the man he has appointed. He has given proof of this to everyone by raising him from the dead."

Romans 3:24
and all are **justified** freely by his grace through the redemption that came by Christ Jesus.

Romans 3:26
he did it to demonstrate his righteousness at the present time, so as to be **just** and the one who **justifies** those who have faith in Jesus.

Romans 3:30
since there is only one God, who will **justify** the circumcised by faith and the uncircumcised through that same faith.

Romans 4:5
However, to the one who does not work but trusts God who **justifies** the ungodly, their faith is credited as righteousness.

Romans 4:25
He was delivered over to death for our sins and was raised to life for our **justification**.

Romans 5:1
Therefore, since we have been **justified** through faith, we have peace with God through our Lord Jesus Christ,

Romans 5:9
Since we have now been **justified** by his blood, how much more shall we be saved from God's wrath through him!

Romans 8:30
And those he predestined, he also called; those he called, he also **justified**; those he **justified**, he also glorified.

Romans 8:33
Who will bring any charge against those whom God has chosen? It is God who **justifies**.

1 Corinthians 6:11
And that is what some of you were. But you were washed, you were sanctified, you were **justified** in the name of the Lord Jesus Christ and by the Spirit of our God.

Galatians 2:16
know that a person is not **justified** by the works of the law, but by faith in Jesus Christ. So we, too, have put our faith in Christ Jesus that we may be **justified** by faith in Christ and not by the works of the law, because by the works of the law no one will be **justified**.

Galatians 3:8
Scripture foresaw that God would **justify** the Gentiles by faith, and announced the gospel in advance to Abraham: "All nations will be blessed through you."

Galatians 3:24
So the law was our guardian until Christ came that we might be **justified** by faith.

2 Thessalonians 1:6
God is **just**: He will pay back trouble to those who trouble you

Titus 3:7
so that, having been **justified** by his grace, we might become heirs having the hope of eternal life.

Hebrews 1:8
But about the Son he says, "Your throne, O God, will last for ever and ever; a scepter of **justice** will be the scepter of your kingdom.

Hebrews 11:33
who through faith conquered kingdoms, administered **justice**, and gained what was promised; who shut the mouths of lions,

1 Peter 2:23
When they hurled their insults at him, he did not retaliate; when he suffered, he made no threats. Instead, he entrusted himself to him who judges **justly**.

1 John 1:9
If we confess our sins, he is faithful and **just** and will forgive us our sins and purify us from all unrighteousness.

Revelation 15:3
and sang the song of God's servant Moses and of the Lamb: "Great and marvelous are your deeds, Lord God Almighty. **Just** and true are your ways, King of the nations.

Revelation 16:5
Then I heard the angel in charge of the waters say: "You are **just** in these judgments, O Holy One, you who are and who were;

God is Just

Revelation 16:7
And I heard the altar respond: "Yes, Lord God Almighty, true and **just** are your judgments."

Revelation 19:2
for true and **just** are his judgments. He has condemned the great prostitute who corrupted the earth by her adulteries. He has avenged on her the blood of his servants."

Revelation 19:11
[*The Heavenly Warrior Defeats the Beast*] I saw heaven standing open and there before me was a white horse, whose rider is called Faithful and True. With **justice** he judges and wages war.

God is Kind
Showing Kindness

Kind:
Being gentle and considerate in one's manner or conduct toward others.

*I led them with cords of human **kindness**, with ties of love. To them I was like one who lifts a little child to the cheek, and I bent down to feed them.*

- Hosea 11:4

God is Kind

1. DEFINE KIND USING YOUR OWN WORDS, SYNONYMS, OR DESCRIPTIONS:

_____

_____

_____

2. LUKE 6:35 SAYS GOD "IS KIND TO THE UNGRATEFUL AND WICKED". HE ALSO WANTS HIS CHILDREN TO BE LIKE HIM BY LOVING PEOPLE WHO HATE THEM AND DOING GOOD WITHOUT EXPECTATION OF GETTING ANYTHING IN RETURN. THIS IS GOOD ADVICE FOR US, BUT WHAT DOES THIS TELL YOU ABOUT GOD?

_____

_____

_____

3. DO YOU HAVE ANY OBSERVATIONS ABOUT THIS CHARACTER TRAIT OF GOD OR WHY GOD WANTS US TO KNOW THAT HE IS KIND AND SHOWS KINDNESS?

_____

_____

_____

_____

_____

The word "grace" emphasizes at one and the same time the helpless poverty of man and limitless kindness of God.

- William Barclay

The kindness of God is reason enough to never desire His wrath.

NOTES:

God is Kind

Genesis 24:14
By this I will know that you have shown **kindness** to my master."

Genesis 24:27
saying, "Praise be to the LORD, the God of my master Abraham, who has not abandoned his **kindness** and faithfulness to my master.

Genesis 24:49
Now if you will show **kindness** and faithfulness to my master, tell me; and if not, tell me, so I may know which way to turn."

Genesis 32:10
I am unworthy of all the **kindness** and faithfulness you have shown your servant.

Genesis 39:21
the LORD was with him; he showed him **kindness** and granted him favor in the eyes of the prison warden.

Exodus 1:20
So God was **kind** to the midwives and the people increased and became even more numerous.

1 Samuel 20:14
But show me unfailing **kindness** like the LORD's **kindness** as long as I live, so that I may not be killed,

2 Samuel 2:6
May the LORD now show you **kindness** and faithfulness,

2 Samuel 9:3
The king asked, "Is there no one still alive from the house of Saul to whom I can show God's **kindness**?"

2 Samuel 15:20
May the LORD show you **kindness** and faithfulness."

2 Samuel 22:51
"He gives his king great victories; he shows unfailing **kindness** to his anointed, to David and his descendants forever."

2 Chronicles 1:8
Solomon answered God, "You have shown great **kindness** to David my father and have made me king in his place.

2 Chronicles 32:25
But Hezekiah's heart was proud and he did not respond to the **kindness** shown him; therefore the LORD's wrath was on him and on Judah and Jerusalem.

Ezra 9:9
Though we are slaves, our God has not forsaken us in our bondage. He has shown us **kindness** in the sight of the kings of Persia:

Psalm 106:7
When our ancestors were in Egypt, they gave no thought to your miracles; they did not remember your many **kindnesses**, and they rebelled by the sea, the Red Sea.

Psalm 138:6
Though the LORD is exalted, he looks **kindly** on the lowly; though lofty, he sees them from afar.

Isaiah 54:8
In a surge of anger I hid my face from you for a moment, but with everlasting **kindness** I will have compassion on you," says the LORD your Redeemer.

Isaiah 63:7
I will tell of the **kindnesses** of the LORD, the deeds for which he is to be praised, according to all the LORD has done for us— yes, the many good things he has done for Israel, according to his compassion and many **kindnesses**.

Jeremiah 9:24
but let the one who boasts boast about this: that they have the understanding to know me, that I am the LORD, who exercises **kindness**, justice and righteousness on earth, for in these I delight," declares the LORD.

Jeremiah 31:3
The LORD appeared to us in the past, saying: "I have loved you with an everlasting love; I have drawn you with unfailing **kindness**.

Hosea 11:4
I led them with cords of human **kindness**, with ties of love. To them I was like one who lifts a little child to the cheek, and I bent down to feed them.

Zechariah 1:13
So the LORD spoke **kind** and comforting words to the angel who talked with me.

Luke 6:35
But love your enemies, do good to them, and lend to them without expecting to get anything back. Then your reward will be great, and you will be children of the Most High, because he is **kind** to the ungrateful and wicked.

Acts 14:17
Yet he has not left himself without testimony: He has shown **kindness** by giving you rain from heaven and crops in their seasons; he provides you with plenty of food and fills your hearts with joy."

Romans 11:22
Consider therefore the **kindness** and sternness of God: sternness to those who fell, but kindness to you, provided that you continue in his **kindness**.

1 Corinthians 13:4
Love is patient, love is **kind**. It does not envy, it does not boast, it is not proud.

Galatians 5:22
But the fruit of the Spirit is love, joy, peace, forbearance, **kindness**, goodness, faithfulness,

Ephesians 2:7
in order that in the coming ages he might show the incomparable riches of his grace, expressed in his **kindness** to us in Christ Jesus.

Ephesians 4:32
Be **kind** and compassionate to one another, forgiving each other, just as in Christ God forgave you.

Titus 3:4
But when the **kindness** and love of God our Savior appeared,

God Our King
Sovereign Majesty; Ruler Overseeing a Kingdom

King or Sovereign:
A supreme ruler with right to the throne and able to make a decree or declaration; Possessing independent power and authority above others.

On his robe and on his thigh he has this name written:
__KING__ OF KINGS AND LORD OF LORDS.

- Revelation 19:16

God Our King

1. DEFINE KING USING YOUR OWN WORDS, SYNONYMS, OR DESCRIPTIONS:

_____

_____

_____

2. BY FAR, THERE ARE MORE REFERENCES TO GOD AS KING THAN ANY OTHER OF HIS CHARACTER TRAITS. WHY DO YOU THINK IT WAS IMPORTANT FOR GOD TO EMPHASIZE HIS SOVEREIGNTY IN THE BIBLE?

_____

_____

_____

3. IN THE BOOK OF EZEKIEL, THE PHRASE "THIS IS WHAT THE SOVEREIGN LORD SAYS" IS REPEATED MANY TIMES. LOOK UP SOME OF THE THINGS THE SOVEREIGN LORD SAYS.

_____

_____

_____

4. READ DANIEL CHAPTER 4. SEE HOW THE MOST POWERFUL KING IN THE WORLD AT THE TIME, NEBUCHADNEZZAR, WAS HUMBLED BY GOD AND CONCLUDES FINALLY, "NOW, I, NEBUCHADNEZZAR, PRAISE AND EXALT AND GLORIFY THE KING OF HEAVEN, BECAUSE EVERYTHING HE DOES IS RIGHT AND ALL HIS WAYS ARE JUST. AND THOSE WHO WALK IN PRIDE HE IS ABLE TO HUMBLE."

_____

_____

_____

5. DO YOU HAVE ANY OBSERVATIONS ABOUT THIS CHARACTER TRAIT OF GOD OR WHY GOD WANTS US TO KNOW THAT HE IS OUR KING, SOVEREIGN, RULER, MAJESTY AND OVERSEES A KINGDOM?

_____

_____

_____

_____

I have lived a long time, sir, and the longer I live the more convincing proofs I see of this truth -- that God governs in the affairs of men.

- Benjamin Franklin

NOTES:

God Our King

Genesis 15:2
But Abram said, "**Sovereign** LORD, what can you give me since I remain childless and the one who will inherit my estate is Eliezer of Damascus?"

Genesis 15:8
But Abram said, "**Sovereign** LORD, how can I know that I will gain possession of it?"

Exodus 15:6
Your right hand, LORD, was **majestic** in power.

Exodus 15:7
"In the greatness of your **majesty** you threw down those who opposed you.

Exodus 15:11
Who among the gods is like you, LORD? Who is like you— **majestic** in holiness, awesome in glory, working wonders?

Exodus 23:17
"Three times a year all the men are to appear before the **Sovereign** LORD.

Exodus 34:23
Three times a year all your men are to appear before the **Sovereign** LORD, the God of Israel.

Deuteronomy 3:24
"**Sovereign** LORD, you have begun to show to your servant your greatness and your strong hand. For what god is there in heaven or on earth who can do the deeds and mighty works you do?

Deuteronomy 5:24
And you said, "The LORD our God has shown us his glory and his **majesty,**

Deuteronomy 9:26
I prayed to the LORD and said, "**Sovereign** LORD, do not destroy your people, your own inheritance that you redeemed by your great power and brought out of Egypt with a mighty hand.

Deuteronomy 11:2
Remember today that your children were not the ones who saw and experienced the discipline of the LORD your God: his **majesty,** his mighty hand, his outstretched arm;

Deuteronomy 33:26
"There is no one like God, who rides across the heavens to help you and on the clouds in his **majesty**.

Joshua 7:7
And Joshua said, "Alas, **Sovereign** LORD, why did you ever bring this people across the Jordan to deliver us into the hands of the Amorites to destroy us? If only we had been content to stay on the other side of the Jordan!

Judges 6:22
When Gideon realized that it was the angel of the LORD, he exclaimed, "Alas, **Sovereign** LORD! I have seen the angel of the LORD face to face!"

Judges 16:28
Then Samson prayed to the LORD, "**Sovereign** LORD, remember me. Please, God, strengthen me just once more, and let me with one blow get revenge on the Philistines for my two eyes."

2 Samuel 7:18
Then King David went in and sat before the LORD, and he said: "Who am I, **Sovereign** LORD, and what is my family, that you have brought me this far?

2 Samuel 7:19
And as if this were not enough in your sight, **Sovereign** LORD, you have also spoken about the future of the house of your servant—and this decree, **Sovereign** LORD, is for a mere human!

2 Samuel 7:20
"What more can David say to you? For you know your servant, **Sovereign** LORD.

2 Samuel 7:22
"How great you are, **Sovereign** LORD! There is no one like you, and there is no God but you, as we have heard with our own ears.

2 Samuel 7:28
Sovereign LORD, you are God! Your covenant is trustworthy, and you have promised these good things to your servant.

2 Samuel 7:29
Now be pleased to bless the house of your servant, that it may continue forever in your sight; for you, **Sovereign** LORD, have spoken, and with your blessing the house of your servant will be blessed forever."

1 Kings 2:26
To Abiathar the priest the king said, "Go back to your fields in Anathoth. You deserve to die, but I will not put you to death now, because you carried the ark of the **Sovereign** LORD before my father David and shared all my father's hardships."

1 Kings 8:53
For you singled them out from all the nations of the world to be your own inheritance, just as you declared through your servant Moses when you, **Sovereign** LORD, brought our ancestors out of Egypt."

1 Chronicles 16:27
Splendor and **majesty** are before him; strength and joy are in his dwelling place.

1 Chronicles 29:11
Yours, LORD, is the greatness and the power and the glory and the **majesty** and the splendor, for everything in heaven and earth is yours. Yours, LORD, is the **kingdom**; you are exalted as head over all.

Job 37:22
God comes in awesome **majesty**.

Psalm 2:6
"I have installed my **king** on Zion, my holy mountain."

Psalm 2:11
Serve the LORD with fear and celebrate his **rule** with trembling.

Psalm 5:2
Hear my cry for help, my **King** and my God, for to you I pray.

Psalm 8:1
LORD, our Lord, how **majestic** is your name in all the earth! You have set your glory in the heavens.

Psalm 8:9
LORD, our Lord, how **majestic** is your name in all the earth!

Psalm 9:8
He **rules** the world in righteousness and judges the peoples with equity.

Psalm 10:16
The LORD is **King** for ever and ever; the nations will perish from his land.

Psalm 22:28
for dominion belongs to the LORD and he **rules** over the nations.

Psalm 24:7
Lift up your heads, you gates; be lifted up, you ancient doors, that the **King** of glory may come in.

God Our King

Psalm 24:8
Who is this **King** of glory? The LORD strong and mighty, the LORD mighty in battle.

Psalm 24:9
Lift up your heads, you gates; lift them up, you ancient doors, that the **King** of glory may come in.

Psalm 24:10
Who is he, this **King** of glory? The LORD Almighty— he is the **King** of glory.

Psalm 29:4
The voice of the LORD is powerful; the voice of the LORD is **majestic**.

Psalm 29:10
The LORD sits enthroned over the flood; the LORD is enthroned as **King** forever.

Psalm 44:4
You are my **King** and my God, who decrees victories for Jacob.

Psalm 45:6
Your **throne**, O God, will last for ever and ever; a scepter of justice will be the scepter of your **kingdom**.

Psalm 47:2
For the LORD Most High is awesome, the great **King** over all the earth.

Psalm 47:6
Sing praises to God, sing praises; sing praises to our **King**, sing praises.

Psalm 47:7
For God is the **King** of all the earth; sing to him a psalm of praise.

Psalm 48:2
Beautiful in its loftiness, the joy of the whole earth, like the heights of Zaphon is Mount Zion, the city of the Great **King**.

Psalm 59:13
Then it will be known to the ends of the earth that God **rules** over Jacob.

Psalm 66:7
He **rules** forever by his power, his eyes watch the nations—

Psalm 67:4
May the nations be glad and sing for joy, for you **rule** the peoples with equity and guide the nations of the earth.

Psalm 68:20
Our God is a God who saves; from the **Sovereign** LORD comes escape from death.

Psalm 68:24
Your procession, God, has come into view, the procession of my God and **King** into the sanctuary.

Psalm 68:34
Proclaim the power of God, whose **majesty** is over Israel, whose power is in the heavens.

Psalm 71:5
For you have been my hope, **Sovereign** LORD, my confidence since my youth.

Psalm 71:16
I will come and proclaim your mighty acts, **Sovereign** LORD; I will proclaim your righteous deeds, yours alone.

Psalm 73:28
But as for me, it is good to be near God. I have made the **Sovereign** LORD my refuge; I will tell of all your deeds.

Psalm 74:12
But God is my **King** from long ago; he brings salvation on the earth.

Psalm 76:4
You are radiant with light, more **majestic** than mountains rich with game.

Psalm 84:3
Even the sparrow has found a home, and the swallow a nest for herself, where she may have her young— a place near your altar, LORD Almighty, my **King** and my God.

Psalm 89:9
You **rule** over the surging sea; when its waves mount up, you still them.

Psalm 93:1
The LORD **reigns**, he is robed in **majesty**; the LORD is robed in **majesty** and armed with strength; indeed, the world is established, firm and secure.

Psalm 95:3
For the LORD is the great God, the great **King** above all gods.

Psalm 96:6
Splendor and **majesty** are before him; strength and glory are in his sanctuary.

Psalm 98:6
with trumpets and the blast of the ram's horn— shout for joy before the LORD, the **King**.

Psalm 99:4
The **King** is mighty, he loves justice— you have established equity; in Jacob you have done what is just and right.

Psalm 103:19
The LORD has established his **throne** in heaven, and his **kingdom** rules over all.

Psalm 104:1
Praise the LORD, my soul. LORD my God, you are very great; you are clothed with splendor and **majesty**.

Psalm 109:21
But you, **Sovereign** LORD, help me for your name's sake; out of the goodness of your love, deliver me.

Psalm 111:3
Glorious and **majestic** are his deeds, and his righteousness endures forever.

Psalm 140:7
Sovereign LORD, my strong deliverer, you shield my head in the day of battle.

Psalm 141:8
But my eyes are fixed on you, **Sovereign** LORD; in you I take refuge—do not give me over to death.

Psalm 145:1
I will exalt you, my God the **King**; I will praise your name for ever and ever.

Psalm 145:5
They speak of the glorious splendor of your **majesty**— and I will meditate on your wonderful works.

Psalm 145:11
They tell of the glory of your **kingdom** and speak of your might,

Psalm 145:12
so that all people may know of your mighty acts and the glorious splendor of your **kingdom**.

Psalm 145:13
Your **kingdom** is an everlasting **kingdom**, and your **dominion** endures through all generations.

God Our King

Psalm 149:2
Let Israel rejoice in their Maker; let the people of Zion be glad in their **King**.

Song of Solomon 6:10
Who is this that appears like the dawn, fair as the moon, bright as the sun, **majestic** as the stars in procession?

Isaiah 2:10
Go into the rocks, hide in the ground from the fearful presence of the LORD and the splendor of his **majesty**!

Isaiah 2:19
People will flee to caves in the rocks and to holes in the ground from the fearful presence of the LORD and the splendor of his **majesty**, when he rises to shake the earth.

Isaiah 2:21
They will flee to caverns in the rocks and to the overhanging crags from the fearful presence of the LORD and the splendor of his **majesty**, when he rises to shake the earth.

Isaiah 6:5
"Woe to me!" I cried. "I am ruined! For I am a man of unclean lips, and I live among a people of unclean lips, and my eyes have seen the **King**, the LORD Almighty."

Isaiah 7:7
Yet this is what the **Sovereign** LORD says: "'It will not take place, it will not happen,

Isaiah 9:7
Of the greatness of his government and peace there will be no end. He will **reign** on David's throne and over his **kingdom**, establishing and upholding it with justice and righteousness from that time on and forever.

Isaiah 24:14
They raise their voices, they shout for joy; from the west they acclaim the LORD's **majesty**.

Isaiah 25:8
The **Sovereign** LORD will wipe away the tears from all faces; he will remove his people's disgrace from all the earth.

Isaiah 26:10
But when grace is shown to the wicked, they do not learn righteousness; even in a land of uprightness they go on doing evil and do not regard the **majesty** of the LORD.

Isaiah 28:16
So this is what the **Sovereign** LORD says: "See, I lay a stone in Zion, a tested stone, a precious cornerstone for a sure foundation; the one who relies on it will never be stricken with panic.

Isaiah 30:15
This is what the **Sovereign** LORD, the Holy One of Israel, says: "In repentance and rest is your salvation, in quietness and trust is your strength, but you would have none of it.

Isaiah 30:30
The LORD will cause people to hear his **majestic** voice and will make them see his arm coming down with raging anger and consuming fire, with cloudburst, thunderstorm and hail.

Isaiah 32:1
[*The Kingdom of Righteousness*] See, a **king** will **reign** in righteousness and rulers will rule with justice.

Isaiah 33:17
Your eyes will see the **king** in his beauty and view a land that stretches afar.

Isaiah 33:22
For the LORD is our judge, the LORD is our lawgiver, the LORD is our **king**; it is he who will save us.

Isaiah 37:16
"LORD Almighty, the God of Israel, **enthroned** between the cherubim, you alone are God over all the kingdoms of the earth. You have made heaven and earth.

Isaiah 40:10
See, the **Sovereign** LORD comes with power, and he **rules** with a mighty arm.

Isaiah 41:21
"Present your case," says the LORD. "Set forth your arguments," says Jacob's **King**.

Isaiah 43:15
I am the LORD, your Holy One, Israel's Creator, your **King**."

Isaiah 44:6
"This is what the LORD says— Israel's **King** and Redeemer, the LORD Almighty: I am the first and I am the last; apart from me there is no God.

Isaiah 48:16
"Come near me and listen to this: "From the first announcement I have not spoken in secret; at the time it happens, I am there." And now the **Sovereign** LORD has sent me, endowed with his Spirit.

Isaiah 49:22
This is what the **Sovereign** LORD says: "See, I will beckon to the nations, I will lift up my banner to the peoples;

Isaiah 50:4
The **Sovereign** LORD has given me a well-instructed tongue, to know the word that sustains the weary.

Isaiah 50:5
The **Sovereign** LORD has opened my ears; I have not been rebellious, I have not turned away.

Isaiah 50:7
Because the **Sovereign** LORD helps me, I will not be disgraced.

Isaiah 50:9
It is the **Sovereign** LORD who helps me. Who will condemn me? They will all wear out like a garment; the moths will eat them up.

Isaiah 51:22
This is what your **Sovereign** LORD says, your God, who defends his people:

Isaiah 52:4
For this is what the **Sovereign** LORD says: "At first my people went down to Egypt to live; lately, Assyria has oppressed them.

Isaiah 56:8
The **Sovereign** LORD declares— he who gathers the exiles of Israel: "I will gather still others to them besides those already gathered."

Isaiah 61:1
The Spirit of the **Sovereign** LORD is on me, because the LORD has anointed me to proclaim good news to the poor. He has sent me to bind up the brokenhearted, to proclaim freedom for the captives and release from darkness for the prisoners,

Isaiah 61:11
For as the soil makes the sprout come up and a garden causes seeds to grow, so the **Sovereign** LORD will make righteousness and praise spring up before all nations.

Isaiah 65:13
Therefore this is what the **Sovereign** LORD says: "My servants will eat, but you will go hungry; my servants will drink, but you will go thirsty; my servants will rejoice, but you will be put to shame.

Isaiah 65:15
You will leave your name for my chosen ones to use in their curses; the **Sovereign** LORD will put you to death, but to his servants he will give another name.

Jeremiah 1:6
"Alas, **Sovereign** LORD," I said, "I do not know how to speak; I am too young."

God Our King

Jeremiah 2:22
Although you wash yourself with soap and use an abundance of cleansing powder, the stain of your guilt is still before me," declares the **Sovereign** LORD.

Jeremiah 4:10
Then I said, "Alas, **Sovereign** LORD! How completely you have deceived this people and Jerusalem by saying, 'You will have peace,' when the sword is at our throats!"

Jeremiah 7:20
"'Therefore this is what the **Sovereign** LORD says: My anger and my wrath will be poured out on this place—on man and beast, on the trees of the field and on the crops of your land—and it will burn and not be quenched.

Jeremiah 10:7
Who should not fear you, **King** of the nations? This is your due. Among all the wise leaders of the nations and in all their kingdoms, there is no one like you.

Jeremiah 10:10
But the LORD is the true God; he is the living God, the eternal **King**. When he is angry, the earth trembles; the nations cannot endure his wrath.

Jeremiah 14:13
But I said, "Alas, **Sovereign** LORD! The prophets keep telling them, 'You will not see the sword or suffer famine.

Jeremiah 23:5
"The days are coming," declares the LORD, "when I will raise up for David a righteous Branch, a **King** who will reign wisely and do what is just and right in the land.

Jeremiah 32:17
"Ah, **Sovereign** LORD, you have made the heavens and the earth by your great power and outstretched arm. Nothing is too hard for you.

Jeremiah 32:25
And though the city will be given into the hands of the Babylonians, you, **Sovereign** LORD, say to me, 'Buy the field with silver and have the transaction witnessed.'"

Jeremiah 44:26
But hear the word of the LORD, all you Jews living in Egypt: 'I swear by my great name,' says the LORD, 'that no one from Judah living anywhere in Egypt will ever again invoke my name or swear, "As surely as the **Sovereign** LORD lives."

Jeremiah 46:18
"As surely as I live," declares the **King**, whose name is the LORD Almighty, "one will come who is like Tabor among the mountains, like Carmel by the sea.

Jeremiah 48:15
her finest young men will go down in the slaughter," declares the **King**, whose name is the LORD Almighty.

Jeremiah 50:25
The LORD has opened his arsenal and brought out the weapons of his wrath, for the **Sovereign** LORD Almighty has work to do in the land of the Babylonians.

Jeremiah 51:57
I will make her officials and wise men drunk, her governors, officers and warriors as well; they will sleep forever and not awake," declares the **King**, whose name is the LORD Almighty.

Ezekiel 2:4
The people to whom I am sending you are obstinate and stubborn. Say to them, 'This is what the **Sovereign** LORD says.'

Ezekiel 3:11
Say to them, 'This is what the **Sovereign** LORD says,' whether they listen or fail to listen."

Ezekiel 3:27
But when I speak to you, I will open your mouth and you shall say to them, 'This is what the **Sovereign** LORD says.' Whoever will listen let them listen, and whoever will refuse let them refuse; for they are a rebellious people.

Ezekiel 4:14
Then I said, "Not so, **Sovereign** LORD! I have never defiled myself.

Ezekiel 5:5
"This is what the **Sovereign** LORD says: This is Jerusalem, which I have set in the center of the nations, with countries all around her.

Ezekiel 5:7
"Therefore this is what the **Sovereign** LORD says: You have been more unruly than the nations around you and have not followed my decrees or kept my laws. You have not even conformed to the standards of the nations around you.

Ezekiel 5:8
"Therefore this is what the **Sovereign** LORD says: I myself am against you, Jerusalem, and I will inflict punishment on you in the sight of the nations.

Ezekiel 5:11
Therefore as surely as I live, declares the **Sovereign** LORD, because you have defiled my sanctuary with all your vile images and detestable practices, I myself will shave you; I will not look on you with pity or spare you.

Ezekiel 6:3
and say: 'You mountains of Israel, hear the word of the **Sovereign** LORD. This is what the **Sovereign** LORD says to the mountains and hills, to the ravines and valleys: I am about to bring a sword against you, and I will destroy your high places.

Ezekiel 6:11
"'This is what the **Sovereign** LORD says: Strike your hands together and stamp your feet and cry out "Alas!" because of all the wicked and detestable practices of the people of Israel, for they will fall by the sword, famine and plague.

Ezekiel 7:2
"Son of man, this is what the **Sovereign** LORD says to the land of Israel: "'The end! The end has come upon the four corners of the land!

Ezekiel 7:5
"This is what the **Sovereign** LORD says: "'Disaster! Unheard-of disaster! See, it comes!

Ezekiel 8:1
In the sixth year, in the sixth month on the fifth day, while I was sitting in my house and the elders of Judah were sitting before me, the hand of the **Sovereign** LORD came on me there.

Ezekiel 9:8
While they were killing and I was left alone, I fell facedown, crying out, "Alas, **Sovereign** LORD! Are you going to destroy the entire remnant of Israel in this outpouring of your wrath on Jerusalem?"

Ezekiel 11:7
"Therefore this is what the **Sovereign** LORD says: The bodies you have thrown there are the meat and this city is the pot, but I will drive you out of it.

Ezekiel 11:8
You fear the sword, and the sword is what I will bring against you, declares the **Sovereign** LORD.

Ezekiel 11:13
Now as I was prophesying, Pelatiah son of Benaiah died. Then I fell facedown and cried out in a loud voice, "Alas, **Sovereign** LORD! Will you completely destroy the remnant of Israel?"

Ezekiel 11:16
"Therefore say: 'This is what the **Sovereign** LORD says: Although I sent them far away among the nations and scattered them among the countries, yet for a little while I have been a sanctuary for them in the countries where they have gone.'

God Our King

Ezekiel 11:17
"Therefore say: 'This is what the **Sovereign** LORD says: I will gather you from the nations and bring you back from the countries where you have been scattered, and I will give you back the land of Israel again.'

Ezekiel 11:21
But as for those whose hearts are devoted to their vile images and detestable idols, I will bring down on their own heads what they have done, declares the **Sovereign** LORD."

Ezekiel 12:10
"Say to them, 'This is what the **Sovereign** LORD says: This prophecy concerns the prince in Jerusalem and all the Israelites who are there.'

Ezekiel 12:19
Say to the people of the land: 'This is what the **Sovereign** LORD says about those living in Jerusalem and in the land of Israel:

Ezekiel 12:23
Say to them, 'This is what the **Sovereign** LORD says: I am going to put an end to this proverb, and they will no longer quote it in Israel.' Say to them, 'The days are near when every vision will be fulfilled.

Ezekiel 12:25
For in your days, you rebellious people, I will fulfill whatever I say, declares the **Sovereign** LORD.'"

Ezekiel 12:28
"Therefore say to them, 'This is what the **Sovereign** LORD says: None of my words will be delayed any longer; whatever I say will be fulfilled, declares the **Sovereign** LORD.'"

Ezekiel 13:3
This is what the **Sovereign** LORD says: Woe to the foolish prophets who follow their own spirit and have seen nothing!

Ezekiel 13:8
"'Therefore this is what the **Sovereign** LORD says: Because of your false words and lying visions, I am against you, declares the **Sovereign** LORD.

Ezekiel 13:9
Then you will know that I am the **Sovereign** LORD.

Ezekiel 13:13
"'Therefore this is what the **Sovereign** LORD says: In my wrath I will unleash a violent wind, and in my anger hailstones and torrents of rain will fall with destructive fury.

Ezekiel 13:16
those prophets of Israel who prophesied to Jerusalem and saw visions of peace for her when there was no peace, declares the **Sovereign** LORD.'"

Ezekiel 13:18
and say, 'This is what the **Sovereign** LORD says: Woe to the women who sew magic charms on all their wrists and make veils of various lengths for their heads in order to ensnare people.

Ezekiel 13:20
"'Therefore this is what the **Sovereign** LORD says: I am against your magic charms with which you ensnare people like birds and I will tear them from your arms; I will set free the people that you ensnare like birds.

Ezekiel 14:4
Therefore speak to them and tell them, 'This is what the **Sovereign** LORD says: When any of the Israelites set up idols in their hearts and put a wicked stumbling block before their faces and then go to a prophet, I the LORD will answer them myself in keeping with their great idolatry.

Ezekiel 14:6
"Therefore say to the people of Israel, 'This is what the **Sovereign** LORD says: Repent! Turn from your idols and renounce all your detestable practices!

Ezekiel 14:11
They will be my people, and I will be their God, declares the **Sovereign** LORD.'"

Ezekiel 14:14
even if these three men—Noah, Daniel and Job—were in it, they could save only themselves by their righteousness, declares the **Sovereign** LORD.

Ezekiel 14:16
as surely as I live, declares the **Sovereign** LORD, even if these three men were in it, they could not save their own sons or daughters. They alone would be saved, but the land would be desolate.

Ezekiel 14:18
as surely as I live, declares the **Sovereign** LORD, even if these three men were in it, they could not save their own sons or daughters. They alone would be saved.

Ezekiel 14:20
as surely as I live, declares the **Sovereign** LORD, even if Noah, Daniel and Job were in it, they could save neither son nor daughter. They would save only themselves by their righteousness.

Ezekiel 14:21
"For this is what the **Sovereign** LORD says: How much worse will it be when I send against Jerusalem my four dreadful judgments—sword and famine and wild beasts and plague—to kill its men and their animals!

Ezekiel 14:23
You will be consoled when you see their conduct and their actions, for you will know that I have done nothing in it without cause, declares the **Sovereign** LORD."

Ezekiel 15:6
"Therefore this is what the **Sovereign** LORD says: As I have given the wood of the vine among the trees of the forest as fuel for the fire, so will I treat the people living in Jerusalem.

Ezekiel 15:8
I will make the land desolate because they have been unfaithful, declares the **Sovereign** LORD."

Ezekiel 16:3
and say, 'This is what the **Sovereign** LORD says to Jerusalem: Your ancestry and birth were in the land of the Canaanites; your father was an Amorite and your mother a Hittite.

Ezekiel 16:8
I gave you my solemn oath and entered into a covenant with you, declares the **Sovereign** LORD, and you became mine.

Ezekiel 16:14
And your fame spread among the nations on account of your beauty, because the splendor I had given you made your beauty perfect, declares the **Sovereign** LORD.

Ezekiel 16:19
That is what happened, declares the **Sovereign** LORD.

Ezekiel 16:23
"'Woe! Woe to you, declares the **Sovereign** LORD. In addition to all your other wickedness,

Ezekiel 16:30
"'I am filled with fury against you, declares the **Sovereign** LORD, when you do all these things, acting like a brazen prostitute!

Ezekiel 16:36
This is what the **Sovereign** LORD says: Because you poured out your lust and exposed your naked body in your promiscuity with your lovers, and because of all your detestable idols, and because you gave them your children's blood,

Ezekiel 16:43
"'Because you did not remember the days of your youth but enraged me with all these things, I will surely bring down on your head what you have done, declares the **Sovereign** LORD. Did you not add lewdness to all your other detestable practices?

God Our King

Ezekiel 16:48
As surely as I live, declares the **Sovereign** LORD, your sister Sodom and her daughters never did what you and your daughters have done.

Ezekiel 16:59
"'This is what the **Sovereign** LORD says: I will deal with you as you deserve, because you have despised my oath by breaking the covenant.

Ezekiel 16:63
Then, when I make atonement for you for all you have done, you will remember and be ashamed and never again open your mouth because of your humiliation, declares the **Sovereign** LORD.'"

Ezekiel 17:3
Say to them, 'This is what the **Sovereign** LORD says: A great eagle with powerful wings, long feathers and full plumage of varied colors came to Lebanon.

Ezekiel 17:9
"Say to them, 'This is what the **Sovereign** LORD says: Will it thrive? Will it not be uprooted and stripped of its fruit so that it withers? All its new growth will wither. It will not take a strong arm or many people to pull it up by the roots.

Ezekiel 17:16
"'As surely as I live, declares the **Sovereign** LORD, he shall die in Babylon, in the land of the king who put him on the throne, whose oath he despised and whose treaty he broke.

Ezekiel 17:19
"'Therefore this is what the **Sovereign** LORD says: As surely as I live, I will repay him for despising my oath and breaking my covenant.

Ezekiel 17:22
"'This is what the **Sovereign** LORD says: I myself will take a shoot from the very top of a cedar and plant it;

Ezekiel 18:3
"As surely as I live, declares the **Sovereign** LORD, you will no longer quote this proverb in Israel.

Ezekiel 18:9
He follows my decrees and faithfully keeps my laws. That man is righteous; he will surely live, declares the **Sovereign** LORD.

Ezekiel 18:23
Do I take any pleasure in the death of the wicked? declares the **Sovereign** LORD.

Ezekiel 18:30
"Therefore, you Israelites, I will judge each of you according to your own ways, declares the **Sovereign** LORD. Repent! Turn away from all your offenses; then sin will not be your downfall.

Ezekiel 18:32
For I take no pleasure in the death of anyone, declares the **Sovereign** LORD. Repent and live!

Ezekiel 20:3
"Son of man, speak to the elders of Israel and say to them, 'This is what the **Sovereign** LORD says: Have you come to inquire of me? As surely as I live, I will not let you inquire of me, declares the **Sovereign** LORD.'

Ezekiel 20:5
and say to them: 'This is what the **Sovereign** LORD says: On the day I chose Israel, I swore with uplifted hand to the descendants of Jacob and revealed myself to them in Egypt. With uplifted hand I said to them, "I am the LORD your God."

Ezekiel 20:27
"Therefore, son of man, speak to the people of Israel and say to them, 'This is what the **Sovereign** LORD says: In this also your ancestors blasphemed me by being unfaithful to me:

Ezekiel 20:30
"Therefore say to the Israelites: 'This is what the **Sovereign** LORD says: Will you defile yourselves the way your ancestors did and lust after their vile images?

God Our King

Ezekiel 20:31
As surely as I live, declares the **Sovereign** LORD, I will not let you inquire of me.

Ezekiel 20:33
As surely as I live, declares the **Sovereign** LORD, I will **reign** over you with a mighty hand and an outstretched arm and with outpoured wrath.

Ezekiel 20:36
As I judged your ancestors in the wilderness of the land of Egypt, so I will judge you, declares the **Sovereign** LORD.

Ezekiel 20:39
"'As for you, people of Israel, this is what the **Sovereign** LORD says: Go and serve your idols, every one of you! But afterward you will surely listen to me and no longer profane my holy name with your gifts and idols.

Ezekiel 20:40
For on my holy mountain, the high mountain of Israel, declares the **Sovereign** LORD, there in the land all the people of Israel will serve me, and there I will accept them.

Ezekiel 20:44
You will know that I am the LORD, when I deal with you for my name's sake and not according to your evil ways and your corrupt practices, you people of Israel, declares the **Sovereign** LORD.'"

Ezekiel 20:47
Say to the southern forest: 'Hear the word of the LORD. This is what the **Sovereign** LORD says: I am about to set fire to you, and it will consume all your trees, both green and dry.

Ezekiel 20:49
Then I said, "**Sovereign** LORD, they are saying of me, 'Isn't he just telling parables?'"

Ezekiel 21:7
It is coming! It will surely take place, declares the **Sovereign** LORD."

Ezekiel 21:13
"'Testing will surely come. And what if even the scepter, which the sword despises, does not continue? declares the **Sovereign** LORD.'

Ezekiel 21:24
"Therefore this is what the **Sovereign** LORD says: 'Because you people have brought to mind your guilt by your open rebellion, revealing your sins in all that you do—because you have done this, you will be taken captive.

Ezekiel 21:26
this is what the **Sovereign** LORD says: Take off the turban, remove the crown. It will not be as it was: The lowly will be exalted and the exalted will be brought low.

Ezekiel 21:28
"And you, son of man, prophesy and say, 'This is what the **Sovereign** LORD says about the Ammonites and their insults:

Ezekiel 22:3
and say: 'This is what the **Sovereign** LORD says: You city that brings on herself doom by shedding blood in her midst and defiles herself by making idols,

Ezekiel 22:12
In you are people who accept bribes to shed blood; you take interest and make a profit from the poor. You extort unjust gain from your neighbors. And you have forgotten me, declares the **Sovereign** LORD.

Ezekiel 22:19
Therefore this is what the **Sovereign** LORD says: 'Because you have all become dross, I will gather you into Jerusalem.

Ezekiel 22:28
Her prophets whitewash these deeds for them by false visions and lying divinations. They say, 'This is what the **Sovereign** LORD says'—when the LORD has not spoken.

God Our King

Ezekiel 22:31
So I will pour out my wrath on them and consume them with my fiery anger, bringing down on their own heads all they have done, declares the **Sovereign** LORD."

Ezekiel 23:22
"Therefore, Oholibah, this is what the **Sovereign** LORD says: I will stir up your lovers against you, those you turned away from in disgust, and I will bring them against you from every side—

Ezekiel 23:28
"For this is what the **Sovereign** LORD says: I am about to deliver you into the hands of those you hate, to those you turned away from in disgust.

Ezekiel 23:32
"This is what the **Sovereign** LORD says: "You will drink your sister's cup, a cup large and deep;

Ezekiel 23:34
I have spoken, declares the **Sovereign** LORD.

Ezekiel 23:35
"Therefore this is what the **Sovereign** LORD says: Since you have forgotten me and turned your back on me, you must bear the consequences of your lewdness and prostitution."

Ezekiel 23:46
"This is what the **Sovereign** LORD says: Bring a mob against them and give them over to terror and plunder.

Ezekiel 23:49
Then you will know that I am the **Sovereign** LORD."

Ezekiel 24:3
'This is what the **Sovereign** LORD says: "'Put on the cooking pot; put it on and pour water into it.

Ezekiel 24:6
"'For this is what the **Sovereign** LORD says: "'Woe to the city of bloodshed, to the pot now encrusted, whose deposit will not go away! Take the meat out piece by piece in whatever order it comes.

Ezekiel 24:9
"'Therefore this is what the **Sovereign** LORD says: "'Woe to the city of bloodshed! I, too, will pile the wood high.

Ezekiel 24:14
You will be judged according to your conduct and your actions, declares the **Sovereign** LORD.'"

Ezekiel 24:21
Say to the people of Israel, 'This is what the **Sovereign** LORD says: I am about to desecrate my sanctuary—the stronghold in which you take pride, the delight of your eyes, the object of your affection.

Ezekiel 24:24
When this happens, you will know that I am the **Sovereign** LORD.'

Ezekiel 25:3
Say to them, 'Hear the word of the **Sovereign** LORD. This is what the **Sovereign** LORD says: Because you said "Aha!" over my sanctuary when it was desecrated and over the land of Israel when it was laid waste and over the people of Judah when they went into exile,

Ezekiel 25:6
For this is what the **Sovereign** LORD says: Because you have clapped your hands and stamped your feet, rejoicing with all the malice of your heart against the land of Israel,

Ezekiel 25:8
"This is what the **Sovereign** LORD says: 'Because Moab and Seir said, "Look, Judah has become like all the other nations,"

Ezekiel 25:12
"This is what the **Sovereign** LORD says: 'Because Edom took revenge on Judah and became very guilty by doing so,

Ezekiel 25:13
therefore this is what the **Sovereign** LORD says: I will stretch out my hand against Edom and kill both man and beast.

Ezekiel 25:14
they will know my vengeance, declares the **Sovereign** LORD.'"

Ezekiel 25:15
This is what the **Sovereign** LORD says: 'Because the Philistines acted in vengeance and took revenge with malice in their hearts, and with ancient hostility sought to destroy Judah,

Ezekiel 25:16
therefore this is what the **Sovereign** LORD says: I am about to stretch out my hand against the Philistines, and I will wipe out the Kerethites and destroy those remaining along the coast.

Ezekiel 26:3
therefore this is what the **Sovereign** LORD says: I am against you, Tyre, and I will bring many nations against you, like the sea casting up its waves.

Ezekiel 26:5
Out in the sea she will become a place to spread fishnets, for I have spoken, declares the **Sovereign** LORD.

Ezekiel 26:7
"For this is what the **Sovereign** LORD says: From the north I am going to bring against Tyre Nebuchadnezzar king of Babylon, king of kings, with horses and chariots, with horsemen and a great army.

Ezekiel 26:14
You will never be rebuilt, for I the LORD have spoken, declares the **Sovereign** LORD.

Ezekiel 26:15
"This is what the **Sovereign** LORD says to Tyre: Will not the coastlands tremble at the sound of your fall, when the wounded groan and the slaughter takes place in you?

Ezekiel 26:19
"This is what the **Sovereign** LORD says: When I make you a desolate city, like cities no longer inhabited, and when I bring the ocean depths over you and its vast waters cover you,

Ezekiel 26:21
You will be sought, but you will never again be found, declares the **Sovereign** LORD."

Ezekiel 27:3
'This is what the **Sovereign** LORD says: "'You say, Tyre, "I am perfect in beauty."

Ezekiel 28:2
"Son of man, say to the ruler of Tyre, 'This is what the **Sovereign** LORD says: "'In the pride of your heart you say, "I am a god; I sit on the throne of a god in the heart of the seas." But you are a mere mortal and not a god, though you think you are as wise as a god.

Ezekiel 28:6
"'Therefore this is what the **Sovereign** LORD says: "'Because you think you are wise, as wise as a god,

Ezekiel 28:10
You will die the death of the uncircumcised at the hands of foreigners. I have spoken, declares the **Sovereign** LORD.'"

Ezekiel 28:12
'This is what the **Sovereign** LORD says: "'You were the seal of perfection, full of wisdom and perfect in beauty.

Ezekiel 28:22
and say: 'This is what the **Sovereign** LORD says: "'I am against you, Sidon, and among you I will display my glory.

Ezekiel 28:24
Then they will know that I am the **Sovereign** LORD.

God Our King

Ezekiel 28:25
"'This is what the **Sovereign** LORD says: When I gather the people of Israel from the nations where they have been scattered, I will be proved holy through them in the sight of the nations.

Ezekiel 29:3
'This is what the **Sovereign** LORD says: "'I am against you, Pharaoh king of Egypt, you great monster lying among your streams. You say, "The Nile belongs to me; I made it for myself."

Ezekiel 29:8
"'Therefore this is what the **Sovereign** LORD says: I will bring a sword against you and kill both man and beast.

Ezekiel 29:13
"'Yet this is what the **Sovereign** LORD says: At the end of forty years I will gather the Egyptians from the nations where they were scattered.

Ezekiel 29:16
Then they will know that I am the **Sovereign** LORD.'"

Ezekiel 29:19
Therefore this is what the **Sovereign** LORD says: I am going to give Egypt to Nebuchadnezzar king of Babylon, and he will carry off its wealth.

Ezekiel 29:20
I have given him Egypt as a reward for his efforts because he and his army did it for me, declares the **Sovereign** LORD.

Ezekiel 30:2
"Son of man, prophesy and say: 'This is what the **Sovereign** LORD says: "'Wail and say, "Alas for that day!"

Ezekiel 30:6
From Migdol to Aswan they will fall by the sword within her, declares the **Sovereign** LORD.

Ezekiel 30:10
"'This is what the **Sovereign** LORD says: "'I will put an end to the hordes of Egypt by the hand of Nebuchadnezzar king of Babylon.

Ezekiel 30:13
"'This is what the **Sovereign** LORD says: "'I will destroy the idols and put an end to the images in Memphis.

Ezekiel 30:22
Therefore this is what the **Sovereign** LORD says: I am against Pharaoh king of Egypt.

Ezekiel 31:10
"'Therefore this is what the **Sovereign** LORD says: Because the great cedar towered over the thick foliage, and because it was proud of its height,

Ezekiel 31:15
"'This is what the **Sovereign** LORD says: On the day it was brought down to the realm of the dead I covered the deep springs with mourning for it;

Ezekiel 31:18
"'Which of the trees of Eden can be compared with you in splendor and **majesty**? Yet you, too, will be brought down with the trees of Eden to the earth below; you will lie among the uncircumcised, with those killed by the sword. "'This is Pharaoh and all his hordes, declares the **Sovereign** LORD.'"

Ezekiel 32:3
"'This is what the **Sovereign** LORD says: "'With a great throng of people I will cast my net over you, and they will haul you up in my net.

Ezekiel 32:8
All the shining lights in the heavens I will darken over you; I will bring darkness over your land, declares the **Sovereign** LORD.

Ezekiel 32:11
"'For this is what the **Sovereign** LORD says: "'The sword of the king of Babylon will come against you.

Ezekiel 32:14
Then I will let her waters settle and make her streams flow like oil, declares the **Sovereign** LORD.

Ezekiel 32:16
for Egypt and all her hordes they will chant it, declares the **Sovereign** LORD."

Ezekiel 32:31
"Pharaoh—he and all his army—will see them and he will be consoled for all his hordes that were killed by the sword, declares the **Sovereign** LORD.

Ezekiel 32:32
Although I had him spread terror in the land of the living, Pharaoh and all his hordes will be laid among the uncircumcised, with those killed by the sword, declares the **Sovereign** LORD."

Ezekiel 33:11
Say to them, 'As surely as I live, declares the **Sovereign** LORD, I take no pleasure in the death of the wicked, but rather that they turn from their ways and live. Turn! Turn from your evil ways! Why will you die, people of Israel?'

Ezekiel 33:25
Therefore say to them, 'This is what the **Sovereign** LORD says: Since you eat meat with the blood still in it and look to your idols and shed blood, should you then possess the land?

Ezekiel 33:27
'This is what the **Sovereign** LORD says: As surely as I live, those who are left in the ruins will fall by the sword, those out in the country I will give to the wild animals to be devoured, and those in strongholds and caves will die of a plague.

Ezekiel 34:2
'This is what the **Sovereign** LORD says: Woe to you shepherds of Israel who only take care of yourselves!

Ezekiel 34:8
As surely as I live, declares the **Sovereign** LORD, because my flock lacks a shepherd and so has been plundered and has become food for all the wild animals, and because my shepherds did not search for my flock but cared for themselves rather than for my flock,

Ezekiel 34:10
This is what the **Sovereign** LORD says: I am against the shepherds and will hold them accountable for my flock.

Ezekiel 34:11
"'For this is what the **Sovereign** LORD says: I myself will search for my sheep and look after them.

Ezekiel 34:15
I myself will tend my sheep and have them lie down, declares the **Sovereign** LORD.

Ezekiel 34:17
"'As for you, my flock, this is what the **Sovereign** LORD says: I will judge between one sheep and another, and between rams and goats.

Ezekiel 34:20
"'Therefore this is what the **Sovereign** LORD says to them: See, I myself will judge between the fat sheep and the lean sheep.

Ezekiel 34:30
Then they will know that I, the LORD their God, am with them and that they, the Israelites, are my people, declares the **Sovereign** LORD.

Ezekiel 34:31
You are my sheep, the sheep of my pasture, and I am your God, declares the **Sovereign** LORD.'"

God Our King

Ezekiel 35:3
and say: 'This is what the **Sovereign** LORD says: I am against you, Mount Seir, and I will stretch out my hand against you and make you a desolate waste.

Ezekiel 35:6
therefore as surely as I live, declares the **Sovereign** LORD, I will give you over to bloodshed and it will pursue you. S

Ezekiel 35:11
therefore as surely as I live, declares the **Sovereign** LORD, I will treat you in accordance with the anger and jealousy you showed in your hatred of them and I will make myself known among them when I judge you.

Ezekiel 35:14
This is what the **Sovereign** LORD says: While the whole earth rejoices, I will make you desolate.

Ezekiel 36:2
This is what the **Sovereign** LORD says: The enemy said of you, "Aha! The ancient heights have become our possession."'

Ezekiel 36:3
Therefore prophesy and say, 'This is what the **Sovereign** LORD says: Because they ravaged and crushed you from every side so that you became the possession of the rest of the nations and the object of people's malicious talk and slander,

Ezekiel 36:4
mountains of Israel, hear the word of the **Sovereign** LORD: This is what the **Sovereign** LORD says to the mountains and hills,

Ezekiel 36:5
this is what the **Sovereign** LORD says: In my burning zeal I have spoken against the rest of the nations,

Ezekiel 36:6
'This is what the **Sovereign** LORD says: I speak in my jealous wrath because you have suffered the scorn of the nations.

Ezekiel 36:7
Therefore this is what the **Sovereign** LORD says: I swear with uplifted hand that the nations around you will also suffer scorn.

Ezekiel 36:13
"'This is what the **Sovereign** LORD says: Because some say to you, "You devour people and deprive your nation of its children,"

Ezekiel 36:14
therefore you will no longer devour people or make your nation childless, declares the **Sovereign** LORD.

Ezekiel 36:15
No longer will I make you hear the taunts of the nations, and no longer will you suffer the scorn of the peoples or cause your nation to fall, declares the **Sovereign** LORD.'"

Ezekiel 36:22
"Therefore say to the Israelites, 'This is what the **Sovereign** LORD says: It is not for your sake, people of Israel, that I am going to do these things, but for the sake of my holy name, which you have profaned among the nations where you have gone.

Ezekiel 36:23
Then the nations will know that I am the LORD, declares the **Sovereign** LORD, when I am proved holy through you before their eyes.

Ezekiel 36:32
I want you to know that I am not doing this for your sake, declares the **Sovereign** LORD.

Ezekiel 36:33
"'This is what the **Sovereign** LORD says: On the day I cleanse you from all your sins,

Ezekiel 36:37
"This is what the **Sovereign** LORD says: Once again I will yield to Israel's plea and do this for them:

Ezekiel 37:3
He asked me, "Son of man, can these bones live?" I said, "**Sovereign** LORD, you alone know."

Ezekiel 37:5
This is what the **Sovereign** LORD says to these bones: I will make breath enter you, and you will come to life.

Ezekiel 37:9
'This is what the **Sovereign** LORD says: Come, breath, from the four winds and breathe into these slain, that they may live.'"

Ezekiel 37:12
'This is what the **Sovereign** LORD says: My people, I am going to open your graves and bring you up from them;

Ezekiel 37:19
'This is what the **Sovereign** LORD says: I am going to take the stick of Joseph—which is in Ephraim's hand—and of the Israelite tribes associated with him, and join it to Judah's stick.

Ezekiel 37:21
'This is what the **Sovereign** LORD says: I will take the Israelites out of the nations where they have gone.

Ezekiel 38:3
'This is what the **Sovereign** LORD says: I am against you, Gog, chief prince of Meshek and Tubal.

Ezekiel 38:10
"'This is what the **Sovereign** LORD says: On that day thoughts will come into your mind and you will devise an evil scheme.

Ezekiel 38:14
'This is what the **Sovereign** LORD says: In that day, when my people Israel are living in safety, will you not take notice of it?

Ezekiel 38:17
"'This is what the **Sovereign** LORD says: You are the one I spoke of in former days by my servants the prophets of Israel.

Ezekiel 38:18
When Gog attacks the land of Israel, my hot anger will be aroused, declares the **Sovereign** LORD.

Ezekiel 38:21
I will summon a sword against Gog on all my mountains, declares the **Sovereign** LORD. E

Ezekiel 39:1
'This is what the **Sovereign** LORD says: I am against you, Gog, chief prince of Meshek and Tubal.

Ezekiel 39:5
You will fall in the open field, for I have spoken, declares the **Sovereign** LORD.

Ezekiel 39:8
It is coming! It will surely take place, declares the **Sovereign** LORD. This is the day I have spoken of.

Ezekiel 39:10
And they will plunder those who plundered them and loot those who looted them, declares the **Sovereign** LORD.

Ezekiel 39:13
and the day I display my glory will be a memorable day for them, declares the **Sovereign** LORD.

Ezekiel 39:17
"Son of man, this is what the **Sovereign** LORD says: Call out to every kind of bird and all the wild animals:

Ezekiel 39:20
At my table you will eat your fill of horses and riders, mighty men and soldiers of every kind,' declares the **Sovereign** LORD.

Ezekiel 39:25
"Therefore this is what the **Sovereign** LORD says: I will now restore the fortunes of Jacob and will have compassion on all the people of Israel, and I will be zealous for my holy name.

God Our King

Ezekiel 39:29
I will no longer hide my face from them, for I will pour out my Spirit on the people of Israel, declares the **Sovereign** LORD."

Ezekiel 43:18
Then he said to me, "Son of man, this is what the **Sovereign** LORD says: These will be the regulations for sacrificing burnt offerings and splashing blood against the altar when it is built:

Ezekiel 43:19
You are to give a young bull as a sin offering to the Levitical priests of the family of Zadok, who come near to minister before me, declares the **Sovereign** LORD.

Ezekiel 43:27
Then I will accept you, declares the **Sovereign** LORD."

Ezekiel 44:6
Say to rebellious Israel, 'This is what the **Sovereign** LORD says: Enough of your detestable practices, people of Israel!

Ezekiel 44:9
This is what the **Sovereign** LORD says: No foreigner uncircumcised in heart and flesh is to enter my sanctuary, not even the foreigners who live among the Israelites.

Ezekiel 44:12
But because they served them in the presence of their idols and made the people of Israel fall into sin, therefore I have sworn with uplifted hand that they must bear the consequences of their sin, declares the **Sovereign** LORD.

Ezekiel 44:15
they are to stand before me to offer sacrifices of fat and blood, declares the **Sovereign** LORD.

Ezekiel 44:27
he is to offer a sin offering for himself, declares the **Sovereign** LORD.

Ezekiel 45:9
"'This is what the **Sovereign** LORD says: You have gone far enough, princes of Israel! Give up your violence and oppression and do what is just and right. Stop dispossessing my people, declares the **Sovereign** LORD.

Ezekiel 45:15
These will be used for the grain offerings, burnt offerings and fellowship offerings to make atonement for the people, declares the **Sovereign** LORD.

Ezekiel 45:18
"'This is what the **Sovereign** LORD says: In the first month on the first day you are to take a young bull without defect and purify the sanctuary.

Ezekiel 46:1
"'This is what the **Sovereign** LORD says: The gate of the inner court facing east is to be shut on the six working days, but on the Sabbath day and on the day of the New Moon it is to be opened.

Ezekiel 46:16
"'This is what the **Sovereign** LORD says: If the prince makes a gift from his inheritance to one of his sons, it will also belong to his descendants; it is to be their property by inheritance.

Ezekiel 47:13
This is what the **Sovereign** LORD says: "These are the boundaries of the land that you will divide among the twelve tribes of Israel as their inheritance, with two portions for Joseph.

Ezekiel 47:23
In whatever tribe a foreigner resides, there you are to give them their inheritance," declares the **Sovereign** LORD.

Ezekiel 48:29
"This is the land you are to allot as an inheritance to the tribes of Israel, and these will be their portions," declares the **Sovereign** LORD.

Daniel 4:3
His **kingdom** is an eternal kingdom; his **dominion** endures from generation to generation.

Daniel 4:17
"'The decision is announced by messengers, the holy ones declare the verdict, so that the living may know that the Most High is **sovereign** over all kingdoms on earth and gives them to anyone he wishes and sets over them the lowliest of people.'

Daniel 4:25
Seven times will pass by for you until you acknowledge that the Most High is **sovereign** over all kingdoms on earth and gives them to anyone he wishes.

Daniel 4:26
The command to leave the stump of the tree with its roots means that your kingdom will be restored to you when you acknowledge that Heaven **rules**.

Daniel 4:32
Seven times will pass by for you until you acknowledge that the Most High is **sovereign** over all kingdoms on earth and gives them to anyone he wishes."

Daniel 4:34
Then I praised the Most High; I honored and glorified him who lives forever. His **dominion** is an eternal **dominion**; his **kingdom** endures from generation to generation.

Daniel 4:37
Now I, Nebuchadnezzar, praise and exalt and glorify the **King** of heaven, because everything he does is right and all his ways are just. And those who walk in pride he is able to humble.

Daniel 5:21
until he acknowledged that the Most High God is **sovereign** over all kingdoms on earth and sets over them anyone he wishes.

Daniel 6:26
"For he is the living God and he endures forever; his **kingdom** will not be destroyed, his **dominion** will never end.

Daniel 7:14
He was given authority, glory and **sovereign** power; all nations and peoples of every language worshiped him. His **dominion** is an everlasting **dominion** that will not pass away, and his **kingdom** is one that will never be destroyed.

Daniel 7:18
But the holy people of the Most High will receive the **kingdom** and will possess it forever—yes, for ever and ever.'

Daniel 7:22
until the Ancient of Days came and pronounced judgment in favor of the holy people of the Most High, and the time came when they possessed the **kingdom**.

Daniel 7:27
Then the sovereignty, power and greatness of all the kingdoms under heaven will be handed over to the holy people of the Most High. His **kingdom** will be an everlasting **kingdom**, and all rulers will worship and obey him.'

Daniel 9:25
"Know and understand this: From the time the word goes out to restore and rebuild Jerusalem until the Anointed One, the **ruler**, comes, there will be seven 'sevens,' and sixty-two 'sevens.'

Amos 1:8
I will turn my hand against Ekron, till the last of the Philistines are dead," says the **Sovereign** LORD.

Amos 3:7
Surely the **Sovereign** LORD does nothing without revealing his plan to his servants the prophets.

Amos 3:8
The lion has roared— who will not fear? The **Sovereign** LORD has spoken— who can but prophesy?

God Our King

Amos 3:11
Therefore this is what the **Sovereign** LORD says: "An enemy will overrun your land, pull down your strongholds and plunder your fortresses."

Amos 4:2
The **Sovereign** LORD has sworn by his holiness: "The time will surely come when you will be taken away with hooks, the last of you with fishhooks.

Amos 4:5
Burn leavened bread as a thank offering and brag about your freewill offerings— boast about them, you Israelites, for this is what you love to do," declares the **Sovereign** LORD.

Amos 5:3
This is what the **Sovereign** LORD says to Israel: "Your city that marches out a thousand strong will have only a hundred left; your town that marches out a hundred strong will have only ten left."

Amos 6:8
The **Sovereign** LORD has sworn by himself—the LORD God Almighty declares: "I abhor the pride of Jacob and detest his fortresses; I will deliver up the city and everything in it."

Amos 7:1
This is what the **Sovereign** LORD showed me: He was preparing swarms of locusts after the king's share had been harvested and just as the late crops were coming up.

Amos 7:2
When they had stripped the land clean, I cried out, "**Sovereign** LORD, forgive! How can Jacob survive? He is so small!"

Amos 7:4
This is what the **Sovereign** LORD showed me: The **Sovereign** LORD was calling for judgment by fire;

Amos 7:5
Then I cried out, "**Sovereign** LORD, I beg you, stop! How can Jacob survive? He is so small!"

Amos 7:6
So the LORD relented. "This will not happen either," the **Sovereign** LORD said.

Amos 8:1
This is what the **Sovereign** LORD showed me: a basket of ripe fruit.

Amos 8:3
"In that day," declares the **Sovereign** LORD, "the songs in the temple will turn to wailing. Many, many bodies—flung everywhere! Silence!"

Amos 8:9
"In that day," declares the **Sovereign** LORD, "I will make the sun go down at noon and darken the earth in broad daylight.

Amos 8:11
"The days are coming," declares the **Sovereign** LORD, "when I will send a famine through the land— not a famine of food or a thirst for water, but a famine of hearing the words of the LORD.

Amos 9:8
"Surely the eyes of the **Sovereign** LORD are on the sinful kingdom. I will destroy it from the face of the earth. Yet I will not totally destroy the descendants of Jacob," declares the LORD.

Obadiah 1:1
The vision of Obadiah. This is what the **Sovereign** LORD says about Edom—

Obadiah 1:21
Deliverers will go up on Mount Zion to govern the mountains of Esau. And the **kingdom** will be the LORD's.

Micah 1:2
Hear, you peoples, all of you, listen, earth and all who live in it, that the **Sovereign** LORD may bear witness against you, the Lord from his holy temple.

Micah 2:13
Their **King** will pass through before them, the LORD at their head."

Micah 4:7
The LORD will **rule** over them in Mount Zion from that day and forever.

Micah 5:1
They will strike Israel's **ruler** on the cheek with a rod.

Micah 5:2
"But you, Bethlehem Ephrathah, though you are small among the clans of Judah, out of you will come for me one who will be **ruler** over Israel, whose origins are from of old, from ancient times."

Micah 5:4
He will stand and shepherd his flock in the strength of the LORD, in the **majesty** of the name of the LORD his God.

Habakkuk 3:19
The **Sovereign** LORD is my strength; he makes my feet like the feet of a deer, he enables me to tread on the heights.

Zephaniah 1:7
Be silent before the **Sovereign** LORD, for the day of the LORD is near.

Zephaniah 3:15
The LORD, the **King** of Israel, is with you; never again will you fear any harm.

Zechariah 9:9
[*The Coming of Zion's King*] Rejoice greatly, Daughter Zion! Shout, Daughter Jerusalem! See, your **king** comes to you, righteous and victorious, lowly and riding on a donkey, on a colt, the foal of a donkey.

Zechariah 9:14
The **Sovereign** LORD will sound the trumpet; he will march in the storms of the south,

Zechariah 14:9
The LORD will be **king** over the whole earth. On that day there will be one LORD, and his name the only name.

Zechariah 14:16
Then the survivors from all the nations that have attacked Jerusalem will go up year after year to worship the **King**, the LORD Almighty, and to celebrate the Festival of Tabernacles.

Zechariah 14:17
If any of the peoples of the earth do not go up to Jerusalem to worship the **King**, the LORD Almighty, they will have no rain.

Malachi 1:14
For I am a great **king**," says the LORD Almighty, "and my name is to be feared among the nations.

Matthew 2:2
and asked, "Where is the one who has been born **king** of the Jews?

Matthew 2:6
"'But you, Bethlehem, in the land of Judah, are by no means least among the rulers of Judah; for out of you will come a **ruler** who will shepherd my people Israel.' "

Matthew 3:2
and saying, "Repent, for the **kingdom** of heaven has come near."

Matthew 4:17
From that time on Jesus began to preach, "Repent, for the **kingdom** of heaven has come near."

Matthew 4:23
Jesus went throughout Galilee, teaching in their synagogues, proclaiming the good news of the **kingdom**, and healing every disease and sickness among the people.

227

God Our King

Matthew 5:3
"Blessed are the poor in spirit, for theirs is the **kingdom** of heaven.

Matthew 5:10
Blessed are those who are persecuted because of righteousness, for theirs is the **kingdom** of heaven.

Matthew 5:19
Therefore anyone who sets aside one of the least of these commands and teaches others accordingly will be called least in the **kingdom** of heaven, but whoever practices and teaches these commands will be called great in the **kingdom** of heaven.

Matthew 5:20
For I tell you that unless your righteousness surpasses that of the Pharisees and the teachers of the law, you will certainly not enter the **kingdom** of heaven.

Matthew 5:35
or by the earth, for it is his footstool; or by Jerusalem, for it is the city of the Great **King**.

Matthew 6:10
your **kingdom** come, your will be done, on earth as it is in heaven.

Matthew 6:33
But seek first his **kingdom** and his righteousness, and all these things will be given to you as well.

Matthew 7:21
"Not everyone who says to me, 'Lord, Lord,' will enter the **kingdom** of heaven, but only the one who does the will of my Father who is in heaven.

Matthew 8:11
I say to you that many will come from the east and the west, and will take their places at the feast with Abraham, Isaac and Jacob in the **kingdom** of heaven.

Matthew 9:35
Jesus went through all the towns and villages, teaching in their synagogues, proclaiming the good news of the **kingdom** and healing every disease and sickness.

Matthew 10:7
As you go, proclaim this message: 'The **kingdom** of heaven has come near.'

Matthew 11:11
Truly I tell you, among those born of women there has not risen anyone greater than John the Baptist; yet whoever is least in the **kingdom** of heaven is greater than he.

Matthew 12:28
But if it is by the Spirit of God that I drive out demons, then the **kingdom** of God has come upon you.

Matthew 13:11
He replied, "Because the knowledge of the secrets of the **kingdom** of heaven has been given to you, but not to them.

Matthew 13:24
Jesus told them another parable: "The **kingdom** of heaven is like a man who sowed good seed in his field.

Matthew 13:31
He told them another parable: "The **kingdom** of heaven is like a mustard seed, which a man took and planted in his field.

Matthew 13:33
He told them still another parable: "The **kingdom** of heaven is like yeast that a woman took and mixed into about sixty pounds of flour until it worked all through the dough."

Matthew 13:41
The Son of Man will send out his angels, and they will weed out of his **kingdom** everything that causes sin and all who do evil.

Matthew 13:43
Then the righteous will shine like the sun in the **kingdom** of their Father.

Matthew 13:44
The **kingdom** of heaven is like treasure hidden in a field. When a man found it, he hid it again, and then in his joy went and sold all he had and bought that field.

Matthew 13:45
"Again, the **kingdom** of heaven is like a merchant looking for fine pearls.

Matthew 13:47
"Once again, the **kingdom** of heaven is like a net that was let down into the lake and caught all kinds of fish.

Matthew 13:52
He said to them, "Therefore every teacher of the law who has become a disciple in the **kingdom** of heaven is like the owner of a house who brings out of his storeroom new treasures as well as old."

Matthew 16:19
I will give you the keys of the **kingdom** of heaven; whatever you bind on earth will be bound in heaven, and whatever you loose on earth will be loosed in heaven."

Matthew 16:28
"Truly I tell you, some who are standing here will not taste death before they see the Son of Man coming in his **kingdom**."

Matthew 18:1
At that time the disciples came to Jesus and asked, "Who, then, is the greatest in the **kingdom** of heaven?"

Matthew 18:3
And he said: "Truly I tell you, unless you change and become like little children, you will never enter the **kingdom** of heaven.

Matthew 18:4
Therefore, whoever takes the lowly position of this child is the greatest in the **kingdom** of heaven.

Matthew 18:23
"Therefore, the **kingdom** of heaven is like a king who wanted to settle accounts with his servants.

Matthew 19:12
For there are eunuchs who were born that way, and there are eunuchs who have been made eunuchs by others—and there are those who choose to live like eunuchs for the sake of the **kingdom** of heaven. The one who can accept this should accept it."

Matthew 19:14
Jesus said, "Let the little children come to me, and do not hinder them, for the **kingdom** of heaven belongs to such as these."

Matthew 19:23
Then Jesus said to his disciples, "Truly I tell you, it is hard for someone who is rich to enter the **kingdom** of heaven.

Matthew 19:24
Again I tell you, it is easier for a camel to go through the eye of a needle than for someone who is rich to enter the **kingdom** of God."

Matthew 20:1
"For the **kingdom** of heaven is like a landowner who went out early in the morning to hire workers for his vineyard.

Matthew 21:5
"Say to Daughter Zion, 'See, your **king** comes to you, gentle and riding on a donkey, and on a colt, the foal of a donkey.'"

Matthew 21:31
"Which of the two did what his father wanted?" "The first," they answered. Jesus said to them, "Truly I tell you, the tax collectors and the prostitutes are entering the **kingdom** of God ahead of you.

Matthew 21:43
"Therefore I tell you that the **kingdom** of God will be taken away from you and given to a people who will produce its fruit.

God Our King

Matthew 22:2
"The **kingdom** of heaven is like a king who prepared a wedding banquet for his son.

Matthew 23:13
"Woe to you, teachers of the law and Pharisees, you hypocrites! You shut the door of the **kingdom** of heaven in people's faces. You yourselves do not enter, nor will you let those enter who are trying to.

Matthew 24:14
And this gospel of the **kingdom** will be preached in the whole world as a testimony to all nations, and then the end will come.

Matthew 25:1
"At that time the **kingdom** of heaven will be like ten virgins who took their lamps and went out to meet the bridegroom.

Matthew 25:34
"Then the **King** will say to those on his right, 'Come, you who are blessed by my Father; take your inheritance, the **kingdom** prepared for you since the creation of the world.

Matthew 25:40
"The **King** will reply, 'Truly I tell you, whatever you did for one of the least of these brothers and sisters of mine, you did for me.'

Matthew 26:29
I tell you, I will not drink from this fruit of the vine from now on until that day when I drink it new with you in my Father's **kingdom**."

Matthew 27:11
[*Jesus Before Pilate*] Meanwhile Jesus stood before the governor, and the governor asked him, "Are you the **king** of the Jews?" "You have said so," Jesus replied.

Matthew 27:29
and then twisted together a crown of thorns and set it on his head. They put a staff in his right hand. Then they knelt in front of him and mocked him. "Hail, **king** of the Jews!" they said.

Matthew 27:37
Above his head they placed the written charge against him: THIS IS JESUS, THE **KING** OF THE JEWS.

Mark 1:15
"The time has come," he said. "The **kingdom** of God has come near. Repent and believe the good news!"

Mark 4:11
He told them, "The secret of the **kingdom** of God has been given to you. But to those on the outside everything is said in parables

Mark 4:26
He also said, "This is what the **kingdom** of God is like. A man scatters seed on the ground.

Mark 4:30
Again he said, "What shall we say the **kingdom** of God is like, or what parable shall we use to describe it?

Mark 9:1
And he said to them, "Truly I tell you, some who are standing here will not taste death before they see that the **kingdom** of God has come with power."

Mark 9:47
And if your eye causes you to stumble, pluck it out. It is better for you to enter the **kingdom** of God with one eye than to have two eyes and be thrown into hell,

Mark 10:14
When Jesus saw this, he was indignant. He said to them, "Let the little children come to me, and do not hinder them, for the **kingdom** of God belongs to such as these.

Mark 10:15
Truly I tell you, anyone who will not receive the **kingdom** of God like a little child will never enter it."

Mark 10:23
Jesus looked around and said to his disciples, "How hard it is for the rich to enter the **kingdom** of God!"

Mark 10:24
The disciples were amazed at his words. But Jesus said again, "Children, how hard it is to enter the **kingdom** of God!

Mark 10:25
It is easier for a camel to go through the eye of a needle than for someone who is rich to enter the **kingdom** of God."

Mark 11:10
"Blessed is the coming **kingdom** of our father David!" "Hosanna in the highest heaven!"

Mark 12:34
When Jesus saw that he had answered wisely, he said to him, "You are not far from the **kingdom** of God." And from then on no one dared ask him any more questions.

Mark 14:25
"Truly I tell you, I will not drink again from the fruit of the vine until that day when I drink it new in the **kingdom** of God."

Mark 15:2
"Are you the **king** of the Jews?" asked Pilate. "You have said so," Jesus replied.

Mark 15:12
"What shall I do, then, with the one you call the **king** of the Jews?" Pilate asked them.

Mark 15:18
And they began to call out to him, "Hail, **king** of the Jews!"

Mark 15:26
The written notice of the charge against him read: THE **KING** OF THE JEWS.

Mark 15:43
Joseph of Arimathea, a prominent member of the Council, who was himself waiting for the **kingdom** of God, went boldly to Pilate and asked for Jesus' body.

Luke 1:33
and he will **reign** over Jacob's descendants forever; his **kingdom** will never end."

Luke 2:29
"**Sovereign** Lord, as you have promised, you may now dismiss your servant in peace.

Luke 4:43
But he said, "I must proclaim the good news of the **kingdom** of God to the other towns also, because that is why I was sent."

Luke 6:20
Looking at his disciples, he said: "Blessed are you who are poor, for yours is the **kingdom** of God.

Luke 7:28
I tell you, among those born of women there is no one greater than John; yet the one who is least in the **kingdom** of God is greater than he."

Luke 8:1
After this, Jesus traveled about from one town and village to another, proclaiming the good news of the **kingdom** of God.

Luke 8:10
He said, "The knowledge of the secrets of the **kingdom** of God has been given to you, but to others I speak in parables, so that, "'though seeing, they may not see; though hearing, they may not understand.'

Luke 9:2
and he sent them out to proclaim the **kingdom** of God and to heal the sick.

God Our King

Luke 9:11
but the crowds learned about it and followed him. He welcomed them and spoke to them about the **kingdom** of God, and healed those who needed healing.

Luke 9:27
"Truly I tell you, some who are standing here will not taste death before they see the **kingdom** of God."

Luke 9:60
Jesus said to him, "Let the dead bury their own dead, but you go and proclaim the **kingdom** of God."

Luke 9:62
Jesus replied, "No one who puts a hand to the plow and looks back is fit for service in the **kingdom** of God."

Luke 10:9
Heal the sick who are there and tell them, 'The **kingdom** of God has come near to you.'

Luke 10:11
'Even the dust of your town we wipe from our feet as a warning to you. Yet be sure of this: The **kingdom** of God has come near.'

Luke 11:2
He said to them, "When you pray, say: "'Father, hallowed be your name, your **kingdom** come.

Luke 11:20
But if I drive out demons by the finger of God, then the **kingdom** of God has come upon you.

Luke 12:31
But seek his **kingdom**, and these things will be given to you as well.

Luke 12:32
"Do not be afraid, little flock, for your Father has been pleased to give you the **kingdom**.

Luke 13:18
Then Jesus asked, "What is the **kingdom** of God like? What shall I compare it to?

Luke 13:20
Again he asked, "What shall I compare the **kingdom** of God to?

Luke 13:28
"There will be weeping there, and gnashing of teeth, when you see Abraham, Isaac and Jacob and all the prophets in the **kingdom** of God, but you yourselves thrown out.

Luke 13:29
People will come from east and west and north and south, and will take their places at the feast in the **kingdom** of God.

Luke 14:15
When one of those at the table with him heard this, he said to Jesus, "Blessed is the one who will eat at the feast in the **kingdom** of God."

Luke 17:20
Once, on being asked by the Pharisees when the **kingdom** of God would come, Jesus replied, "The coming of the **kingdom** of God is not something that can be observed,

Luke 17:21
nor will people say, 'Here it is,' or 'There it is,' because the **kingdom** of God is in your midst."

Luke 18:16
But Jesus called the children to him and said, "Let the little children come to me, and do not hinder them, for the **kingdom** of God belongs to such as these.

Luke 18:17
Truly I tell you, anyone who will not receive the **kingdom** of God like a little child will never enter it."

Luke 18:24
Jesus looked at him and said, "How hard it is for the rich to enter the **kingdom** of God!

Luke 18:25
Indeed, it is easier for a camel to go through the eye of a needle than for someone who is rich to enter the **kingdom** of God."

Luke 18:29
"Truly I tell you," Jesus said to them, "no one who has left home or wife or brothers or sisters or parents or children for the sake of the **kingdom** of God

Luke 19:38
"Blessed is the **king** who comes in the name of the Lord!" "Peace in heaven and glory in the highest!"

Luke 21:31
Even so, when you see these things happening, you know that the **kingdom** of God is near.

Luke 22:16
For I tell you, I will not eat it again until it finds fulfillment in the **kingdom** of God."

Luke 22:18
For I tell you I will not drink again from the fruit of the vine until the **kingdom** of God comes."

Luke 22:29
And I confer on you a **kingdom**, just as my Father conferred one on me,

Luke 22:30
so that you may eat and drink at my table in my **kingdom** and sit on thrones, judging the twelve tribes of Israel.

Luke 23:2
And they began to accuse him, saying, "We have found this man subverting our nation. He opposes payment of taxes to Caesar and claims to be Messiah, a **king**."

Luke 23:3
So Pilate asked Jesus, "Are you the **king** of the Jews?" "You have said so," Jesus replied.

Luke 23:37
and said, "If you are the **king** of the Jews, save yourself."

Luke 23:38
There was a written notice above him, which read: THIS IS THE **KING** OF THE JEWS.

Luke 23:42
Then he said, "Jesus, remember me when you come into your **kingdom**. "

Luke 23:51
He came from the Judean town of Arimathea, and he himself was waiting for the **kingdom** of God.

John 1:49
Then Nathanael declared, "Rabbi, you are the Son of God; you are the **king** of Israel."

John 3:3
Jesus replied, "Very truly I tell you, no one can see the **kingdom** of God unless they are born again. "

John 3:5
Jesus answered, "Very truly I tell you, no one can enter the **kingdom** of God unless they are born of water and the Spirit.

John 12:13
They took palm branches and went out to meet him, shouting, "Hosanna! " "Blessed is he who comes in the name of the Lord!" "Blessed is the **king** of Israel!"

John 12:15
"Do not be afraid, Daughter Zion; see, your **king** is coming, seated on a donkey's colt."

God Our King

John 18:36
Jesus said, "My **kingdom** is not of this world. If it were, my servants would fight to prevent my arrest by the Jewish leaders. But now my **kingdom** is from another place."

John 18:37
"You are a **king**, then!" said Pilate. Jesus answered, "You say that I am a **king**. In fact, the reason I was born and came into the world is to testify to the truth. Everyone on the side of truth listens to me."

John 19:3
and went up to him again and again, saying, "Hail, **king** of the Jews!" And they slapped him in the face.

John 19:14
It was the day of Preparation of the Passover; it was about noon. "Here is your **king**," Pilate said to the Jews.

John 19:15
But they shouted, "Take him away! Take him away! Crucify him!" "Shall I crucify your **king**?" Pilate asked. "We have no **king** but Caesar," the chief priests answered.

John 19:19
Pilate had a notice prepared and fastened to the cross. It read: JESUS OF NAZARETH, THE **KING** OF THE JEWS.

John 19:21
The chief priests of the Jews protested to Pilate, "Do not write 'The **King** of the Jews,' but that this man claimed to be king of the Jews."

Acts 1:3
After his suffering, he presented himself to them and gave many convincing proofs that he was alive. He appeared to them over a period of forty days and spoke about the **kingdom** of God.

Acts 1:6
Then they gathered around him and asked him, "Lord, are you at this time going to restore the **kingdom** to Israel?"

Acts 4:24
When they heard this, they raised their voices together in prayer to God. "**Sovereign** Lord," they said, "you made the heavens and the earth and the sea, and everything in them.

Acts 8:12
But when they believed Philip as he proclaimed the good news of the **kingdom** of God and the name of Jesus Christ, they were baptized, both men and women.

Acts 14:22
strengthening the disciples and encouraging them to remain true to the faith. "We must go through many hardships to enter the **kingdom** of God," they said.

Acts 17:7
They are all defying Caesar's decrees, saying that there is another **king**, one called Jesus."

Acts 19:8
Paul entered the synagogue and spoke boldly there for three months, arguing persuasively about the **kingdom** of God.

Acts 20:25
"Now I know that none of you among whom I have gone about preaching the **kingdom** will ever see me again.

Acts 28:23
He witnessed to them from morning till evening, explaining about the **kingdom** of God, and from the Law of Moses and from the Prophets he tried to persuade them about Jesus.

Acts 28:31
He proclaimed the **kingdom** of God and taught about the Lord Jesus Christ—with all boldness and without hindrance!

Romans 14:17
For the **kingdom** of God is not a matter of eating and drinking, but of righteousness, peace and joy in the Holy Spirit,

Romans 15:12
And again, Isaiah says, "The Root of Jesse will spring up, one who will arise to **rule** over the nations; in him the Gentiles will hope."

1 Corinthians 4:20
For the **kingdom** of God is not a matter of talk but of power.

1 Corinthians 6:9
Or do you not know that wrongdoers will not inherit the **kingdom** of God?

1 Corinthians 6:10
nor thieves nor the greedy nor drunkards nor slanderers nor swindlers will inherit the **kingdom** of God.

1 Corinthians 15:24
Then the end will come, when he hands over the **kingdom** to God the Father after he has destroyed all dominion, authority and power.

1 Corinthians 15:50
I declare to you, brothers and sisters, that flesh and blood cannot inherit the **kingdom** of God, nor does the perishable inherit the imperishable.

Galatians 5:21
I warn you, as I did before, that those who live like this will not inherit the **kingdom** of God.

Ephesians 5:5
For of this you can be sure: No immoral, impure or greedy person—such a person is an idolater—has any inheritance in the **kingdom** of Christ and of God.

Colossians 1:12
and giving joyful thanks to the Father, who has qualified you to share in the inheritance of his holy people in the **kingdom** of light.

Colossians 1:13
For he has rescued us from the dominion of darkness and brought us into the **kingdom** of the Son he loves,

Colossians 3:15
Let the peace of Christ **rule** in your hearts, since as members of one body you were called to peace.

Colossians 4:11
These are the only Jews among my co-workers for the **kingdom** of God, and they have proved a comfort to me.

1 Thessalonians 2:12
encouraging, comforting and urging you to live lives worthy of God, who calls you into his **kingdom** and glory.

2 Thessalonians 1:5
All this is evidence that God's judgment is right, and as a result you will be counted worthy of the **kingdom** of God, for which you are suffering.

1 Timothy 1:17
Now to the **King** eternal, immortal, invisible, the only God, be honor and glory for ever and ever. Amen.

1 Timothy 6:15
which God will bring about in his own time—God, the blessed and only **Ruler**, the **King** of kings and Lord of lords,

2 Timothy 4:1
In the presence of God and of Christ Jesus, who will judge the living and the dead, and in view of his appearing and his **kingdom**, I give you this charge:

2 Timothy 4:18
The Lord will rescue me from every evil attack and will bring me safely to his heavenly **kingdom**. To him be glory for ever and ever. Amen.

Hebrews 1:3
After he had provided purification for sins, he sat down at the right hand of the **Majesty** in heaven.

Hebrews 1:8
But about the Son he says, "Your **throne**, O God, will last for ever and ever; a scepter of justice will be the scepter of your **kingdom**.

Hebrews 8:1
We do have such a high priest, who sat down at the right hand of the throne of the **Majesty** in heaven,

Hebrews 12:28
Therefore, since we are receiving a **kingdom** that cannot be shaken,

God Our King

James 2:5
Listen, my dear brothers and sisters: Has not God chosen those who are poor in the eyes of the world to be rich in faith and to inherit the **kingdom** he promised those who love him?

2 Peter 1:11
and you will receive a rich welcome into the eternal **kingdom** of our Lord and Savior Jesus Christ.

2 Peter 1:16
For we did not follow cleverly devised stories when we told you about the coming of our Lord Jesus Christ in power, but we were eyewitnesses of his **majesty**.

2 Peter 1:17
He received honor and glory from God the Father when the voice came to him from the **Majestic** Glory, saying, "This is my Son, whom I love; with him I am well pleased."

2 Peter 2:1
But there were also false prophets among the people, just as there will be false teachers among you. They will secretly introduce destructive heresies, even denying the **sovereign** Lord who bought them—bringing swift destruction on themselves.

Jude 1:4
They are ungodly people, who pervert the grace of our God into a license for immorality and deny Jesus Christ our only **Sovereign** and Lord.

Jude 1:25
to the only God our Savior be glory, **majesty**, power and authority, through Jesus Christ our Lord, before all ages, now and forevermore! Amen.

Revelation 1:5
and from Jesus Christ, who is the faithful witness, the firstborn from the dead, and the **ruler** of the kings of the earth.

Revelation 1:6
and has made us to be a **kingdom** and priests to serve his God and Father—to him be glory and power for ever and ever!

Revelation 5:10
You have made them to be a **kingdom** and priests to serve our God, and they will **reign** on the earth."

Revelation 6:10
They called out in a loud voice, "How long, **Sovereign** Lord, holy and true, until you judge the inhabitants of the earth and avenge our blood?"

Revelation 11:15
The seventh angel sounded his trumpet, and there were loud voices in heaven, which said: "The kingdom of the world has become the **kingdom** of our Lord and of his Messiah, and he will **reign** for ever and ever."

Revelation 12:10
Then I heard a loud voice in heaven say: "Now have come the salvation and the power and the **kingdom** of our God, and the authority of his Messiah. For the accuser of our brothers and sisters, who accuses them before our God day and night, has been hurled down.

Revelation 15:3
and sang the song of God's servant Moses and of the Lamb: "Great and marvelous are your deeds, Lord God Almighty. Just and true are your ways, **King** of the nations.

Revelation 17:14
They will wage war against the Lamb, but the Lamb will triumph over them because he is Lord of lords and **King** of kings—and with him will be his called, chosen and faithful followers."

Revelation 19:16
On his robe and on his thigh he has this name written: **KING** OF KINGS AND LORD OF LORDS.

God is Light
Lamp; Brightness
Having No Darkness

Light:
Allowing an unobstructed or unobscured view; Something clearly shown; The absence of darkness; Something that exposes or reveals.

*You, Lord, are my **lamp**; the Lord turns my darkness into **light**.*

- II Samuel 22:29

God is Light

1. DEFINE LIGHT USING YOUR OWN WORDS, SYNONYMS, OR DESCRIPTIONS:

_____

_____

_____

2. PSALM 104:2 SAYS, "THE LORD WRAPS HIMSELF IN LIGHT AS WITH A GARMENT" AND PEOPLE WHO HAVE SEEN GOD DESCRIBE HIS APPEARANCE AS BRILLIANT OR RADIANT LIGHT. WHAT IS THE SIGNIFICANCE OF THAT?

_____

_____

_____

3. IN EXODUS 10:21-23, GOD CAUSED A PLAGUE OF DARKNESS OVER EGYPT -- SO DARK THAT IT WAS SAID IT COULD "BE FELT" AND NO ONE COULD SEE EACH OTHER. HOWEVER, THINGS WERE QUITE DIFFERENT FOR GOD'S PEOPLE: "YET ALL THE ISRAELITES HAD LIGHT IN THE PLACES WHERE THEY LIVED." THINK OF HOW AMAZING THAT MUST HAVE BEEN AND SYMBOLISM IT STILL REPRESENTS TO US ABOUT GOD.

_____

_____

_____

4. DO YOU HAVE ANY OBSERVATIONS ABOUT THIS CHARACTER TRAIT OF GOD OR WHY GOD WANTS US TO KNOW THAT HE IS LIGHT OR OUR LAMP, POSSESSES BRIGHTNESS AND IS ABSENT OF DARKNESS?

_____

_____

_____

_____

When we try to focus our thought upon One who is pure uncreated being we may see nothing at all, for He dwelleth in light that no man can approach unto. Only by faith and love are we able to glimpse Him as He passes by our shelter in the cleft of the rock.

- A. W. Tozer

NOTES:

God is Light

Genesis 1:3
And God said, "Let there be **light**," and there was **light**.

Exodus 13:21
By day the LORD went ahead of them in a pillar of cloud to guide them on their way and by night in a pillar of fire to give them **light**, so that they could travel by day or night.

2 Samuel 22:13
Out of the **brightness** of his presence bolts of lightning blazed forth.

2 Samuel 22:29
You, LORD, are my **lamp**; the LORD turns my darkness into **light**.

2 Samuel 23:4
he is like the **light** of morning at sunrise on a cloudless morning, like the **brightness** after rain that brings grass from the earth.'

Nehemiah 9:12
By day you led them with a pillar of cloud, and by night with a pillar of fire to give them **light** on the way they were to take.

Psalm 4:6
Many, LORD, are asking, "Who will bring us prosperity?" Let the **light** of your face shine on us.

Psalm 18:12
Out of the **brightness** of his presence clouds advanced, with hailstones and bolts of lightning.

Psalm 18:28
You, LORD, keep my **lamp** burning; my God turns my darkness into **light**.

Psalm 19:8
The commands of the LORD are radiant, giving **light** to the eyes.

Psalm 27:1
The LORD is my **light** and my salvation—whom shall I fear? The LORD is the stronghold of my life—of whom shall I be afraid?

Psalm 36:9
For with you is the fountain of life; in your **light** we see **light**.

Psalm 43:3
Send me your **light** and your faithful care, let them lead me;

Psalm 44:3
It was not by their sword that they won the land, nor did their arm bring them victory; it was your right hand, your arm, and the **light** of your face, for you loved them.

Psalm 76:4
You are radiant with **light**, more majestic than mountains rich with game.

Psalm 77:18
Your thunder was heard in the whirlwind, your lightning **lit up** the world;

Psalm 78:14
He guided them with the cloud by day and with **light** from the fire all night.

Psalm 89:15
Blessed are those who have learned to acclaim you, who walk in the **light** of your presence, LORD.

Psalm 90:8
You have set our iniquities before you, our secret sins in the **light** of your presence.

Psalm 97:4
His lightning **lights up** the world;

Psalm 104:2
The LORD wraps himself in **light** as with a garment;

Psalm 105:39
He spread out a cloud as a covering, and a fire to give **light** at night.

Psalm 118:27
The LORD is God, and he has made his **light** shine on us.

Psalm 119:105
Your word is a **lamp** for my feet, a **light** on my path.

Psalm 119:130
The unfolding of your words gives **light**; it gives understanding to the simple.

Psalm 136:7
who made the great **lights**— His love endures forever.

Psalm 139:12
even the **darkness will not be dark** to you; the night will shine like the day, for **darkness is as light** to you.

Proverbs 6:23
For this command is a **lamp,** this teaching is a **light,** and correction and instruction are the way to life,

Proverbs 20:27
The human spirit is the **lamp** of the LORD that sheds **light** on one's inmost being.

Isaiah 2:5
Come, descendants of Jacob, let us walk in the **light** of the LORD.

Isaiah 9:2
The people walking in darkness have seen a great **light**; on those living in the land of deep darkness a **light** has dawned.

Isaiah 10:17
The **Light** of Israel will become a fire, their Holy One a flame;

Isaiah 42:16
I will lead the blind by ways they have not known, along unfamiliar paths I will guide them; I will turn the darkness into **light** before them and make the rough places smooth.

Isaiah 45:7
I form the **light** and create darkness, I bring prosperity and create disaster; I, the LORD, do all these things.

Isaiah 51:4
"Listen to me, my people; hear me, my nation: Instruction will go out from me; my justice will become a **light** to the nations.

Isaiah 53:11
After he has suffered, he will see the **light** of life and be satisfied; by his knowledge my righteous servant will justify many, and he will bear their iniquities.

Isaiah 58:8
Then your **light** will break forth like the dawn, and your healing will quickly appear; then your righteousness will go before you, and the glory of the LORD will be your rear guard.

Isaiah 60:1
"Arise, shine, for your **light** has come, and the glory of the LORD rises upon you.

God is Light

Isaiah 60:3
Nations will come to your **light**, and kings to the **brightness** of your dawn.

Isaiah 60:19
The sun will no more be your light by day, nor will the brightness of the moon shine on you, for the LORD will be your everlasting **light**, and your God will be your glory.

Isaiah 60:20
Your sun will never set again, and your moon will wane no more; the LORD will be your everlasting **light**, and your days of sorrow will end.

Ezekiel 1:27
I saw that from what appeared to be his waist up he looked like glowing metal, as if full of fire, and that from there down he looked like fire; and brilliant **light** surrounded him.

Daniel 2:22
He reveals deep and hidden things; he knows what lies in darkness, and **light** dwells with him.

Micah 7:8
Do not gloat over me, my enemy! Though I have fallen, I will rise. Though I sit in darkness, the LORD will be my **light**.

Micah 7:9
He will bring me out into the **light**; I will see his righteousness.

Matthew 4:16
the people living in darkness have seen a great **light**; on those living in the land of the shadow of death a **light** has dawned."

Matthew 17:2
[*Jesus' transfiguration*] There he was transfigured before them. His face shone like the sun, and his clothes became as white as the **light**.

Luke 2:32
a **light** for revelation to the Gentiles, and the glory of your people Israel."

John 1:4
In him was life, and that life was the **light** of all mankind.

John 1:5
The **light** shines in the darkness, and the darkness has not overcome it.

John 1:7
[*The ministry of John the Baptist*] He came as a witness to testify concerning that **light**, so that through him all might believe.

John 1:8
He himself was not the light; he came only as a witness to the **light**.

John 1:9
The true **light** that gives **light** to everyone was coming into the world.

John 3:19
This is the verdict: **Light** has come into the world, but people loved darkness instead of **light** because their deeds were evil.

John 3:20
Everyone who does evil hates the **light**, and will not come into the **light** for fear that their deeds will be exposed.

John 3:21
But whoever lives by the truth comes into the **light**, so that it may be seen plainly that what they have done has been done in the sight of God.

John 8:12
When Jesus spoke again to the people, he said, "I am the **light** of the world. Whoever follows me will never walk in darkness, but will have the **light** of life."

John 9:5
While I am in the world, I am the **light** of the world."

John 12:35
Then Jesus told them, "You are going to have the **light** just a little while longer. Walk while you have the **light**, before darkness overtakes you.

John 12:36
Believe in the **light** while you have the **light**, so that you may become children of **light**."

John 12:46
I have come into the world as a **light**, so that no one who believes in me should stay in darkness.

Acts 26:18
to open their eyes and turn them from darkness to **light**, and from the power of Satan to God,

Acts 26:23
that the Messiah would suffer and, as the first to rise from the dead, would bring the message of **light** to his own people and to the Gentiles."

1 Corinthians 4:5
He will bring to **light** what is hidden in darkness and will expose the motives of the heart.

2 Corinthians 4:4
The god of this age has blinded the minds of unbelievers, so that they cannot see the **light** of the gospel that displays the glory of Christ, who is the image of God.

2 Corinthians 4:6
For God, who said, "Let **light** shine out of darkness," made his **light** shine in our hearts to give us the **light** of the knowledge of God's glory displayed in the face of Christ.

Ephesians 5:8
For you were once darkness, but now you are **light** in the Lord. Live as children of **light**

Colossians 1:12
and giving joyful thanks to the Father, who has qualified you to share in the inheritance of his holy people in the kingdom of **light**.

1 Thessalonians 5:5
You are all children of the **light** and children of the day. We do not belong to the night or to the darkness.

1 Timothy 6:16
who alone is immortal and who lives in unapproachable **light**, whom no one has seen or can see.

2 Timothy 1:10
but it has now been revealed through the appearing of our Savior, Christ Jesus, who has destroyed death and has brought life and immortality to **light** through the gospel.

James 1:17
Every good and perfect gift is from above, coming down from the Father of the heavenly **lights**, who does not change like shifting shadows.

1 Peter 2:9
But you are a chosen people, a royal priesthood, a holy nation, God's special possession, that you may declare the praises of him who called you out of darkness into his wonderful **light**.

1 John 1:5
This is the message we have heard from him and declare to you: God is **light**; in him there is **no darkness** at all.

1 John 1:7
But if we walk in the **light**, as he is in the **light**, we have fellowship with one another, and the blood of Jesus, his Son, purifies us from all sin.

God is Light

1 John 2:8
Yet I am writing you a new command; its truth is seen in him and in you, because the darkness is passing and the true **light** is already shining.

1 John 2:9
Anyone who claims to be in the **light** but hates a brother or sister is still in the darkness.

1 John 2:10
Anyone who loves their brother and sister lives in the **light**, and there is nothing in them to make them stumble.

Revelation 21:23
The city does not need the sun or the moon to shine on it, for the glory of God gives it **light**, and the Lamb is its **lamp**.

Revelation 21:24
The nations will walk by its **light**, and the kings of the earth will bring their splendor into it.

Revelation 22:5
There will be **no more night**. They will **not need the light** of a **lamp** or the light of the sun, for the Lord God will give them **light**. And they will reign for ever and ever.

God is Love

Love:
Extreme devotion or affection.

For as high as the heavens are above the earth, so great is his **love** *for those who fear him.*

- Psalm 103:11

God is Love

1. DEFINE LOVE USING YOUR OWN WORDS, SYNONYMS, OR DESCRIPTIONS:

_____

_____

_____

2. SOME HAVE SAID THAT GOD WAS A GOD OF WRATH IN THE OLD TESTAMENT BUT A GOD OF LOVE IN THE NEW TESTAMENT. DOES THAT SEEM TRUE AFTER LOOKING AT WHAT THE BIBLE SHOWS US ABOUT GOD?

_____

_____

_____

3. LOOK AT THE VERSES, MOSTLY IN THE PSALMS, THAT SPEAK OF GOD'S _UNFAILING_ LOVE. WHAT DOES IT MEAN THAT GOD'S LOVE IS UNFAILING AND DOES IT NOT SHOW THE GREAT DEPTH OF GOD'S LOVE FOR US?

_____

_____

_____

4. DO YOU HAVE ANY OBSERVATIONS ABOUT THIS CHARACTER TRAIT OF GOD OR WHY GOD WANTS US TO KNOW THAT HE IS LOVE?

_____

_____

_____

_____

_____

God loves each of us as if there were only one of us.
— _Augustine_

The love of God is one of the greatest realities of the universe, a pillar upon which the hope of the world rests. But it is a personal, intimate thing too. God does not love populations, He loves people. He does not love masses, but men.
— _A. W. Tozer_

NOTES:

God is Love

Exodus 15:13
In your unfailing **love** you will lead the people you have redeemed. In your strength you will guide them to your holy dwelling.

Exodus 20:6
but showing **love** to a thousand generations of those who love me and keep my commandments.

Exodus 34:6
And he passed in front of Moses, proclaiming, "The LORD, the LORD, the compassionate and gracious God, slow to anger, abounding in **love** and faithfulness,

Exodus 34:7
maintaining **love** to thousands, and forgiving wickedness, rebellion and sin. Yet he does not leave the guilty unpunished;

Numbers 14:18
'The LORD is slow to anger, abounding in **love** and forgiving sin and rebellion. Yet he does not leave the guilty unpunished;

Numbers 14:19
In accordance with your great **love**, forgive the sin of these people, just as you have pardoned them from the time they left Egypt until now."

Deuteronomy 4:37
Because he **loved** your ancestors and chose their descendants after them, he brought you out of Egypt by his Presence and his great strength,

Deuteronomy 5:10
but showing **love** to a thousand generations of those who love me and keep my commandments.

Deuteronomy 7:8
But it was because the LORD **loved** you and kept the oath he swore to your ancestors that he brought you out with a mighty hand and redeemed you from the land of slavery, from the power of Pharaoh king of Egypt.

Deuteronomy 7:9
Know therefore that the LORD your God is God; he is the faithful God, keeping his covenant of **love** to a thousand generations of those who love him and keep his commandments.

Deuteronomy 7:12
If you pay attention to these laws and are careful to follow them, then the LORD your God will keep his covenant of **love** with you, as he swore to your ancestors.

Deuteronomy 7:13
He will **love** you and bless you and increase your numbers. He will bless the fruit of your womb, the crops of your land—

Deuteronomy 10:15
Yet the LORD set his affection on your ancestors and **loved** them, and he chose you, their descendants, above all the nations—as it is today.

Deuteronomy 10:18
He defends the cause of the fatherless and the widow, and **loves** the foreigner residing among you, giving them food and clothing.

Deuteronomy 23:5
However, the LORD your God would not listen to Balaam but turned the curse into a blessing for you, because the LORD your God **loves** you.

Deuteronomy 33:3
Surely it is you who **love** the people; all the holy ones are in your hand.

Deuteronomy 33:12
About Benjamin he said: "Let the beloved of the LORD rest secure in him, for he shields him all day long, and the one the LORD **loves** rests between his shoulders."

2 Samuel 7:15
[*God's love for David*] But my **love** will never be taken away from him, as I took it away from Saul, whom I removed from before you.

2 Samuel 12:24
She gave birth to a son, and they named him Solomon. The LORD **loved** him;

2 Samuel 12:25
and because the LORD **loved** him, he sent word through Nathan the prophet to name him Jedidiah.

1 Kings 8:23
and said: "LORD, the God of Israel, there is no God like you in heaven above or on earth below—you who keep your covenant of **love** with your servants who continue wholeheartedly in your way.

1 Kings 10:9
Praise be to the LORD your God, who has delighted in you and placed you on the throne of Israel. Because of the LORD's eternal **love** for Israel, he has made you king to maintain justice and righteousness."

1 Chronicles 16:34
Give thanks to the LORD, for he is good; his **love** endures forever.

1 Chronicles 16:41
With them were Heman and Jeduthun and the rest of those chosen and designated by name to give thanks to the LORD, "for his **love** endures forever."

1 Chronicles 17:13
I will be his father, and he will be my son. I will never take my **love** away from him, as I took it away from your predecessor.

2 Chronicles 2:11
Hiram king of Tyre replied by letter to Solomon: "Because the LORD **loves** his people, he has made you their king."

2 Chronicles 5:13
The trumpeters and musicians joined in unison to give praise and thanks to the LORD. Accompanied by trumpets, cymbals and other instruments, the singers raised their voices in praise to the LORD and sang: "He is good; his **love** endures forever."

2 Chronicles 6:14
He said: "LORD, the God of Israel, there is no God like you in heaven or on earth—you who keep your covenant of **love** with your servants who continue wholeheartedly in your way.

2 Chronicles 6:42
LORD God, do not reject your anointed one. Remember the great **love** promised to David your servant."

2 Chronicles 7:3
When all the Israelites saw the fire coming down and the glory of the LORD above the temple, they knelt on the pavement with their faces to the ground, and they worshiped and gave thanks to the LORD, saying, "He is good; his **love** endures forever."

2 Chronicles 7:6
The priests took their positions, as did the Levites with the LORD's musical instruments, which King David had made for praising the LORD and which were used when he gave thanks, saying, "His **love** endures forever."

2 Chronicles 9:8
Because of the **love** of your God for Israel and his desire to uphold them forever, he has made you king over them, to maintain justice and righteousness."

2 Chronicles 20:21
After consulting the people, Jehoshaphat appointed men to sing to the LORD and to praise him for the splendor of his holiness as they went out at the head of the army, saying: "Give thanks to the LORD, for his **love** endures forever."

Ezra 3:11
With praise and thanksgiving they sang to the LORD: "He is good; his **love** toward Israel endures forever."

God is Love

Nehemiah 1:5
Then I said: "LORD, the God of heaven, the great and awesome God, who keeps his covenant of **love** with those who love him and keep his commandments,

Nehemiah 9:17
But you are a forgiving God, gracious and compassionate, slow to anger and abounding in **love**.

Nehemiah 9:32
"Now therefore, our God, the great God, mighty and awesome, who keeps his covenant of **love**, do not let all this hardship seem trifling in your eyes—

Nehemiah 13:22
Remember me for this also, my God, and show mercy to me according to your great **love**.

Nehemiah 13:26
Was it not because of marriages like these that Solomon king of Israel sinned? Among the many nations there was no king like him. He was **loved** by his God, and God made him king over all Israel, but even he was led into sin by foreign women.

Psalm 5:7
But I, by your great **love**, can come into your house; in reverence I bow down toward your holy temple.

Psalm 6:4
Turn, LORD, and deliver me; save me because of your unfailing **love**.

Psalm 13:5
But I trust in your unfailing **love**; my heart rejoices in your salvation.

Psalm 17:7
Show me the wonders of your great **love**, you who save by your right hand those who take refuge in you from their foes.

Psalm 18:50
He gives his king great victories; he shows unfailing **love** to his anointed, to David and to his descendants forever.

Psalm 21:7
For the king trusts in the LORD; through the unfailing **love** of the Most High he will not be shaken.

Psalm 23:6
Surely your goodness and **love** will follow me all the days of my life, and I will dwell in the house of the LORD forever.

Psalm 25:6
Remember, LORD, your great mercy and **love**, for they are from of old.

Psalm 25:7
Do not remember the sins of my youth and my rebellious ways; according to your **love** remember me, for you, LORD, are good.

Psalm 26:3
for I have always been mindful of your unfailing **love** and have lived in reliance on your faithfulness.

Psalm 31:7
I will be glad and rejoice in your **love**, for you saw my affliction and knew the anguish of my soul.

Psalm 31:16
Let your face shine on your servant; save me in your unfailing **love**.

Psalm 31:21
Praise be to the LORD, for he showed me the wonders of his **love** when I was in a city under siege.

Psalm 32:10
Many are the woes of the wicked, but the LORD's unfailing **love** surrounds the one who trusts in him

Psalm 33:18
But the eyes of the LORD are on those who fear him, on those whose hope is in his unfailing **love**,

Psalm 33:22
May your unfailing **love** be with us, LORD, even as we put our hope in you.

Psalm 36:5
Your **love**, LORD, reaches to the heavens, your faithfulness to the skies.

Psalm 36:7
How priceless is your unfailing **love**, O God!

Psalm 36:10
Continue your **love** to those who know you, your righteousness to the upright in heart.

Psalm 37:28
For the LORD **loves** the just and will not forsake his faithful ones.

Psalm 40:10
I do not conceal your **love** and your faithfulness from the great assembly.

Psalm 40:11
Do not withhold your mercy from me, LORD; may your **love** and faithfulness always protect me.

Psalm 42:8
By day the LORD directs his **love**, at night his song is with me— a prayer to the God of my life.

Psalm 44:3
It was not by their sword that they won the land, nor did their arm bring them victory; it was your right hand, your arm, and the light of your face, for you **loved** them.

Psalm 44:26
Rise up and help us; rescue us because of your unfailing **love**.

Psalm 47:4
He chose our inheritance for us, the pride of Jacob, whom he **loved**.

Psalm 48:9
Within your temple, O God, we meditate on your unfailing **love**.

Psalm 51:1
Have mercy on me, O God, according to your unfailing **love**; according to your great compassion blot out my transgressions.

Psalm 52:8
But I am like an olive tree flourishing in the house of God; I trust in God's unfailing **love** for ever and ever.

Psalm 57:3
He sends from heaven and saves me, rebuking those who hotly pursue me— God sends forth his **love** and his faithfulness.

Psalm 57:10
For great is your **love**, reaching to the heavens; your faithfulness reaches to the skies.

Psalm 59:16
But I will sing of your strength, in the morning I will sing of your **love**; for you are my fortress, my refuge in times of trouble.

Psalm 61:7
May he be enthroned in God's presence forever; appoint your **love** and faithfulness to protect him.

Psalm 62:12
and with you, Lord, is unfailing **love**"; and, "You reward everyone according to what they have done."

Psalm 63:3
Because your **love** is better than life, my lips will glorify you.

God is Love

Psalm 66:20
Praise be to God, who has not rejected my prayer or withheld his **love** from me!

Psalm 69:13
But I pray to you, LORD, in the time of your favor; in your great **love**, O God, answer me with your sure salvation.

Psalm 69:16
Answer me, LORD, out of the goodness of your **love**; in your great mercy turn to me.

Psalm 78:68
but he chose the tribe of Judah, Mount Zion, which he **loved**.

Psalm 85:7
Show us your unfailing **love**, LORD, and grant us your salvation.

Psalm 85:10
Love and faithfulness meet together; righteousness and peace kiss each other.

Psalm 86:5
You, Lord, are forgiving and good, abounding in **love** to all who call to you.

Psalm 86:13
For great is your **love** toward me; you have delivered me from the depths, from the realm of the dead.

Psalm 86:15
But you, Lord, are a compassionate and gracious God, slow to anger, abounding in **love** and faithfulness.

Psalm 87:2
The LORD **loves** the gates of Zion more than all the other dwellings of Jacob.

Psalm 89:1
I will sing of the LORD's great **love** forever; with my mouth I will make your faithfulness known through all generations.

Psalm 89:2
I will declare that your **love** stands firm forever, that you have established your faithfulness in heaven itself.

Psalm 89:14
Righteousness and justice are the foundation of your throne; **love** and faithfulness go before you.

Psalm 89:24
[*God's covenant with David*] My faithful **love** will be with him, and through my name his horn will be exalted.

Psalm 89:28
I will maintain my **love** to him forever, and my covenant with him will never fail.

Psalm 89:33
but I will not take my **love** from him, nor will I ever betray my faithfulness.

Psalm 90:14
Satisfy us in the morning with your unfailing **love**, that we may sing for joy and be glad all our days.

Psalm 92:2
proclaiming your **love** in the morning and your faithfulness at night,

Psalm 94:18
When I said, "My foot is slipping," your unfailing **love**, LORD, supported me.

Psalm 98:3
He has remembered his **love** and his faithfulness to Israel; all the ends of the earth have seen the salvation of our God.

Psalm 99:4
The King is mighty, he **loves** justice— you have established equity; in Jacob you have done what is just and right.

Psalm 100:5
For the LORD is good and his **love** endures forever; his faithfulness continues through all generations.

Psalm 101:1
I will sing of your **love** and justice; to you, LORD, I will sing praise.

Psalm 103:4
who redeems your life from the pit and crowns you with **love** and compassion,

Psalm 103:8
The LORD is compassionate and gracious, slow to anger, abounding in **love**.

Psalm 103:11
For as high as the heavens are above the earth, so great is his **love** for those who fear him;

Psalm 103:17
But from everlasting to everlasting the LORD's **love** is with those who fear him, and his righteousness with their children's children—

Psalm 106:1
Praise the LORD. Give thanks to the LORD, for he is good; his **love** endures forever.

Psalm 106:45
for their sake he remembered his covenant and out of his great **love** he relented.

Psalm 107:1
Give thanks to the LORD, for he is good; his **love** endures forever.

Psalm 107:8, 15, 21, 31
Let them give thanks to the LORD for his unfailing **love** and his wonderful deeds for mankind,

Psalm 108:4
For great is your **love**, higher than the heavens; your faithfulness reaches to the skies.

Psalm 108:6
Save us and help us with your right hand, that those you **love** may be delivered.

Psalm 109:21
But you, Sovereign LORD, help me for your name's sake; out of the goodness of your **love**, deliver me.

Psalm 109:26
Help me, LORD my God; save me according to your unfailing **love**.

Psalm 115:1
Not to us, LORD, not to us but to your name be the glory, because of your **love** and faithfulness.

Psalm 117:2
For great is his **love** toward us, and the faithfulness of the LORD endures forever. Praise the LORD.

Psalm 118:1
Give thanks to the LORD, for he is good; his **love** endures forever.

Psalm 118:2
Let Israel say: "His **love** endures forever."

Psalm 118:3
Let the house of Aaron say: "His **love** endures forever."

Psalm 118:4
Let those who fear the LORD say: "His **love** endures forever."

God is Love

Psalm 118:29
Give thanks to the LORD, for he is good; his **love** endures forever.

Psalm 119:41
May your unfailing **love** come to me, LORD, your salvation, according to your promise;

Psalm 119:64
The earth is filled with your **love**, LORD;

Psalm 119:76
May your unfailing **love** be my comfort, according to your promise to your servant.

Psalm 119:88
In your unfailing **love** preserve my life, that I may obey the statutes of your mouth.

Psalm 119:124
Deal with your servant according to your **love** and teach me your decrees.

Psalm 119:149
Hear my voice in accordance with your **love**; preserve my life, LORD, according to your laws.

Psalm 127:2
In vain you rise early and stay up late, toiling for food to eat— for he grants sleep to those he **loves**.

Psalm 130:7
Israel, put your hope in the LORD, for with the LORD is unfailing **love** and with him is full redemption.

Psalm 136:1
Give thanks to the LORD, for he is good. His **love** endures forever.

Psalm 136:2
Give thanks to the God of gods. His **love** endures forever.

Psalm 136:3
Give thanks to the Lord of lords: His **love** endures forever.

Psalm 136:4
to him who alone does great wonders, His **love** endures forever.

Psalm 136:5
who by his understanding made the heavens, His **love** endures forever.

Psalm 136:6
who spread out the earth upon the waters, His **love** endures forever.

Psalm 136:7
who made the great lights— His **love** endures forever.

Psalm 136:8
the sun to govern the day, His **love** endures forever.

Psalm 136:9
the moon and stars to govern the night; His **love** endures forever.

Psalm 136:10
to him who struck down the firstborn of Egypt His **love** endures forever.

Psalm 136:11
and brought Israel out from among them His **love** endures forever.

Psalm 136:12
with a mighty hand and outstretched arm; His **love** endures forever.

Psalm 136:13
to him who divided the Red Sea asunder His **love** endures forever.

Psalm 136:14
and brought Israel through the midst of it, His **love** endures forever.

Psalm 136:15
but swept Pharaoh and his army into the Red Sea; His **love** endures forever.

Psalm 136:16
to him who led his people through the wilderness; His **love** endures forever.

Psalm 136:17
to him who struck down great kings, His **love** endures forever.

Psalm 136:18
and killed mighty kings— His **love** endures forever.

Psalm 136:19
Sihon king of the Amorites His **love** endures forever.

Psalm 136:20
and Og king of Bashan— His **love** endures forever.

Psalm 136:21
and gave their land as an inheritance, His **love** endures forever.

Psalm 136:22
an inheritance to his servant Israel. His **love** endures forever.

Psalm 136:23
He remembered us in our low estate His **love** endures forever.

Psalm 136:24
and freed us from our enemies. His **love** endures forever.

Psalm 136:25
He gives food to every creature. His **love** endures forever.

Psalm 136:26
Give thanks to the God of heaven. His **love** endures forever.

Psalm 138:2
I will bow down toward your holy temple and will praise your name for your unfailing **love** and your faithfulness,

Psalm 138:8
The LORD will vindicate me; your **love**, LORD, endures forever—

Psalm 143:8
Let the morning bring me word of your unfailing **love**, for I have put my trust in you. Show me the way I should go, for to you I entrust my life.

Psalm 143:12
In your unfailing **love**, silence my enemies; destroy all my foes, for I am your servant.

Psalm 145:8
The LORD is gracious and compassionate, slow to anger and rich in **love**.

Psalm 146:8
the LORD gives sight to the blind, the LORD lifts up those who are bowed down, the LORD **loves** the righteous.

God is Love

Psalm 147:11
the LORD delights in those who fear him, who put their hope in his unfailing **love**.

Proverbs 3:12
because the LORD disciplines those he **loves**, as a father the son he delights in.

Proverbs 15:9
The LORD detests the way of the wicked, but he **loves** those who pursue righteousness.

Proverbs 16:6
Through **love** and faithfulness sin is atoned for;

Isaiah 38:17
In your **love** you kept me from the pit of destruction; you have put all my sins behind your back.

Isaiah 43:4
Since you are precious and honored in my sight, and because I **love** you, I will give people in exchange for you, nations in exchange for your life.

Isaiah 54:10
Though the mountains be shaken and the hills be removed, yet my unfailing **love** for you will not be shaken nor my covenant of peace be removed," says the LORD, who has compassion on you.

Isaiah 55:3
I will make an everlasting covenant with you, my faithful **love** promised to David.

Isaiah 61:8
"For I, the LORD, **love** justice; I hate robbery and wrongdoing.

Isaiah 63:9
In his **love** and mercy he redeemed them;

Jeremiah 12:7
"I will forsake my house, abandon my inheritance; I will give the one I **love** into the hands of her enemies.

Jeremiah 16:5
For this is what the LORD says: "Do not enter a house where there is a funeral meal; do not go to mourn or show sympathy, because I have withdrawn my blessing, my **love** and my pity from this people," declares the LORD.

Jeremiah 31:3
The LORD appeared to us in the past, saying: "I have **loved** you with an everlasting love; I have drawn you with unfailing kindness.

Jeremiah 33:11
"Give thanks to the LORD Almighty, for the LORD is good; his **love** endures forever."

Lamentations 3:22
Because of the LORD's great **love** we are not consumed, for his compassions never fail.

Lamentations 3:32
Though he brings grief, he will show compassion, so great is his unfailing **love**.

Daniel 9:4
I prayed to the LORD my God and confessed: "Lord, the great and awesome God, who keeps his covenant of **love** with those who love him and keep his commandments,

Hosea 1:7
Yet I will show **love** to Judah; and I will save them—not by bow, sword or battle, or by horses and horsemen, but I, the LORD their God, will save them."

Hosea 2:4
I will not show my **love** to her children, because they are the children of adultery.

Hosea 2:23
I will plant her for myself in the land; I will show my **love** to the one I called 'Not my loved one.' I will say to those called 'Not my people,' 'You are my people'; and they will say, 'You are my God.'"

Hosea 3:1
Love her as the LORD **loves** the Israelites, though they turn to other gods and love the sacred raisin cakes."

Hosea 11:1
"When Israel was a child, I **loved** him, and out of Egypt I called my son.

Hosea 11:4
I led them with cords of human kindness, with ties of **love**. To them I was like one who lifts a little child to the cheek, and I bent down to feed them.

Hosea 14:4
"I will heal their waywardness and **love** them freely, for my anger has turned away from them.

Joel 2:13
Rend your heart and not your garments. Return to the LORD your God, for he is gracious and compassionate, slow to anger and abounding in **love**, and he relents from sending calamity.

Jonah 2:8
"Those who cling to worthless idols turn away from God's **love** for them.

Jonah 4:2
I knew that you are a gracious and compassionate God, slow to anger and abounding in **love**, a God who relents from sending calamity.

Micah 7:20
You will be faithful to Jacob, and show **love** to Abraham, as you pledged on oath to our ancestors in days long ago.

Zephaniah 3:17
The LORD your God is with you, the Mighty Warrior who saves. He will take great delight in you; in his **love** he will no longer rebuke you, but will rejoice over you with singing."

Malachi 1:2
"I have **loved** you," says the LORD. "But you ask, 'How have you **loved** us?' "Was not Esau Jacob's brother?" declares the LORD. "Yet I have **loved** Jacob,

Matthew 3:17
And a voice from heaven said, "This is my Son, whom I **love**; with him I am well pleased."

Matthew 12:18
"Here is my servant whom I have chosen, the one I **love**, in whom I delight; I will put my Spirit on him, and he will proclaim justice to the nations.

Matthew 17:5
While he was still speaking, a bright cloud covered them, and a voice from the cloud said, "This is my Son, whom I **love**; with him I am well pleased. Listen to him!"

Mark 1:11
And a voice came from heaven: "You are my Son, whom I **love**; with you I am well pleased."

Mark 9:7
Then a cloud appeared and covered them, and a voice came from the cloud: "This is my Son, whom I **love**. Listen to him!"

Mark 10:21
Jesus looked at him and **loved** him.

Luke 3:22
and the Holy Spirit descended on him in bodily form like a dove. And a voice came from heaven: "You are my Son, whom I **love**; with you I am well pleased."

God is Love

Luke 11:42
"Woe to you Pharisees, because you give God a tenth of your mint, rue and all other kinds of garden herbs, but you neglect justice and the **love** of God.

John 3:16
For God so **loved** the world that he gave his one and only Son, that whoever believes in him shall not perish but have eternal life.

John 3:35
The Father **loves** the Son and has placed everything in his hands.

John 5:20
For the Father **loves** the Son and shows him all he does.

John 10:17
The reason my Father **loves** me is that I lay down my life—only to take it up again.

John 11:3
So the sisters sent word to Jesus, "Lord, the one you **love** is sick."

John 11:5
Now Jesus **loved** Martha and her sister and Lazarus.

John 11:36
Then the Jews said, "See how he **loved** him!"

John 13:1
Jesus knew that the hour had come for him to leave this world and go to the Father. Having **loved** his own who were in the world, he **loved** them to the end.

John 13:23
One of them, the disciple whom Jesus **loved**, was reclining next to him.

John 13:34
"A new command I give you: Love one another. As I have **loved** you, so you must love one another.

John 14:21
The one who loves me will be **loved** by my Father, and I too will **love** them and show myself to them."

John 14:23
Jesus replied, "Anyone who loves me will obey my teaching. My Father will **love** them, and we will come to them and make our home with them.

John 14:31
but he comes so that the world may learn that I **love** the Father and do exactly what my Father has commanded me.

John 15:9
"As the Father has **loved** me, so have I **loved** you.

John 15:12
My command is this: Love each other as I have **loved** you.

John 16:27
No, the Father himself **loves** you because you have loved me and have believed that I came from God.

John 17:23
[*Jesus praying to the Father*] I in them and you in me—so that they may be brought to complete unity. Then the world will know that you sent me and have **loved** them even as you have **loved** me.

God is Love

John 17:24
"Father, I want those you have given me to be with me where I am, and to see my glory, the glory you have given me because you **loved** me before the creation of the world.

John 17:26
I have made you known to them, and will continue to make you known in order that the **love** you have for me may be in them and that I myself may be in them."

John 19:26
When Jesus saw his mother there, and the disciple whom he **loved** standing nearby, he said to her, "Woman, here is your son,"

John 20:2
So she came running to Simon Peter and the other disciple, the one Jesus **loved**, and said, "They have taken the Lord out of the tomb, and we don't know where they have put him!"

John 21:7
Then the disciple whom Jesus **loved** said to Peter, "It is the Lord!"

John 21:20
Peter turned and saw that the disciple whom Jesus **loved** was following them.

Romans 1:7
To all in Rome who are **loved** by God and called to be his holy people:

Romans 5:5
And hope does not put us to shame, because God's **love** has been poured out into our hearts through the Holy Spirit, who has been given to us.

Romans 5:8
But God demonstrates his own **love** for us in this: While we were still sinners, Christ died for us.

Romans 8:35
Who shall separate us from the **love** of Christ?

Romans 8:37
No, in all these things we are more than conquerors through him who **loved** us.

Romans 8:39
neither height nor depth, nor anything else in all creation, will be able to separate us from the **love** of God that is in Christ Jesus our Lord.

Romans 9:13
Just as it is written: "Jacob I **loved**, but Esau I hated."

Romans 9:25
As he says in Hosea: "I will call them 'my people' who are not my people; and I will call her 'my **loved** one' who is not my loved one,"

Romans 15:30
I urge you, brothers and sisters, by our Lord Jesus Christ and by the **love** of the Spirit,

2 Corinthians 5:14
For Christ's **love** compels us, because we are convinced that one died for all, and therefore all died.

2 Corinthians 9:7
Each of you should give what you have decided in your heart to give, not reluctantly or under compulsion, for God **loves** a cheerful giver.

2 Corinthians 13:11
And the God of **love** and peace will be with you.

God is Love

2 Corinthians 13:14
May the grace of the Lord Jesus Christ, and the **love** of God, and the fellowship of the Holy Spirit be with you all.

Galatians 2:20
The life I now live in the body, I live by faith in the Son of God, who **loved** me and gave himself for me.

Galatians 5:22
But the fruit of the Spirit is **love**, joy, peace, forbearance, kindness, goodness, faithfulness,

Ephesians 1:4-6
For he chose us in him before the creation of the world to be holy and blameless in his sight. In **love** he predestined us for adoption to sonship through Jesus Christ, in accordance with his pleasure and will—to the praise of his glorious grace, which he has freely given us in the One he **loves**.

Ephesians 2:4
But because of his great **love** for us, God, who is rich in mercy,

Ephesians 3:18
may have power, together with all the Lord's holy people, to grasp how wide and long and high and deep is the **love** of Christ,

Ephesians 3:19
and to know this **love** that surpasses knowledge—that you may be filled to the measure of all the fullness of God.

Ephesians 5:1
Follow God's example, therefore, as dearly **loved** children

Ephesians 5:2
and walk in the way of love, just as Christ **loved** us and gave himself up for us as a fragrant offering and sacrifice to God.

Ephesians 5:25
Husbands, love your wives, just as Christ **loved** the church and gave himself up for her

Philippians 2:1
Therefore if you have any encouragement from being united with Christ, if any comfort from his **love**, if any common sharing in the Spirit, if any tenderness and compassion,

Colossians 1:13
For he has rescued us from the dominion of darkness and brought us into the kingdom of the Son he **loves**,

Colossians 3:12
Therefore, as God's chosen people, holy and dearly **loved**,

1 Thessalonians 1:4
For we know, brothers and sisters **loved** by God, that he has chosen you,

1 Thessalonians 4:9
Now about your love for one another we do not need to write to you, for you yourselves have been taught by God to **love** each other.

2 Thessalonians 2:13
But we ought always to thank God for you, brothers and sisters **loved** by the Lord, because God chose you as firstfruits to be saved through the sanctifying work of the Spirit and through belief in the truth.

2 Thessalonians 2:16
May our Lord Jesus Christ himself and God our Father, who **loved** us and by his grace gave us eternal encouragement and good hope,

2 Thessalonians 3:5
May the Lord direct your hearts into God's **love** and Christ's perseverance.

1 Timothy 1:14
The grace of our Lord was poured out on me abundantly, along with the faith and **love** that are in Christ Jesus.

2 Timothy 1:7
For the Spirit God gave us does not make us timid, but gives us power, **love** and self-discipline.

Titus 3:4
But when the kindness and **love** of God our Savior appeared,

Hebrews 12:6
because the Lord disciplines the one he **loves**, and he chastens everyone he accepts as his son."

2 Peter 1:17
He received honor and glory from God the Father when the voice came to him from the Majestic Glory, saying, "This is my Son, whom I **love**; with him I am well pleased."

1 John 3:1
See what great **love** the Father has lavished on us, that we should be called children of God!

1 John 3:16
This is how we know what **love** is: Jesus Christ laid down his life for us.

1 John 4:7
Dear friends, let us love one another, for **love** comes from God.

1 John 4:8
Whoever does not love does not know God, because God is **love**.

1 John 4:9
This is how God showed his **love** among us: He sent his one and only Son into the world that we might live through him.

1 John 4:10
This is **love**: not that we loved God, but that he **loved** us and sent his Son as an atoning sacrifice for our sins.

1 John 4:11
Dear friends, since God so **loved** us, we also ought to love one another.

1 John 4:12
No one has ever seen God; but if we love one another, God lives in us and his **love** is made complete in us.

1 John 4:16
And so we know and rely on the **love** God has for us. God is **love**. Whoever lives in love lives in God, and God in them.

1 John 4:19
We love because he first **loved** us.

Jude 1:1
To those who have been called, who are **loved** in God the Father and kept for Jesus Christ:

Jude 1:21
keep yourselves in God's **love** as you wait for the mercy of our Lord Jesus Christ to bring you to eternal life.

God is Love

Revelation 1:5
and from Jesus Christ, who is the faithful witness, the firstborn from the dead, and the ruler of the kings of the earth. To him who **loves** us and has freed us from our sins by his blood,

Revelation 3:19
Those whom I **love** I rebuke and discipline. So be earnest and repent.

God is Merciful
Showing Mercy

Merciful:
Refraining from inflicting punishment or pain on an offender.

*The Lord is full of compassion and **mercy**.*
- James 5:11

God is Merciful

1. DEFINE MERCIFUL USING YOUR OWN WORDS, SYNONYMS, OR DESCRIPTIONS:

_____

_____

_____

2. IN 2 SAMUEL 24:10-17 THERE IS AN INTERESTING ACCOUNT. KING DAVID SINS AGAINST GOD BUT COMES TO REALIZE AND ADMIT HIS WRONGDOING. GOD GIVES HIM THREE CHOICES FOR PUNISHMENT. READ VERSES 14-16 TO SEE DAVID'S CHOICE AND WHAT HAPPENED AS A CONSEQUENCE. WHAT DID DAVID KNOW ABOUT GOD'S CHARACTER THAT HELPED HIM CHOOSE THE WAY HE DID?

_____

_____

_____

3. DO YOU HAVE ANY OBSERVATIONS ABOUT THIS CHARACTER TRAIT OF GOD OR WHY GOD WANTS US TO KNOW THAT HE IS MERCIFUL AND SHOWS MERCY?

_____

_____

_____

_____

_____

Only God can throw the first stone -- and he doesn't.
- Albert Wells, Jr.

NOTES:

God is Merciful

Genesis 19:16
[*Lot saved from destruction of Sodom*] When he hesitated, the men grasped his hand and the hands of his wife and of his two daughters and led them safely out of the city, for the LORD was **merciful** to them.

Genesis 43:14
And may God Almighty grant you **mercy** before the man so that he will let your other brother and Benjamin come back with you.

Exodus 33:19
And the LORD said, "I will cause all my goodness to pass in front of you, and I will proclaim my name, the LORD, in your presence. I will have **mercy** on whom I will have **mercy**, and I will have compassion on whom I will have compassion.

Deuteronomy 4:31
For the LORD your God is a **merciful** God; he will not abandon or destroy you or forget the covenant with your ancestors, which he confirmed to them by oath.

Deuteronomy 13:17
Then the LORD will turn from his fierce anger, will show you **mercy**, and will have compassion on you.

2 Samuel 24:14
Let us fall into the hands of the LORD, for his **mercy** is great;

1 Kings 8:28
Yet give attention to your servant's prayer and his plea for **mercy**, LORD my God.

1 Kings 8:50
And forgive your people, who have sinned against you; forgive all the offenses they have committed against you, and cause their captors to show them **mercy**;

1 Chronicles 21:13
Let me fall into the hands of the LORD, for his **mercy** is very great;

Nehemiah 9:31
But in your great **mercy** you did not put an end to them or abandon them, for you are a gracious and **merciful** God.

Nehemiah 13:22
Remember me for this also, my God, and show **mercy** to me according to your great love.

Psalm 4:1
Answer me when I call to you, my righteous God. Give me relief from my distress; have **mercy** on me and hear my prayer.

Psalm 6:2
Have **mercy** on me, LORD, for I am faint; heal me, LORD, for my bones are in agony.

Psalm 9:13
LORD, see how my enemies persecute me! Have **mercy** and lift me up from the gates of death,

Psalm 25:6
Remember, LORD, your great **mercy** and love, for they are from of old.

Psalm 26:11
I lead a blameless life; deliver me and be **merciful** to me.

Psalm 27:7
Hear my voice when I call, LORD; be **merciful** to me and answer me.

Psalm 28:6
Praise be to the LORD, for he has heard my cry for **mercy**.

Psalm 30:10
Hear, LORD, and be **merciful** to me; LORD, be my help."

Psalm 31:9
Be **merciful** to me, LORD, for I am in distress;

Psalm 40:11
Do not withhold your **mercy** from me, LORD; may your love and faithfulness always protect me.

Psalm 41:4
I said, "Have **mercy** on me, LORD; heal me, for I have sinned against you."

Psalm 41:10
But may you have **mercy** on me, LORD; raise me up, that I may repay them.

Psalm 51:1
Have **mercy** on me, O God, according to your unfailing love; according to your great compassion blot out my transgressions.

Psalm 56:1
Be **merciful** to me, my God, for my enemies are in hot pursuit; all day long they press their attack.

Psalm 57:1
Have **mercy** on me, my God, have **mercy** on me, for in you I take refuge.

Psalm 69:16
Answer me, LORD, out of the goodness of your love; in your great **mercy** turn to me.

Psalm 78:38
Yet he was **merciful**; he forgave their iniquities and did not destroy them. Time after time he restrained his anger and did not stir up his full wrath.

Psalm 79:8
Do not hold against us the sins of past generations; may your **mercy** come quickly to meet us, for we are in desperate need.

Psalm 86:3
have **mercy** on me, Lord, for I call to you all day long.

Psalm 86:16
Turn to me and have **mercy** on me;

Psalm 106:46
He caused all who held them captive to show them **mercy**.

Psalm 116:1
I love the LORD, for he heard my voice; he heard my cry for **mercy**.

Psalm 119:132
Turn to me and have **mercy** on me, as you always do to those who love your name.

Psalm 123:2
so our eyes look to the LORD our God, till he shows us his **mercy**.

Psalm 123:3
Have mercy on us, LORD, have **mercy** on us, for we have endured no end of contempt.

Psalm 130:2
Lord, hear my voice. Let your ears be attentive to my cry for **mercy**.

Psalm 140:6
I say to the LORD, "You are my God." Hear, LORD, my cry for **mercy**.

Psalm 142:1
I cry aloud to the LORD; I lift up my voice to the LORD for **mercy**.

God is Merciful

Psalm 143:1
LORD, hear my prayer, listen to my cry for **mercy**; in your faithfulness and righteousness come to my relief.

Proverbs 28:13
Whoever conceals their sins does not prosper, but the one who confesses and renounces them finds **mercy**.

Isaiah 55:7
Let them turn to the LORD, and he will have **mercy** on them, and to our God, for he will freely pardon.

Isaiah 63:9
In his love and **mercy** he redeemed them; he lifted them up and carried them all the days of old.

Daniel 9:9
The Lord our God is **merciful** and forgiving, even though we have rebelled against him;

Daniel 9:18
We do not make requests of you because we are righteous, but because of your great **mercy**.

Amos 5:15
Perhaps the LORD God Almighty will have **mercy** on the remnant of Joseph.

Micah 7:18
Who is a God like you, who pardons sin and forgives the transgression of the remnant of his inheritance? You do not stay angry forever but delight to show **mercy**.

Habakkuk 3:2
LORD, I have heard of your fame; I stand in awe of your deeds, LORD. Repeat them in our day, in our time make them known; in wrath remember **mercy**.

Zechariah 1:16
"Therefore this is what the LORD says: 'I will return to Jerusalem with **mercy**, and there my house will be rebuilt.

Matthew 5:7
Blessed are the merciful, for they will be shown **mercy**.

Matthew 9:27
As Jesus went on from there, two blind men followed him, calling out, "Have **mercy** on us, Son of David!"

Matthew 15:22
A Canaanite woman from that vicinity came to him, crying out, "Lord, Son of David, have **mercy** on me!

Matthew 17:15
"Lord, have **mercy** on my son," he said.

Matthew 20:30
Two blind men were sitting by the roadside, and when they heard that Jesus was going by, they shouted, "Lord, Son of David, have **mercy** on us!"

Matthew 20:31
The crowd rebuked them and told them to be quiet, but they shouted all the louder, "Lord, Son of David, have **mercy** on us!"

Mark 5:19
Jesus did not let him, but said, "Go home to your own people and tell them how much the Lord has done for you, and how he has had **mercy** on you."

Mark 10:47
When he heard that it was Jesus of Nazareth, he began to shout, "Jesus, Son of David, have **mercy** on me!"

Mark 10:48
Many rebuked him and told him to be quiet, but he shouted all the more, "Son of David, have **mercy** on me!"

God is Merciful

Luke 1:50
His **mercy** extends to those who fear him, from generation to generation.

Luke 1:54
He has helped his servant Israel, remembering to be **merciful**

Luke 1:58
Her neighbors and relatives heard that the Lord had shown her great **mercy**, and they shared her joy.

Luke 1:72
to show **mercy** to our ancestors and to remember his holy covenant,

Luke 1:78
because of the tender **mercy** of our God, by which the rising sun will come to us from heaven

Luke 6:36
Be merciful, just as your Father is **merciful**.

Luke 18:13
"But the tax collector stood at a distance. He would not even look up to heaven, but beat his breast and said, 'God, have **mercy** on me, a sinner.'

Luke 18:38
He called out, "Jesus, Son of David, have **mercy** on me!"

Luke 18:39
Those who led the way rebuked him and told him to be quiet, but he shouted all the more, "Son of David, have **mercy** on me!"

Romans 9:15
For he says to Moses, "I will have **mercy** on whom I have **mercy**, and I will have compassion on whom I have compassion."

Romans 9:16
It does not, therefore, depend on human desire or effort, but on God's **mercy**.

Romans 9:18
Therefore God has **mercy** on whom he wants to have **mercy**,

Romans 9:23
What if he did this to make the riches of his glory known to the objects of his **mercy**, whom he prepared in advance for glory—

Romans 11:32
For God has bound everyone over to disobedience so that he may have **mercy** on them all.

Romans 12:1
Therefore, I urge you, brothers and sisters, in view of God's **mercy**,

Romans 15:9
and, moreover, that the Gentiles might glorify God for his **mercy**.

1 Corinthians 7:25
but I give a judgment as one who by the Lord's **mercy** is trustworthy.

2 Corinthians 4:1
Therefore, since through God's **mercy** we have this ministry, we do not lose heart.

Ephesians 2:4
But because of his great love for us, God, who is rich in **mercy**,

Philippians 2:27
Indeed he was ill, and almost died. But God had **mercy** on him,

God is Merciful

1 Timothy 1:2
Grace, **mercy** and peace from God the Father and Christ Jesus our Lord.

1 Timothy 1:13
Even though I was once a blasphemer and a persecutor and a violent man, I was shown **mercy** because I acted in ignorance and unbelief.

1 Timothy 1:16
But for that very reason I was shown **mercy** so that in me, the worst of sinners, Christ Jesus might display his immense patience as an example for those who would believe in him and receive eternal life.

2 Timothy 1:2
Grace, **mercy** and peace from God the Father and Christ Jesus our Lord.

2 Timothy 1:16
May the Lord show **mercy** to the household of Onesiphorus,

2 Timothy 1:18
May the Lord grant that he will find **mercy** from the Lord on that day!

Titus 3:5
he saved us, not because of righteous things we had done, but because of his **mercy**.

Hebrews 4:16
Let us then approach God's throne of grace with confidence, so that we may receive **mercy** and find grace to help us in our time of need.

James 3:17
But the wisdom that comes from heaven is first of all pure; then peace-loving, considerate, submissive, full of **mercy** and good fruit, impartial and sincere.

James 5:11
The Lord is full of compassion and **mercy**.

1 Peter 1:3
Praise be to the God and Father of our Lord Jesus Christ! In his great **mercy** he has given us new birth into a living hope through the resurrection of Jesus Christ from the dead,

1 Peter 2:10
Once you were not a people, but now you are the people of God; once you had not received mercy, but now you have received **mercy**.

2 John 1:3
Grace, **mercy** and peace from God the Father and from Jesus Christ, the Father's Son,

Jude 1:21
keep yourselves in God's love as you wait for the **mercy** of our Lord Jesus Christ to bring you to eternal life.

God is Patient
Showing Patience
Slow to Anger
Forebearing

Patient:
Calm endurance of hardship, annoyance or delay.

*The Lord is not slow in keeping his promise, as some understand slowness. Instead he is **patient** with you, not wanting anyone to perish, but everyone to come to repentance.*

- II Peter 3:9

God is Patient

1. DEFINE PATIENT USING YOUR OWN WORDS, SYNONYMS, OR DESCRIPTIONS:

_____

_____

_____

2. IN 1 PETER 3:20 AND AGAIN IN 2 PETER 3:8-9, IT STATES THAT GOD'S PATIENCE IN THE DAYS OF NOAH AS WELL TODAY ARE TO GIVE TIME FOR PEOPLE TO COME TO SALVATION; GOD DOESN'T WANT TO SEE ANYONE PERISH. WHAT DOES THIS SHOW YOU ABOUT THE FOUNDATION OF GOD'S PATIENCE?

_____

_____

_____

3. 2 PETER 3:8, "WITH THE LORD A DAY IS LIKE A THOUSAND YEARS, AND A THOUSAND YEARS ARE LIKE A DAY." THIS WAS SAID IN REFERENCE TO GOD'S PATIENCE. EXPLAIN WHAT IT MEANS.

_____

_____

_____

4. DO YOU HAVE ANY OBSERVATIONS ABOUT THIS CHARACTER TRAIT OF GOD OR WHY GOD WANTS US TO KNOW THAT HE IS PATIENT, FOREBEARING AND SLOW TO ANGER?

_____

_____

_____

_____

_____

The best things are never arrived at in haste. God is in no hurry; His plans are never rushed.
- Michael Phillips

NOTES:

God is Patient

Exodus 34:6
And he passed in front of Moses, proclaiming, "The LORD, the LORD, the compassionate and gracious God, **slow to anger**, abounding in love and faithfulness,

Numbers 14:18
'The LORD is **slow to anger**, abounding in love and forgiving sin and rebellion.

Nehemiah 9:17
you are a forgiving God, gracious and compassionate, **slow to anger** and abounding in love.

Nehemiah 9:30
For many years you were **patient** with them. By your Spirit you warned them through your prophets.

Psalm 86:15
But you, Lord, are a compassionate and gracious God, **slow to anger**, abounding in love and faithfulness.

Psalm 103:8
The LORD is compassionate and gracious, **slow to anger**, abounding in love.

Psalm 145:8
The LORD is gracious and compassionate, **slow to anger** and rich in love.

Joel 2:13
Return to the LORD your God, for he is gracious and compassionate, **slow to anger** and abounding in love, and he relents from sending calamity.

Jonah 4:2
I knew that you are a gracious and compassionate God, **slow to anger** and abounding in love, a God who relents from sending calamity.

Nahum 1:3
The LORD is **slow to anger** but great in power; the LORD will not leave the guilty unpunished.

Romans 2:4
Or do you show contempt for the riches of his kindness, **forbearance and patience**, not realizing that God's kindness is intended to lead you to repentance?

Romans 9:22
What if God, although choosing to show his wrath and make his power known, bore with great **patience** the objects of his wrath—prepared for destruction?

1 Corinthians 13:4
Love is **patient**, love is kind.

1 Timothy 1:16
But for that very reason I was shown mercy so that in me, the worst of sinners, Christ Jesus might display his immense **patience** as an example for those who would believe in him and receive eternal life.

1 Peter 3:20
to those who were disobedient long ago when God waited **patiently** in the days of Noah while the ark was being built.

2 Peter 3:9
The Lord is not slow in keeping his promise, as some understand slowness. Instead he is **patient** with you, not wanting anyone to perish, but everyone to come to repentance.

2 Peter 3:15
Bear in mind that our Lord's **patience** means salvation,

God Our Peace
Peaceful
Giving Peace

Peaceful:
Freedom from anxiety; quiet; calm; A state of harmony; Absence of strife; Cessation of war.

*For to us a child is born, to us a son is given, and the government will be on his shoulders. And he will be called Wonderful Counselor, Mighty God, Everlasting Father, Prince of **Peace**. Of the greatness of his government and **peace** there will be no end.*

- Isaiah 9:6-7

God Our Peace

1. DEFINE PEACE USING YOUR OWN WORDS, SYNONYMS, OR DESCRIPTIONS:

_____

_____

_____

2. SCRIPTURE SEEMS TO INDICATE THAT PEACE IS A RESULT OF WALKING IN OBEDIENCE TO GOD. CAN YOU FIND THE VERSES THAT INDICATE THIS?

_____

_____

_____

3. ROMANS 16:20, "THE GOD OF PEACE WILL SOON CRUSH SATAN UNDER YOUR FEET." AT FIRST GLANCE, THIS STATEMENT MIGHT SEEM CONTRADICTORY BUT EXPLAIN WHY IT IS NOT.

_____

_____

_____

4. DO YOU HAVE ANY OBSERVATIONS ABOUT THIS CHARACTER TRAIT OF GOD OR WHY GOD WANTS US TO KNOW THAT HE IS OUR PEACE, PEACEFUL AND GIVES PEACE?

_____

_____

_____

_____

_____

All men desire peace, but very few desire those things that make for peace.
— _Thomas Kempis_

Alexander, Caesar, Charlemagne, and I myself have founded great empires ... But Jesus alone founded His empire on love, and to this very day, millions would die for Him. Jesus Christ was more than a man.
— _Napolean_

The peace of the celestial city is the perfectly ordered and hormonious enjoyment of God, and of one another in God.
— _St. Augustine_

NOTES:

God Our Peace

Leviticus 26:6
"'I will grant **peace** in the land, and you will lie down and no one will make you afraid.

Numbers 6:26
the LORD turn his face toward you and give you **peace.**'"

Numbers 25:12
Therefore tell him I am making my covenant of **peace** with him.

Judges 6:23
But the LORD said to him, "**Peace**! Do not be afraid. You are not going to die."

Judges 6:24
So Gideon built an altar to the LORD there and called it The LORD Is **Peace**.

1 Kings 2:33
But on David and his descendants, his house and his throne, may there be the LORD's **peace** forever."

1 Chronicles 22:9
But you will have a son who will be a man of peace and rest, and I will give him rest from all his enemies on every side. His name will be Solomon, and I will grant Israel **peace** and quiet during his reign.

2 Chronicles 20:30
And the kingdom of Jehoshaphat was at **peace**, for his God had given him rest on every side.

Psalm 4:8
In **peace** I will lie down and sleep, for you alone, LORD, make me dwell in safety.

Psalm 29:11
The LORD gives strength to his people; the LORD blesses his people with **peace**.

Psalm 37:11
But the meek will inherit the land and enjoy **peace** and prosperity.

Psalm 85:8
I will listen to what God the LORD says; he promises **peace** to his people, his faithful servants—

Psalm 85:10
Love and faithfulness meet together; righteousness and **peace** kiss each other.

Psalm 119:165
Great **peace** have those who love your law, and nothing can make them stumble.

Psalm 122:6
Pray for the **peace** of Jerusalem: "May those who love you be secure.

Psalm 147:14
He grants **peace** to your borders and satisfies you with the finest of wheat.

Proverbs 16:7
When the LORD takes pleasure in anyone's way, he causes their enemies to make **peace** with them.

Isaiah 9:6
For to us a child is born, to us a son is given, and the government will be on his shoulders. And he will be called Wonderful Counselor, Mighty God, Everlasting Father, Prince of **Peace**.

Isaiah 9:7
Of the greatness of his government and **peace** there will be no end.

Isaiah 26:3
You will keep in perfect **peace** those whose minds are steadfast, because they trust in you.

Isaiah 26:12
LORD, you establish **peace** for us; all that we have accomplished you have done for us.

Isaiah 32:17
The fruit of that righteousness will be **peace**; its effect will be quietness and confidence forever.

Isaiah 33:20
Look on Zion, the city of our festivals; your eyes will see Jerusalem, a **peaceful** abode, a tent that will not be moved; its stakes will never be pulled up, nor any of its ropes broken.

Isaiah 48:18
If only you had paid attention to my commands, your **peace** would have been like a river, your well-being like the waves of the sea.

Isaiah 53:5
But he was pierced for our transgressions, he was crushed for our iniquities; the punishment that brought us **peace** was on him, and by his wounds we are healed.

Isaiah 54:10
Though the mountains be shaken and the hills be removed, yet my unfailing love for you will not be shaken nor my covenant of **peace** be removed," says the LORD, who has compassion on you.

Isaiah 54:13
All your children will be taught by the LORD, and great will be their **peace**.

Isaiah 55:12
You will go out in joy and be led forth in **peace**;

Isaiah 57:19
Peace, **peace**, to those far and near," says the LORD. "And I will heal them."

Isaiah 60:17
I will make **peace** your governor and well-being your ruler.

Isaiah 66:12
For this is what the LORD says: "I will extend **peace** to her like a river, and the wealth of nations like a flooding stream;

Jeremiah 30:10
Jacob will again have **peace** and security, and no one will make him afraid.

Jeremiah 33:6
"'Nevertheless, I will bring health and healing to it; I will heal my people and will let them enjoy abundant **peace** and security.

Jeremiah 33:9
Then this city will bring me renown, joy, praise and honor before all nations on earth that hear of all the good things I do for it; and they will be in awe and will tremble at the abundant prosperity and **peace** I provide for it.'

Jeremiah 46:27
Jacob will again have **peace** and security, and no one will make him afraid.

Ezekiel 34:25
"'I will make a covenant of **peace** with them and rid the land of savage beasts so that they may live in the wilderness and sleep in the forests in safety.

Ezekiel 37:26
I will make a covenant of **peace** with them; it will be an everlasting covenant.

Micah 5:5
And he will be our **peace** when the Assyrians invade our land and march through our fortresses.

God Our Peace

Nahum 1:15
Look, there on the mountains, the feet of one who brings good news, who proclaims **peace**! Celebrate your festivals, Judah, and fulfill your vows. No more will the wicked invade you; they will be completely destroyed.

Haggai 2:9
And in this place I will grant **peace**,' declares the LORD Almighty."

Zechariah 9:10
He will proclaim **peace** to the nations. His rule will extend from sea to sea and from the River to the ends of the earth.

Malachi 2:5
"My covenant was with him, a covenant of life and **peace**, and I gave them to him; this called for reverence and he revered me and stood in awe of my name.

Matthew 5:9
Blessed are the **peacemakers**, for they will be called children of God.

Mark 5:34
He said to her, "Daughter, your faith has healed you. Go in **peace** and be freed from your suffering."

Luke 1:79
to shine on those living in darkness and in the shadow of death, to guide our feet into the path of **peace**."

Luke 2:14
"Glory to God in the highest heaven, and on earth **peace** to those on whom his favor rests."

Luke 2:29
"Sovereign Lord, as you have promised, you may now dismiss your servant in **peace**.

Luke 7:50
Jesus said to the woman, "Your faith has saved you; go in **peace**."

Luke 8:48
Then he said to her, "Daughter, your faith has healed you. Go in **peace**."

Luke 19:38
"Blessed is the king who comes in the name of the Lord!" "**Peace** in heaven and glory in the highest!"

Luke 24:36
Jesus himself stood among them and said to them, "**Peace** be with you."

John 14:27
Peace I leave with you; my **peace** I give you. I do not give to you as the world gives. Do not let your hearts be troubled and do not be afraid.

John 16:33
"I have told you these things, so that in me you may have **peace**. In this world you will have trouble. But take heart! I have overcome the world."

John 20:19
Jesus came and stood among them and said, "**Peace** be with you!"

John 20:21
Again Jesus said, "**Peace** be with you!

John 20:26
Though the doors were locked, Jesus came and stood among them and said, "**Peace** be with you!"

Acts 10:36
You know the message God sent to the people of Israel, announcing the good news of **peace** through Jesus Christ, who is Lord of all.

Romans 1:7
Grace and **peace** to you from God our Father and from the Lord Jesus Christ.

Romans 5:1
Therefore, since we have been justified through faith, we have **peace** with God through our Lord Jesus Christ,

Romans 8:6
The mind governed by the flesh is death, but the mind governed by the Spirit is life and **peace**.

Romans 14:17
For the kingdom of God is not a matter of eating and drinking, but of righteousness, **peace** and joy in the Holy Spirit,

Romans 15:13
May the God of hope fill you with all joy and **peace** as you trust in him, so that you may overflow with hope by the power of the Holy Spirit.

Romans 15:33
The God of **peace** be with you all.

Romans 16:20
The God of **peace** will soon crush Satan under your feet.

1 Corinthians 1:3
Grace and **peace** to you from God our Father and the Lord Jesus Christ.

1 Corinthians 14:33
For God is not a God of disorder but of **peace**—

2 Corinthians 1:2
Grace and **peace** to you from God our Father and the Lord Jesus Christ.

2 Corinthians 13:11
And the God of love and **peace** will be with you.

Galatians 1:3
Grace and **peace** to you from God our Father and the Lord Jesus Christ,

Galatians 5:22
But the fruit of the Spirit is love, joy, **peace**, forbearance, kindness, goodness, faithfulness,

Ephesians 1:2
Grace and **peace** to you from God our Father and the Lord Jesus Christ.

Ephesians 2:14
For he himself is our **peace**,

Ephesians 2:15
His purpose was to create in himself one new humanity out of the two, thus making **peace**,

Ephesians 2:17
He came and preached **peace** to you who were far away and **peace** to those who were near.

Ephesians 6:15
and with your feet fitted with the readiness that comes from the gospel of **peace**.

Philippians 1:2
Grace and **peace** to you from God our Father and the Lord Jesus Christ.

Philippians 4:7
And the **peace** of God, which transcends all understanding, will guard your hearts and your minds in Christ Jesus.

God Our Peace

Philippians 4:9
And the God of **peace** will be with you.

Colossians 1:2
Grace and **peace** to you from God our Father.

Colossians 1:20
and through him to reconcile to himself all things, whether things on earth or things in heaven, by making **peace** through his blood, shed on the cross.

Colossians 3:15
Let the peace of Christ rule in your hearts, since as members of one body you were called to **peace**.

1 Thessalonians 5:23
May God himself, the God of **peace**, sanctify you through and through.

2 Thessalonians 1:2
Grace and **peace** to you from God the Father and the Lord Jesus Christ.

2 Thessalonians 3:16
Now may the Lord of **peace** himself give you **peace** at all times and in every way.

1 Timothy 1:2
Grace, mercy and **peace** from God the Father and Christ Jesus our Lord.

2 Timothy 1:2
Grace, mercy and **peace** from God the Father and Christ Jesus our Lord.

Titus 1:4
Grace and **peace** from God the Father and Christ Jesus our Savior.

Philemon 1:3
Grace and **peace** to you from God our Father and the Lord Jesus Christ.

Hebrews 13:20
Now may the God of **peace**, who through the blood of the eternal covenant brought back from the dead our Lord Jesus, that great Shepherd of the sheep,

James 3:17
But the wisdom that comes from heaven is first of all pure; then **peace**-loving, considerate, submissive, full of mercy and good fruit, impartial and sincere.

2 John 1:3
Grace, mercy and **peace** from God the Father and from Jesus Christ, the Father's Son, will be with us in truth and love.

Revelation 1:4
Grace and **peace** to you from him who is, and who was, and who is to come,

God is Perfect
Without Blemish
Flawless; Complete

Perfect:
Faultless; Excellent; Complete; Lacking in nothing; Having all essential qualities.

*As for God, his way is **perfect**: The Lord's word is **flawless**.*

- II Samuel 22:31

God is Perfect

1. DEFINE PERFECT USING YOUR OWN WORDS, SYNONYMS, OR DESCRIPTIONS:

_____

_____

_____

2. THE BIBLE SAYS GOD IS PERFECT -- THAT HIS WORKS, LAW AND WORD ARE PERFECT. WHAT DOES THIS SAY ABOUT GOD AS THE ONE BY WHOM ALL OTHERS ARE MEASURED?

_____

_____

_____

3. DO YOU HAVE ANY OBSERVATIONS ABOUT THIS CHARACTER TRAIT OF GOD OR WHY GOD WANTS US TO KNOW THAT HE IS PERFECT, FLAWLESS, COMPLETE AND WITHOUT BLEMISH?

_____

_____

_____

_____

_____

Angels had fallen, men have sinned. It does not mean that God has failed.
- Toba Beta

God will not fail, because He cannot fail.
- Joy Dawson

*Christian perfection is not so severe, tiresome and constraining as we think.
It asks us only to be God's from the bottom of our hearts.*
- Francois Fenelon

NOTES:

God is Perfect

Deuteronomy 32:4
He is the Rock, his works are **perfect**, and all his ways are just. A faithful God who does no wrong, upright and just is he.

2 Samuel 22:31
"As for God, his way is **perfect**: The LORD's word is **flawless**;

Psalm 18:30
As for God, his way is **perfect**: The LORD's word is **flawless**;

Psalm 19:7
The law of the LORD is **perfect**,

Psalm 50:2
From Zion, **perfect** in beauty, God shines forth.

Proverbs 30:5
"Every word of God is **flawless**;

Isaiah 25:1
LORD, you are my God; I will exalt you and praise your name, for in **perfect** faithfulness you have done wonderful things, things planned long ago.

Isaiah 26:3
You will keep in **perfect** peace those whose minds are steadfast, because they trust in you.

Matthew 5:48
Be perfect, therefore, as your heavenly Father is **perfect**.

Romans 12:2
Do not conform to the pattern of this world, but be transformed by the renewing of your mind. Then you will be able to test and approve what God's will is—his good, pleasing and **perfect** will.

1 Corinthians 13:10
but when **completeness** comes, what is in part disappears.

Hebrews 2:10
In bringing many sons and daughters to glory, it was fitting that God, for whom and through whom everything exists, should make the pioneer of their salvation **perfect** through what he suffered.

Hebrews 5:9
and, once made **perfect**, he became the source of eternal salvation for all who obey him

Hebrews 7:25
Therefore he is able to save **completely** those who come to God through him, because he always lives to intercede for them.

Hebrews 7:28
For the law appoints as high priests men in all their weakness; but the oath, which came after the law, appointed the Son, who has been made **perfect** forever.

Hebrews 9:11
[*The Blood of Christ*] But when Christ came as high priest of the good things that are now already here, he went through the greater and more **perfect** tabernacle that is not made with human hands, that is to say, is not a part of this creation.

Hebrews 10:14
For by one sacrifice he has made **perfect** forever those who are being made holy.

Hebrews 12:2
fixing our eyes on Jesus, the pioneer and **perfecter** of faith.

James 1:17
Every good and **perfect** gift is from above, coming down from the Father of the heavenly lights, who does not change like shifting shadows.

James 1:25
But whoever looks intently into the **perfect** law that gives freedom,

1 Peter 1:19
but with the precious blood of Christ, a lamb **without blemish or defect**.

1 John 4:12
No one has ever seen God; but if we love one another, God lives in us and his love is made **complete** in us.

1 John 4:17
This is how love is made **complete** among us so that we will have confidence on the day of judgment: In this world we are like Jesus.

God is Powerful
Strong; Mighty
Able to Give (or Take) Strength

Powerful:
Having great power, strength, force or influence; Better in comparison to any contender.

*Be strong and courageous. Do not be afraid or discouraged because of the king of Assyria and the vast army with him, for there is a greater **power** with us than with him.*

- II Chronicles 32:7

God is Powerful

1. DEFINE POWERFUL USING YOUR OWN WORDS, SYNONYMS, OR DESCRIPTIONS:

_____

_____

_____

2. LIST ALL THE VERSES THAT REFER TO THE "MIGHTY HAND" OF GOD. WHAT DO YOU THINK IS THE SIGNIFICANCE OF USING THE WORD "HAND" (ALSO: SOMETIMES "RIGHT HAND" OR "ARM") IN REFERENCE TO GOD'S POWER?

_____

_____

_____

_____

_____

3. IN GENESIS 17, GOD APPEARED TO ABRAHAM WHO WAS 99 YEARS OLD. THE FIRST THING GOD TOLD MOSES IS, I AM GOD ALMIGHTY" AND HE MADE A COVENANT WITH ABRAHAM TO MAKE A GREAT NATION FROM HIM AND HIS WIFE, SARAH, WHO WAS ALSO IN HER 90's. READ GENESIS 17:1-22 AND 21:1-7 TO SEE HOW AN ALL-MIGHTY GOD CHOSE AN OBEDIENT OLD MAN AND WOMAN FROM WHICH TO START A MULTITUDE OF DESCENDANTS.

_____

_____

_____

4. DO YOU HAVE ANY OBSERVATIONS ABOUT THIS CHARACTER TRAIT OF GOD OR WHY GOD WANTS US TO KNOW THAT HE IS POWERFUL, STRONG, MIGHTY AND THE GIVER OF STRENGTH?

_____

_____

_____

_____

_____

NOTES:

God is Powerful

Genesis 49:24
But his bow remained steady, his strong arms stayed limber, because of the hand of the **Mighty** One of Jacob, because of the Shepherd, the Rock of Israel,

Exodus 4:21
The LORD said to Moses, "When you return to Egypt, see that you perform before Pharaoh all the wonders I have given you the **power** to do.

Exodus 6:1
Then the LORD said to Moses, "Now you will see what I will do to Pharaoh: Because of my **mighty** hand he will let them go; because of my **mighty** hand he will drive them out of his country."

Exodus 6:6
"Therefore, say to the Israelites: 'I am the LORD, and I will bring you out from under the yoke of the Egyptians. I will free you from being slaves to them, and I will redeem you with an outstretched arm and with **mighty** acts of judgment.

Exodus 7:4
Then I will lay my hand on Egypt and with **mighty** acts of judgment I will bring out my divisions, my people the Israelites.

Exodus 9:16
But I have raised you up for this very purpose, that I might show you my **power** and that my name might be proclaimed in all the earth.

Exodus 13:3
Then Moses said to the people, "Commemorate this day, the day you came out of Egypt, out of the land of slavery, because the LORD brought you out of it with a **mighty** hand.

Exodus 13:9
For the LORD brought you out of Egypt with his **mighty** hand.

Exodus 13:14
"In days to come, when your son asks you, 'What does this mean?' say to him, 'With a **mighty** hand the LORD brought us out of Egypt, out of the land of slavery.

Exodus 13:16
And it will be like a sign on your hand and a symbol on your forehead that the LORD brought us out of Egypt with his **mighty** hand."

Exodus 14:31
And when the Israelites saw the **mighty** hand of the LORD displayed against the Egyptians, the people feared the LORD and put their trust in him and in Moses his servant.

Exodus 15:2
"The LORD is my **strength** and my defense ; he has become my salvation.

Exodus 15:6
Your right hand, LORD, was majestic in **power**. Your right hand, LORD, shattered the enemy.

Exodus 15:13
In your unfailing love you will lead the people you have redeemed. In your **strength** you will guide them to your holy dwelling.

Exodus 15:16
By the **power** of your arm they will be as still as a stone— until your people pass by, LORD, until the people you bought pass by.

Exodus 32:11
But Moses sought the favor of the LORD his God. "LORD," he said, "why should your anger burn against your people, whom you brought out of Egypt with great **power** and a **mighty** hand?

Numbers 11:17
I will come down and speak with you there, and I will take some of the **power** of the Spirit that is on you and put it on them.

Numbers 11:25
Then the LORD came down in the cloud and spoke with him, and he took some of the **power** of the Spirit that was on him and put it on the seventy elders.

Numbers 14:13
Moses said to the LORD, "Then the Egyptians will hear about it! By your **power** you brought these people up from among them.

Numbers 14:17
"Now may the Lord's **strength** be displayed, just as you have declared:

Deuteronomy 3:24
"Sovereign LORD, you have begun to show to your servant your greatness and your **strong** hand. For what god is there in heaven or on earth who can do the deeds and **mighty** works you do?

Deuteronomy 4:34
Has any god ever tried to take for himself one nation out of another nation, by testings, by signs and wonders, by war, by a **mighty** hand and an outstretched arm, or by great and awesome deeds, like all the things the LORD your God did for you in Egypt before your very eyes?

Deuteronomy 4:37
Because he loved your ancestors and chose their descendants after them, he brought you out of Egypt by his Presence and his great **strength**,

Deuteronomy 5:15
Remember that you were slaves in Egypt and that the LORD your God brought you out of there with a **mighty** hand and an outstretched arm.

Deuteronomy 6:21
"We were slaves of Pharaoh in Egypt, but the LORD brought us out of Egypt with a **mighty** hand.

Deuteronomy 7:8
But it was because the LORD loved you and kept the oath he swore to your ancestors that he brought you out with a **mighty** hand and redeemed you from the land of slavery, from the power of Pharaoh king of Egypt.

Deuteronomy 7:19
You saw with your own eyes the great trials, the signs and wonders, the **mighty** hand and outstretched arm, with which the LORD your God brought you out.

Deuteronomy 9:26
I prayed to the LORD and said, "Sovereign LORD, do not destroy your people, your own inheritance that you redeemed by your great power and brought out of Egypt with a **mighty** hand.

Deuteronomy 9:29
But they are your people, your inheritance that you brought out by your great **power** and your outstretched arm."

Deuteronomy 10:17
For the LORD your God is God of gods and Lord of lords, the great God, **mighty** and awesome, who shows no partiality and accepts no bribes.

Deuteronomy 11:2
Remember today that your children were not the ones who saw and experienced the discipline of the LORD your God: his majesty, his **mighty** hand, his outstretched arm;

Deuteronomy 26:8
So the LORD brought us out of Egypt with a **mighty** hand and an outstretched arm, with great terror and with signs and wonders.

Joshua 4:24
He did this so that all the peoples of the earth might know that the hand of the LORD is **powerful** and so that you might always fear the LORD your God."

God is Powerful

Joshua 22:22
"The **Mighty** One, God, the LORD! The **Mighty** One, God, the LORD!

Judges 14:6
The Spirit of the LORD came **powerfully** upon him so that he tore the lion apart with his bare hands as he might have torn a young goat.

Judges 14:19
Then the Spirit of the LORD came **powerfully** upon him.

Judges 15:14
The Spirit of the LORD came **powerfully** upon him.

Judges 16:28
Then Samson prayed to the LORD, "Sovereign LORD, remember me. Please, God, **strengthen** me just once more,

1 Samuel 2:10
The Most High will thunder from heaven; the LORD will judge the ends of the earth. "He will give **strength** to his king and exalt the horn of his anointed."

1 Samuel 2:31
The time is coming when I will cut short your **strength** and the **strength** of your priestly house,

1 Samuel 2:33
Every one of you that I do not cut off from serving at my altar I will spare only to destroy your sight and sap your **strength**, and all your descendants will die in the prime of life.

1 Samuel 10:6
The Spirit of the LORD will come **powerfully** upon you, and you will prophesy with them;

1 Samuel 10:10
the Spirit of God came **powerfully** upon him, and he joined in their prophesying.

1 Samuel 11:6
When Saul heard their words, the Spirit of God came **powerfully** upon him, and he burned with anger.

1 Samuel 16:13
So Samuel took the horn of oil and anointed him in the presence of his brothers, and from that day on the Spirit of the LORD came **powerfully** upon David.

1 Samuel 30:6
But David found **strength** in the LORD his God.

2 Samuel 22:33
It is God who arms me with **strength** and keeps my way secure.

2 Samuel 22:40
You armed me with **strength** for battle; you humbled my adversaries before me.

1 Kings 8:42
for they will hear of your great name and your **mighty** hand and your outstretched arm—

1 Kings 18:46
The **power** of the LORD came on Elijah and, tucking his cloak into his belt, he ran ahead of Ahab all the way to Jezreel.

2 Kings 17:36
But the LORD, who brought you up out of Egypt with **mighty** power and outstretched arm, is the one you must worship.

1 Chronicles 16:11
Look to the LORD and his **strength**; seek his face always.

1 Chronicles 16:27
Splendor and majesty are before him; **strength** and joy are in his dwelling place.

1 Chronicles 16:28
Ascribe to the LORD, all you families of nations, ascribe to the LORD glory and **strength**.

1 Chronicles 29:11
Yours, LORD, is the greatness and the **power** and the glory and the majesty and the splendor, for everything in heaven and earth is yours.

1 Chronicles 29:12
Wealth and honor come from you; you are the ruler of all things. In your hands are **strength** and **power** to exalt and give strength to all.

2 Chronicles 6:32
"As for the foreigner who does not belong to your people Israel but has come from a distant land because of your great name and your **mighty** hand and your outstretched arm—

2 Chronicles 16:9
For the eyes of the LORD range throughout the earth to **strengthen** those whose hearts are fully committed to him.

2 Chronicles 20:6
"LORD, the God of our ancestors, are you not the God who is in heaven? You rule over all the kingdoms of the nations. **Power** and **might** are in your hand, and no one can withstand you.

2 Chronicles 25:8
Even if you go and fight courageously in battle, God will overthrow you before the enemy, for God has the **power** to help or to overthrow."

2 Chronicles 32:7
"Be strong and courageous. Do not be afraid or discouraged because of the king of Assyria and the vast army with him, for there is a greater **power** with us than with him.

Nehemiah 1:10
"They are your servants and your people, whom you redeemed by your great **strength** and your **mighty** hand.

Nehemiah 6:9
But I prayed, "Now **strengthen** my hands."

Nehemiah 8:10
Nehemiah said, "This day is holy to our Lord. Do not grieve, for the joy of the LORD is your **strength**."

Nehemiah 9:32
"Now therefore, our God, the great God, **mighty** and awesome, who keeps his covenant of love,

Job 9:19
If it is a matter of **strength**, he is **mighty**!

Job 12:13
"To God belong wisdom and **power**; counsel and understanding are his.

Job 36:5
"God is **mighty**, but despises no one; he is **mighty**, and firm in his purpose.

Job 36:22
"God is exalted in his **power**. Who is a teacher like him?

Job 37:23
The Almighty is beyond our reach and exalted in **power**;

Psalm 18:1
I love you, LORD, my **strength**.

God is Powerful

Psalm 18:32
It is God who arms me with **strength** and keeps my way secure.

Psalm 18:39
You armed me with **strength** for battle; you humbled my adversaries before me.

Psalm 20:6
Now this I know: The LORD gives victory to his anointed. He answers him from his heavenly sanctuary with the victorious **power** of his right hand.

Psalm 21:1
The king rejoices in your **strength**, LORD. How great is his joy in the victories you give!

Psalm 21:13
Be exalted in your **strength**, LORD; we will sing and praise your **might**.

Psalm 22:19
But you, LORD, do not be far from me. You are my **strength**;

Psalm 24:8
Who is this King of glory? The LORD **strong** and **mighty**, the LORD **mighty** in battle.

Psalm 28:7
The LORD is my **strength** and my shield; my heart trusts in him, and he helps me.

Psalm 28:8
The LORD is the **strength** of his people, a fortress of salvation for his anointed one.

Psalm 29:1
Ascribe to the LORD, you heavenly beings, ascribe to the LORD glory and **strength**.

Psalm 29:4
The voice of the LORD is **powerful**; the voice of the LORD is majestic.

Psalm 29:11
The LORD gives **strength** to his people; the LORD blesses his people with peace.

Psalm 31:2
Turn your ear to me, come quickly to my rescue; be my rock of refuge, a **strong** fortress to save me.

Psalm 42:4
These things I remember as I pour out my soul: how I used to go to the house of God under the protection of the **Mighty** One with shouts of joy and praise among the festive throng.

Psalm 46:1
God is our refuge and **strength**, an ever-present help in trouble.

Psalm 50:1
The **Mighty** One, God, the LORD, speaks and summons the earth from the rising of the sun to where it sets.

Psalm 59:9
You are my **strength**, I watch for you; you, God, are my fortress,

Psalm 59:16
But I will sing of your **strength**, in the morning I will sing of your love; for you are my fortress, my refuge in times of trouble.

Psalm 59:17
You are my **strength**, I sing praise to you; you, God, are my fortress, my God on whom I can rely.

Psalm 61:3
For you have been my refuge, a **strong** tower against the foe.

Psalm 62:7
My salvation and my honor depend on God ; he is my **mighty** rock, my refuge.

Psalm 62:11
"**Power** belongs to you, God,

Psalm 63:2
I have seen you in the sanctuary and beheld your **power** and your glory.

Psalm 65:6
who formed the mountains by your **power**, having armed yourself with **strength**,

Psalm 66:3
Say to God, "How awesome are your deeds! So great is your **power** that your enemies cringe before you.

Psalm 66:7
He rules forever by his **power**, his eyes watch the nations—

Psalm 68:28
Summon your **power**, God; show us your **strength**, our God, as you have done before.

Psalm 68:33
to him who rides across the highest heavens, the ancient heavens, who thunders with **mighty** voice.

Psalm 68:34
Proclaim the **power** of God, whose majesty is over Israel, whose **power** is in the heavens.

Psalm 68:35
You, God, are awesome in your sanctuary; the God of Israel gives **power** and **strength** to his people. Praise be to God!

Psalm 71:7
you are my **strong** refuge.

Psalm 71:16
I will come and proclaim your **mighty** acts, Sovereign LORD;

Psalm 71:18
Even when I am old and gray, do not forsake me, my God, till I declare your **power** to the next generation, your **mighty** acts to all who are to come.

Psalm 73:26
My flesh and my heart may fail, but God is the **strength** of my heart and my portion forever.

Psalm 74:13
It was you who split open the sea by your **power**;

Psalm 77:12
I will consider all your works and meditate on all your **mighty** deeds."

Psalm 77:14
You are the God who performs miracles; you display your **power** among the peoples.

Psalm 77:15
With your **mighty** arm you redeemed your people, the descendants of Jacob and Joseph.

Psalm 78:4
We will not hide them from their descendants; we will tell the next generation the praiseworthy deeds of the LORD, his **power**, and the wonders he has done.

Psalm 78:26
He let loose the east wind from the heavens and by his **power** made the south wind blow.

God is Powerful

Psalm 78:42
They did not remember his **power**— the day he redeemed them from the oppressor,

Psalm 81:1
Sing for joy to God our **strength**; shout aloud to the God of Jacob!

Psalm 86:16
Turn to me and have mercy on me; show your **strength** in behalf of your servant;

Psalm 89:8
Who is like you, LORD God Almighty? You, LORD, are **mighty,** and your faithfulness surrounds you.

Psalm 89:10
with your **strong** arm you scattered your enemies.

Psalm 89:13
Your arm is endowed with **power**; your hand is **strong,** your right hand exalted.

Psalm 89:17
For you are their glory and **strength,** and by your favor you exalt our horn.

Psalm 89:19
Once you spoke in a vision, to your faithful people you said: "I have bestowed **strength** on a warrior;

Psalm 89:21
My hand will sustain him; surely my arm will **strengthen** him.

Psalm 90:11
If only we knew the **power** of your anger! Your wrath is as great as the fear that is your due.

Psalm 93:1
The LORD reigns, he is robed in majesty; the LORD is robed in majesty and armed with **strength**;

Psalm 93:4
Mightier than the thunder of the great waters, **mightier** than the breakers of the sea— the LORD on high is **mighty.**

Psalm 96:6
Splendor and majesty are before him; **strength** and glory are in his sanctuary.

Psalm 96:7
Ascribe to the LORD, all you families of nations, ascribe to the LORD glory and **strength.**

Psalm 99:4
The King is **mighty,** he loves justice— you have established equity;

Psalm 105:4
Look to the LORD and his **strength**; seek his face always.

Psalm 106:2
Who can proclaim the **mighty** acts of the LORD or fully declare his praise?

Psalm 106:8
Yet he saved them for his name's sake, to make his **mighty** power known.

Psalm 111:6
He has shown his people the **power** of his works,

Psalm 118:14
The LORD is my **strength** and my defense; he has become my salvation.

Psalm 118:15
Shouts of joy and victory resound in the tents of the righteous: "The LORD's right hand has done **mighty** things!

Psalm 118:16
The LORD's right hand is lifted high; the LORD's right hand has done **mighty** things!"

Psalm 119:28
My soul is weary with sorrow; **strengthen** me according to your word.

Psalm 132:2
He swore an oath to the LORD, he made a vow to the **Mighty** One of Jacob:

Psalm 132:5
till I find a place for the LORD, a dwelling for the **Mighty** One of Jacob."

Psalm 136:12
with a **mighty** hand and outstretched arm; His love endures forever.

Psalm 140:7
Sovereign LORD, my **strong** deliverer, you shield my head in the day of battle.

Psalm 145:4
One generation commends your works to another; they tell of your **mighty** acts.

Psalm 145:6
They tell of the **power** of your awesome works— and I will proclaim your great deeds.

Psalm 145:12
so that all people may know of your **mighty** acts and the glorious splendor of your kingdom.

Psalm 147:5
Great is our Lord and mighty in **power**; his understanding has no limit.

Psalm 147:13
He **strengthens** the bars of your gates and blesses your people within you.

Psalm 150:1
Praise the LORD. Praise God in his sanctuary; praise him in his **mighty** heavens.

Psalm 150:2
Praise him for his acts of **power**; praise him for his surpassing greatness.

Proverbs 23:11
for their Defender is **strong**; he will take up their case against you.

Isaiah 1:24
Therefore the Lord, the LORD Almighty, the **Mighty** One of Israel,

Isaiah 8:11
This is what the LORD says to me with his **strong** hand upon me,

Isaiah 9:6
For to us a child is born, to us a son is given, and the government will be on his shoulders. And he will be called Wonderful Counselor, **Mighty** God, Everlasting Father, Prince of Peace.

Isaiah 10:13
For he says: "'By the **strength** of my hand I have done this, and by my wisdom, because I have understanding. I removed the boundaries of nations, I plundered their treasures; like a **mighty** one I subdued their kings.

Isaiah 10:21
A remnant will return, a remnant of Jacob will return to the **Mighty** God.

Isaiah 10:33
See, the Lord, the LORD Almighty, will lop off the boughs with great **power**.

God is Powerful

Isaiah 10:34
He will cut down the forest thickets with an ax; Lebanon will fall before the **Mighty** One.

Isaiah 12:2
The LORD, the LORD himself, is my **strength** and my defense; he has become my salvation."

Isaiah 27:1
In that day, the LORD will punish with his sword— his fierce, great and **powerful** sword—

Isaiah 33:2
LORD, be gracious to us; we long for you. Be our **strength** every morning, our salvation in time of distress.

Isaiah 33:13
You who are far away, hear what I have done; you who are near, acknowledge my **power**!

Isaiah 33:21
There the LORD will be our **Mighty** One.

Isaiah 40:10
See, the Sovereign LORD comes with **power**, and he rules with a **mighty** arm.

Isaiah 40:26
Lift up your eyes and look to the heavens: Who created all these? He who brings out the starry host one by one and calls forth each of them by name. Because of his great **power** and **mighty strength**, not one of them is missing.

Isaiah 40:29
He gives **strength** to the weary and increases the **power** of the weak.

Isaiah 40:31
but those who hope in the LORD will renew their **strength**. They will soar on wings like eagles; they will run and not grow weary, they will walk and not be faint.

Isaiah 41:10
So do not fear, for I am with you; do not be dismayed, for I am your God. I will **strengthen** you and help you; I will uphold you with my righteous right hand.

Isaiah 45:5
I am the LORD, and there is no other; apart from me there is no God. I will **strengthen** you,

Isaiah 45:24
They will say of me, 'In the LORD alone are deliverance and **strength**.'"

Isaiah 49:5
for I am honored in the eyes of the LORD and my God has been my **strength**—

Isaiah 49:26
Then all mankind will know that I, the LORD, am your Savior, your Redeemer, the **Mighty** One of Jacob."

Isaiah 50:2
When I came, why was there no one? When I called, why was there no one to answer? Was my arm too short to deliver you? **Do I lack the strength** to rescue you? By a mere rebuke I dry up the sea, I turn rivers into a desert;

Isaiah 58:11
The LORD will guide you always; he will satisfy your needs in a sun-scorched land and will **strengthen** your frame. You will be like a well-watered garden, like a spring whose waters never fail.

Isaiah 60:16
Then you will know that I, the LORD, am your Savior, your Redeemer, the **Mighty** One of Jacob.

Isaiah 62:8
The LORD has sworn by his right hand and by his **mighty** arm:

Isaiah 63:1
Who is this, robed in splendor, striding forward in the greatness of his **strength**? "It is I, proclaiming victory, **mighty** to save."

Isaiah 63:12
who sent his glorious arm of **power** to be at Moses' right hand, who divided the waters before them, to gain for himself everlasting renown,

Jeremiah 10:6
No one is like you, LORD; you are great, and your name is **mighty** in **power**.

Jeremiah 10:12
But God made the earth by his **power**; he founded the world by his wisdom and stretched out the heavens by his understanding.

Jeremiah 16:19
LORD, my **strength** and my fortress, my refuge in time of distress,

Jeremiah 16:21
"Therefore I will teach them— this time I will teach them my **power** and **might**. Then they will know that my name is the LORD.

Jeremiah 20:11
But the LORD is with me like a **mighty** warrior;

Jeremiah 21:5
I myself will fight against you with an outstretched hand and a **mighty** arm in furious anger and in great wrath.

Jeremiah 27:5
With my great **power** and outstretched arm I made the earth and its people and the animals that are on it, and I give it to anyone I please.

Jeremiah 32:17
"Ah, Sovereign LORD, you have made the heavens and the earth by your great **power** and outstretched arm. Nothing is too hard for you.

Jeremiah 32:18
You show love to thousands but bring the punishment for the parents' sins into the laps of their children after them. Great and **mighty** God, whose name is the LORD Almighty,

Jeremiah 32:19
great are your purposes and **mighty** are your deeds.

Jeremiah 32:21
You brought your people Israel out of Egypt with signs and wonders, by a **mighty** hand and an outstretched arm and with great terror.

Jeremiah 50:34
Yet their Redeemer is **strong**; the LORD Almighty is his name.

Jeremiah 51:15
"He made the earth by his **power**; he founded the world by his wisdom and stretched out the heavens by his understanding.

Ezekiel 3:14
The Spirit then lifted me up and took me away, . . . with the **strong** hand of the LORD on me.

Ezekiel 20:33
As surely as I live, declares the Sovereign LORD, I will reign over you with a **mighty** hand and an outstretched arm and with outpoured wrath.

Ezekiel 20:34
I will bring you from the nations and gather you from the countries where you have been scattered—with a **mighty** hand and an outstretched arm and with outpoured wrath.

God is Powerful

Ezekiel 34:16
I will search for the lost and bring back the strays. I will bind up the injured and **strengthen** the weak,

Daniel 2:20
"Praise be to the name of God for ever and ever; wisdom and **power** are his.

Daniel 2:23
I thank and praise you, God of my ancestors: You have given me wisdom and **power**,

Daniel 4:3
How great are his signs, how **mighty** his wonders! His kingdom is an eternal kingdom; his dominion endures from generation to generation.

Daniel 7:14
He was given authority, glory and sovereign **power**; all nations and peoples of every language worshiped him. His dominion is an everlasting dominion that will not pass away, and his kingdom is one that will never be destroyed.

Daniel 9:15
"Now, Lord our God, who brought your people out of Egypt with a **mighty** hand and who made for yourself a name that endures to this day, we have sinned, we have done wrong.

Hosea 13:14
"I will deliver this people from the **power** of the grave; I will redeem them from death. Where, O death, are your plagues? Where, O grave, is your destruction?

Micah 5:4
He will stand and shepherd his flock in the **strength** of the LORD, in the majesty of the name of the LORD his God.

Nahum 1:3
The LORD is slow to anger but great in **power**;

Habakkuk 3:4
His splendor was like the sunrise; rays flashed from his hand, where his **power** was hidden.

Habakkuk 3:19
The Sovereign LORD is my **strength**; he makes my feet like the feet of a deer, he enables me to tread on the heights.

Zephaniah 1:14
The great day of the LORD is near— near and coming quickly. The cry on the day of the LORD is bitter; the **Mighty** Warrior shouts his battle cry.

Zephaniah 3:17
The LORD your God is with you, the **Mighty** Warrior who saves.

Zechariah 10:6
"I will **strengthen** Judah and save the tribes of Joseph. I will restore them because I have compassion on them. They will be as though I had not rejected them, for I am the LORD their God and I will answer them.

Zechariah 10:12
I will **strengthen** them in the LORD and in his name they will live securely," declares the LORD.

Zechariah 12:5
Then the clans of Judah will say in their hearts, 'The people of Jerusalem are **strong**, because the LORD Almighty is their God.'

Matthew 3:11
[*John the Baptist concerning Jesus*] "I baptize you with water for repentance. But after me comes one who is more **powerful** than I, whose sandals I am not worthy to carry. He will baptize you with the Holy Spirit and fire.

God is Powerful

Matthew 13:54
Coming to his hometown, he began teaching the people in their synagogue, and they were amazed. "Where did this man get this wisdom and these miraculous **powers**?"

Matthew 22:29
Jesus replied, "You are in error because you do not know the Scriptures or the **power** of God.

Matthew 24:30
"Then will appear the sign of the Son of Man in heaven. And then all the peoples of the earth will mourn when they see the Son of Man coming on the clouds of heaven, with **power** and great glory.

Matthew 26:64
"You have said so," Jesus replied. "But I say to all of you: From now on you will see the Son of Man sitting at the right hand of the **Mighty** One and coming on the clouds of heaven."

Mark 1:7
And this was his message: "After me comes the one more **powerful** than I, the straps of whose sandals I am not worthy to stoop down and untie.

Mark 5:30
At once Jesus realized that **power** had gone out from him. He turned around in the crowd and asked, "Who touched my clothes?"

Mark 9:1
And he said to them, "Truly I tell you, some who are standing here will not taste death before they see that the kingdom of God has come with **power**."

Mark 12:24
Jesus replied, "Are you not in error because you do not know the Scriptures or the **power** of God?

Mark 13:26
"At that time people will see the Son of Man coming in clouds with great **power** and glory.

Mark 14:62
"I am," said Jesus. "And you will see the Son of Man sitting at the right hand of the **Mighty** One and coming on the clouds of heaven."

Luke 1:35
"The Holy Spirit will come on you, and the **power** of the Most High will overshadow you. So the holy one to be born will be called the Son of God.

Luke 1:49
for the **Mighty** One has done great things for me— holy is his name.

Luke 1:51
He has performed **mighty** deeds with his arm; he has scattered those who are proud in their inmost thoughts.

Luke 3:16
John answered them all, "I baptize you with water. But one who is more **powerful** than I will come, the straps of whose sandals I am not worthy to untie.

Luke 4:14
Jesus returned to Galilee in the **power** of the Spirit,

Luke 4:36
All the people were amazed and said to each other, "What words these are! With authority and **power** he gives orders to impure spirits and they come out!"

God is Powerful

Luke 5:17
And the **power** of the Lord was with Jesus to heal the sick.

Luke 6:19
and the people all tried to touch him, because **power** was coming from him and healing them all.

Luke 8:46
But Jesus said, "Someone touched me; I know that **powe**r has gone out from me."

Luke 21:27
At that time they will see the Son of Man coming in a cloud with **power** and great glory.

Luke 22:69
But from now on, the Son of Man will be seated at the right hand of the **mighty** God."

Luke 24:19
"About Jesus of Nazareth," they replied. "He was a prophet, **powerful** in word and deed before God and all the people.

John 13:3
Jesus knew that the Father had put all things under his **power**, and that he had come from God and was returning to God;

John 17:11
Holy Father, protect them by the **power** of your name, the name you gave me, so that they may be one as we are one.

Acts 1:8
But you will receive **power** when the Holy Spirit comes on you;

Acts 3:16
By faith in the name of Jesus, this man whom you see and know was made **strong**.

Acts 4:33
And God's grace was so **powerfully** at work in them all

Acts 10:38
how God anointed Jesus of Nazareth with the Holy Spirit and **power**,

Acts 13:17
The God of the people of Israel chose our ancestors; he made the people prosper during their stay in Egypt; with **mighty power** he led them out of that country;

Romans 1:16
For I am not ashamed of the gospel, because it is the **power** of God that brings salvation to everyone who believes:

Romans 1:20
For since the creation of the world God's invisible qualities—his eternal **power** and divine nature—have been clearly seen, being understood from what has been made, so that people are without excuse.

Romans 4:21
being fully persuaded that God had **power** to do what he had promised.

Romans 9:22
What if God, although choosing to show his wrath and make his **power** known,

Romans 15:13
May the God of hope fill you with all joy and peace as you trust in him, so that you may overflow with hope by the **power** of the Holy Spirit.

Romans 15:19
by the power of signs and wonders, through the **power** of the Spirit of God.

1 Corinthians 1:17
lest the cross of Christ be emptied of its **power**.

1 Corinthians 1:18
For the message of the cross is foolishness to those who are perishing, but to us who are being saved it is the **power** of God.

1 Corinthians 1:24
but to those whom God has called, both Jews and Greeks, Christ the **power** of God and the wisdom of God.

1 Corinthians 1:25
For the foolishness of God is wiser than human wisdom, and the weakness of God is **stronger** than human strength.

1 Corinthians 2:4
but with a demonstration of the Spirit's **power**,

1 Corinthians 2:5
so that your faith might not rest on human wisdom, but on God's **power**.

1 Corinthians 4:20
For the kingdom of God is not a matter of talk but of **power**.

1 Corinthians 5:4
So when you are assembled and I am with you in spirit, and the **power** of our Lord Jesus is present,

1 Corinthians 6:14
By his **power** God raised the Lord from the dead, and he will raise us also.

2 Corinthians 4:7
But we have this treasure in jars of clay to show that this all-surpassing **power** is from God and not from us.

2 Corinthians 6:7
in truthful speech and in the **power** of God;

2 Corinthians 10:4
The weapons we fight with are not the weapons of the world. On the contrary, they have divine **power** to demolish strongholds.

2 Corinthians 12:9
But he said to me, "My grace is sufficient for you, for my **power** is made perfect in weakness." Therefore I will boast all the more gladly about my weaknesses, so that Christ's power may rest on me.

2 Corinthians 13:3
He is not weak in dealing with you, but is **powerful** among you.

Galatians 4:29
At that time the son born according to the flesh persecuted the son born by the **power** of the Spirit.

Ephesians 1:18-20
and his incomparably great **power** for us who believe. That **power** is the same as the **mighty strength** he exerted when he raised Christ from the dead and seated him at his right hand in the heavenly realms,

God is Powerful

Ephesians 3:7
I became a servant of this gospel by the gift of God's grace given me through the working of his **power**.

Ephesians 6:10
[*The Armor of God*] Finally, be strong in the Lord and in his **mighty power**.

Philippians 3:10
I want to know Christ—yes, to know the **power** of his resurrection

Philippians 3:21
who, by the **power** that enables him to bring everything under his control,

Philippians 4:13
I can do all this through him who gives me **strength**.

Colossians 1:11
being **strengthened** with all **power** according to his glorious **might**

Colossians 1:29
To this end I strenuously contend with all the energy Christ so **powerfully** works in me.

Colossians 2:10
and in Christ you have been brought to fullness. He is the head over every **power** and authority.

2 Thessalonians 1:11
that our God may make you worthy of his calling, and that by his **power** he may bring to fruition your every desire for goodness

2 Thessalonians 3:3
But the Lord is faithful, and he will **strengthen** you and protect you from the evil one.

1 Timothy 1:12
I thank Christ Jesus our Lord, who has given me **strength**,

2 Timothy 1:7
For the Spirit God gave us does not make us timid, but gives us **power**, love and self-discipline.

2 Timothy 1:8
Rather, join with me in suffering for the gospel, by the **power** of God.

2 Timothy 4:17
But the Lord stood at my side and gave me **strength**,

Hebrews 1:3
The Son is the radiance of God's glory and the exact representation of his being, sustaining all things by his **powerful** word.

1 Peter 1:5
who through faith are shielded by God's **power** until the coming of the salvation that is ready to be revealed in the last time.!

1 Peter 4:11
If anyone serves, they should do so with the **strength** God provides, so that in all things God may be praised through Jesus Christ. To him be the glory and the power for ever and ever.

1 Peter 5:6
Humble yourselves, therefore, under God's **mighty** hand, that he may lift you up in due time.

1 Peter 5:10
And the God of all grace, who called you to his eternal glory in Christ, after you have suffered a little while, will himself restore you and make you **strong**, firm and steadfast.

1 Peter 5:11
To him be the **power** for ever and ever.

2 Peter 1:3
His divine **power** has given us everything we need for a godly life

2 Peter 1:16
we told you about the coming of our Lord Jesus Christ in **power**, but we were eyewitnesses of his majesty.

Jude 1:25
to the only God our Savior be glory, majesty, **power** and authority, through Jesus Christ our Lord, before all ages, now and forevermore!

Revelation 1:6
and has made us to be a kingdom and priests to serve his God and Father—to him be glory and **power** for ever and ever!

Revelation 4:11
"You are worthy, our Lord and God, to receive glory and honor and **power**, for you created all things, and by your will they were created and have their being."

Revelation 5:12
In a loud voice they were saying: "Worthy is the Lamb, who was slain, to receive **power** and wealth and wisdom and strength and honor and glory and praise!"

Revelation 5:13
Then I heard every creature in heaven and on earth and under the earth and on the sea, and all that is in them, saying: "To him who sits on the throne and to the Lamb be praise and honor and glory and **power**, for ever and ever!"

Revelation 7:12
"Amen! Praise and glory and wisdom and thanks and honor and **power** and **strength** be to our God for ever and ever. Amen!"

Revelation 11:17
saying: "We give thanks to you, Lord God Almighty, the One who is and who was, because you have taken your great **power** and have begun to reign.

Revelation 12:10
Then I heard a loud voice in heaven say: "Now have come the salvation and the **power** and the kingdom of our God, and the authority of his Messiah. For the accuser of our brothers and sisters, who accuses them before our God day and night, has been hurled down.

Revelation 15:8
And the temple was filled with smoke from the glory of God and from his **power**,

Revelation 18:8
Therefore in one day her plagues will overtake her: death, mourning and famine. She will be consumed by fire, for **mighty** is the Lord God who judges her.

Revelation 19:1
After this I heard what sounded like the roar of a great multitude in heaven shouting: "Hallelujah! Salvation and glory and **power** belong to our God,

God Our Provider
Able to Provide

Provider:
One who supplies the needs or neccessities of another.

*"Then this city will bring me renown, joy, praise and honor before the nations on earth that hear of all the good things I do for it; and they will be in awe and will tremble at the abundant prosperity and peace I **provide** for it."*

- Jeremiah 33:9

God Our Provider

1. DEFINE PROVIDER USING YOUR OWN WORDS, SYNONYMS, OR DESCRIPTIONS:

_____

_____

_____

2. READ THE VERSES DEALING WITH GOD AS OUR PROVIDER AND LIST ALL THE WAYS HE PROVIDES FOR US.

_____

_____

_____

_____

_____

3. DO YOU HAVE ANY OBSERVATIONS ABOUT THIS CHARACTER TRAIT OF GOD OR WHY GOD WANTS US TO KNOW THAT HE IS OUR PROVIDER?

_____

_____

_____

_____

_____

_____

God will not fail because He cannot fail.
                    - Joy Dawson

NOTES:

God Our Provider

Genesis 22:8
Abraham answered, "God himself will **provide** the lamb for the burnt offering, my son."

Genesis 22:14
So Abraham called that place The LORD Will **Provide**. And to this day it is said, "On the mountain of the LORD it will be **provided**."

Deuteronomy 11:15
I will **provide** grass in the fields for your cattle, and you will eat and be satisfied.

2 Samuel 7:10
And I will **provide** a place for my people Israel and will plant them so that they can have a home of their own and no longer be disturbed.

2 Samuel 22:37
You **provide** a broad path for my feet, so that my ankles do not give way.

2 Kings 13:5
The LORD **provided** a deliverer for Israel,

1 Chronicles 17:9
And I will **provide** a place for my people Israel and will plant them so that they can have a home of their own and no longer be disturbed.

Psalm 18:36
You **provide** a broad path for my feet, so that my ankles do not give way.

Psalm 65:9
You care for the land and water it; you enrich it abundantly. The streams of God are filled with water to **provide** the people with grain, for so you have ordained it.

Psalm 68:10
Your people settled in it, and from your bounty, God, you **provided** for the poor.

Psalm 111:5
He **provides** food for those who fear him; he remembers his covenant forever.

Psalm 111:9
He **provided** redemption for his people; he ordained his covenant forever— holy and awesome is his name.

Psalm 147:9
He **provides** food for the cattle and for the young ravens when they call.

Isaiah 43:20
The wild animals honor me, the jackals and the owls, because I **provide** water in the wilderness and streams in the wasteland, to give drink to my people, my chosen,

Isaiah 61:3
and **provide** for those who grieve in Zion— to bestow on them a crown of beauty instead of ashes, the oil of joy instead of mourning, and a garment of praise instead of a spirit of despair. They will be called oaks of righteousness, a planting of the LORD for the display of his splendor.

Jeremiah 33:9
Then this city will bring me renown, joy, praise and honor before all nations on earth that hear of all the good things I do for it; and they will be in awe and will tremble at the abundant prosperity and peace I **provide** for it.'

Ezekiel 16:19
Also the food I **provided** for you—the flour, olive oil and honey I gave you to eat—you offered as fragrant incense before them. That is what happened, declares the Sovereign LORD.

Ezekiel 34:29
I will **provide** for them a land renowned for its crops, and they will no longer be victims of famine in the land or bear the scorn of the nations.

Jonah 1:17
Now the LORD **provided** a huge fish to swallow Jonah, and Jonah was in the belly of the fish three days and three nights.

Jonah 4:6
Then the LORD God **provided** a leafy plant and made it grow up over Jonah to give shade for his head to ease his discomfort, and Jonah was very happy about the plant.

Acts 14:17
Yet he has not left himself without testimony: He has shown kindness by giving you rain from heaven and crops in their seasons; he **provides** you with plenty of food and fills your hearts with joy."

1 Corinthians 10:13
No temptation has overtaken you except what is common to mankind. And God is faithful; he will not let you be tempted beyond what you can bear. But when you are tempted, he will also **provide** a way out so that you can endure it.

1 Timothy 6:17
Command those who are rich in this present world not to be arrogant nor to put their hope in wealth, which is so uncertain, but to put their hope in God, who richly **provides** us with everything for our enjoyment.

Hebrews 1:3
The Son is the radiance of God's glory and the exact representation of his being, sustaining all things by his powerful word. After he had **provided** purification for sins, he sat down at the right hand of the Majesty in heaven.

1 Peter 4:11
If anyone serves, they should do so with the strength God **provides**, so that in all things God may be praised through Jesus Christ.

God Our Redeemer
Able to Redeem

Redeemer:
One who buys back or recovers something by payment or action and then makes claim to it; Clearing a debt; Making up for deficiencies.

*But now, this is what the Lord says -- he who created you, Jacob, he who formed you, Israel: "Do not fear, for I have **redeemed** you; I have summoned you by name; you are mine."*

- Isaiah 43:1

God Our Redeemer

1. DEFINE REDEEMER USING YOUR OWN WORDS, SYNONYMS, OR DESCRIPTIONS:

_____

_____

_____

2. HOSEA 13:14, "I WILL DELIVER THIS PEOPLE FROM THE POWER OF THE GRAVE; I WILL REDEEM THEM FROM DEATH. WHERE, O DEATH, ARE YOUR PLAGUES? WHERE, O GRAVE, IS YOUR DESTRUCTION?" IT WAS ALWAYS GOD'S PURPOSE TO REDEEM US FROM THE GRASP OF SPIRITUAL DEATH AND TO ETERNAL LIFE WITH HIM. GALATIANS 4:5, "TO REDEEM THOSE UNDER THE LAW, THAT WE MIGHT RECEIVE ADOPTION TO SONSHIP." EXPLAIN HOW GOD'S REDEMPTION MAKES THIS POSSIBLE.

_____

_____

_____

3. DO YOU HAVE ANY OBSERVATIONS ABOUT THIS CHARACTER TRAIT OF GOD OR WHY GOD WANTS US TO KNOW THAT HE IS OUR REDEEMER?

_____

_____

_____

_____

_____

NOTES:

God Our Redeemer

Exodus 6:6
I am the LORD, and I will bring you out from under the yoke of the Egyptians. I will free you from being slaves to them, and I will **redeem** you with an outstretched arm and with mighty acts of judgment.

Exodus 15:13
In your unfailing love you will lead the people you have **redeemed**. In your strength you will guide them to your holy dwelling.

Deuteronomy 7:8
But it was because the LORD loved you and kept the oath he swore to your ancestors that he brought you out with a mighty hand and **redeemed** you from the land of slavery, from the power of Pharaoh king of Egypt.

Deuteronomy 9:26
I prayed to the LORD and said, "Sovereign LORD, do not destroy your people, your own inheritance that you **redeemed** by your great power and brought out of Egypt with a mighty hand.

Deuteronomy 13:5
the LORD your God, who brought you out of Egypt and **redeemed** you from the land of slavery.

Deuteronomy 15:15
Remember that you were slaves in Egypt and the LORD your God **redeemed** you.

Deuteronomy 21:8
Accept this atonement for your people Israel, whom you have **redeemed**, LORD,

Deuteronomy 24:18
Remember that you were slaves in Egypt and the LORD your God **redeemed** you from there.

2 Samuel 7:23
And who is like your people Israel—the one nation on earth that God went out to **redeem** as a people for himself, and to make a name for himself, and to perform great and awesome wonders by driving out nations and their gods from before your people, whom you **redeemed** from Egypt?

1 Chronicles 17:21
And who is like your people Israel—the one nation on earth whose God went out to **redeem** a people for himself, and to make a name for yourself, and to perform great and awesome wonders by driving out nations from before your people, whom you **redeemed** from Egypt?

Nehemiah 1:10
"They are your servants and your people, whom you **redeemed** by your great strength and your mighty hand.

Job 19:25
I know that my **redeemer** lives, and that in the end he will stand on the earth.

Psalm 19:14
May these words of my mouth and this meditation of my heart be pleasing in your sight, LORD, my Rock and my **Redeemer**.

Psalm 49:15
But God will **redeem** me from the realm of the dead; he will surely take me to himself.

Psalm 74:2
Remember the nation you purchased long ago, the people of your inheritance, whom you **redeemed**— Mount Zion, where you dwelt.

Psalm 77:15
With your mighty arm you **redeemed** your people, the descendants of Jacob and Joseph.

Psalm 78:35
They remembered that God was their Rock, that God Most High was their **Redeemer**.

Psalm 78:42
They did not remember his power— the day he **redeemed** them from the oppressor,

Psalm 103:4
who **redeems** your life from the pit and crowns you with love and compassion,

Psalm 106:10
He saved them from the hand of the foe; from the hand of the enemy he **redeemed** them.

Psalm 107:2
Let the **redeemed** of the LORD tell their story— those he **redeemed** from the hand of the foe,

Psalm 119:134
Redeem me from human oppression, that I may obey your precepts.

Psalm 119:154
Defend my cause and **redeem** me; preserve my life according to your promise.

Psalm 130:8
He himself will **redeem** Israel from all their sins.

Isaiah 29:22
Therefore this is what the LORD, who **redeemed** Abraham, says to the descendants of Jacob:

Isaiah 41:14
Do not be afraid, you worm Jacob, little Israel, do not fear, for I myself will help you," declares the LORD, your **Redeemer**, the Holy One of Israel.

Isaiah 43:1
But now, this is what the LORD says— he who created you, Jacob, he who formed you, Israel: "Do not fear, for I have **redeemed** you; I have summoned you by name; you are mine.

Isaiah 43:14
This is what the LORD says— your **Redeemer**, the Holy One of Israel:

Isaiah 44:6
"This is what the LORD says— Israel's King and **Redeemer**, the LORD Almighty: I am the first and I am the last; apart from me there is no God.

Isaiah 44:22
I have swept away your offenses like a cloud, your sins like the morning mist. Return to me, for I have **redeemed** you."

Isaiah 44:23
Burst into song, you mountains, you forests and all your trees, for the LORD has **redeemed** Jacob, he displays his glory in Israel.

Isaiah 44:24
"This is what the LORD says— your **Redeemer**, who formed you in the womb: I am the LORD, the Maker of all things, who stretches out the heavens, who spreads out the earth by myself,

Isaiah 47:4
Our **Redeemer**—the LORD Almighty is his name— is the Holy One of Israel.

Isaiah 48:17
This is what the LORD says— your **Redeemer**, the Holy One of Israel: "I am the LORD your God, who teaches you what is best for you, who directs you in the way you should go.

Isaiah 48:20
Send it out to the ends of the earth; say, "The LORD has **redeemed** his servant Jacob."

Isaiah 49:7
This is what the LORD says— the **Redeemer** and Holy One of Israel—

Isaiah 49:26
Then all mankind will know that I, the LORD, am your Savior, your **Redeemer**, the Mighty One of Jacob."

Isaiah 52:3
For this is what the LORD says: "You were sold for nothing, and without money you will be **redeemed**."

Isaiah 52:9
Burst into songs of joy together, you ruins of Jerusalem, for the LORD has comforted his people, he has **redeemed** Jerusalem.

Isaiah 54:5
For your Maker is your husband— the LORD Almighty is his name— the Holy One of Israel is your **Redeemer**; he is called the God of all the earth.

God Our Redeemer

Isaiah 54:8
In a surge of anger I hid my face from you for a moment, but with everlasting kindness I will have compassion on you," says the LORD your **Redeemer**.

Isaiah 59:20
"The **Redeemer** will come to Zion, to those in Jacob who repent of their sins," declares the LORD.

Isaiah 60:16
Then you will know that I, the LORD, am your Savior, your **Redeemer**, the Mighty One of Jacob.

Isaiah 62:12
They will be called the Holy People, the **Redeemed** of the LORD;

Isaiah 63:9
In his love and mercy he **redeemed** them; he lifted them up and carried them all the days of old.

Isaiah 63:16
you, LORD, are our Father, our **Redeemer** from of old is your name.

Jeremiah 31:11
For the LORD will deliver Jacob and **redeem** them from the hand of those stronger than they.

Jeremiah 50:34
Yet their **Redeemer** is strong; the LORD Almighty is his name. He will vigorously defend their cause

Lamentations 3:58
You, Lord, took up my case; you **redeemed** my life.

Hosea 7:13
Woe to them, because they have strayed from me! Destruction to them, because they have rebelled against me! I long to **redeem** them but they speak about me falsely.

Hosea 13:14
"I will deliver this people from the power of the grave; I will **redeem** them from death. Where, O death, are your plagues? Where, O grave, is your destruction?

Micah 4:10
There the LORD will **redeem** you out of the hand of your enemies.

Micah 6:4
I brought you up out of Egypt and **redeemed** you from the land of slavery.

Zechariah 10:8
I will signal for them and gather them in. Surely I will **redeem** them; they will be as numerous as before.

Luke 1:68
"Praise be to the Lord, the God of Israel, because he has come to his people and **redeemed** them.

Galatians 3:13
Christ **redeemed** us from the curse of the law by becoming a curse for us, for it is written: "Cursed is everyone who is hung on a pole."

Galatians 3:14
He **redeemed** us in order that the blessing given to Abraham might come to the Gentiles through Christ Jesus, so that by faith we might receive the promise of the Spirit.

Galatians 4:5
to **redeem** those under the law, that we might receive adoption to sonship.

Titus 2:14
who gave himself for us to **redeem** us from all wickedness and to purify for himself a people that are his very own,

1 Peter 1:18
For you know that it was not with perishable things such as silver or gold that you were **redeemed** from the empty way of life handed down to you from your ancestors,

Revelation 14:3
And they sang a new song before the throne and before the four living creatures and the elders. No one could learn the song except the 144,000 who had been **redeemed** from the earth.

God Our Refuge

Refuge:
A shelter from pursuit, danger or trouble; A place of protection.

*The eternal God is your **refuge**, and underneath are the everlasting arms.*

- Deuteronomy 33:27

God Our Refuge

1. DEFINE REFUGE USING YOUR OWN WORDS, SYNONYMS, OR DESCRIPTIONS:

_____

_____

_____

2. WHAT DOES IT MAKE YOU THINK TO HEAR GOD "SHIELDS THOSE WHO TAKE REFUGE IN HIM" AND WE CAN "TAKE REFUGE IN THE SHELTER OF HIS WINGS" OR THAT HE IS OUR "ROCK OF REFUGE"?

_____

_____

_____

3. DO YOU HAVE ANY OBSERVATIONS ABOUT THIS CHARACTER TRAIT OF GOD OR WHY GOD WANTS US TO KNOW THAT HE IS OUR REFUGE?

_____

_____

_____

_____

_____

_____

The gardener is never so near as when pruning.

NOTES:

God Our Refuge

Deuteronomy 33:27
The eternal God is your **refuge**, and underneath are the everlasting arms.

Ruth 2:12
May you be richly rewarded by the LORD, the God of Israel, under whose wings you have come to take **refuge**."

2 Samuel 22:3
my God is my rock, in whom I take **refuge**, my shield and the horn of my salvation. He is my stronghold, my **refuge** and my savior—

2 Samuel 22:31
"As for God, his way is perfect: The LORD's word is flawless; he shields all who take **refuge** in him.

Psalm 2:12
Blessed are all who take **refuge** in him.

Psalm 5:11
But let all who take **refuge** in you be glad; let them ever sing for joy. Spread your protection over them, that those who love your name may rejoice in you.

Psalm 7:1
LORD my God, I take **refuge** in you; save and deliver me from all who pursue me,

Psalm 9:9
The LORD is a **refuge** for the oppressed, a stronghold in times of trouble.

Psalm 11:1
In the LORD I take **refuge**.

Psalm 14:6
You evildoers frustrate the plans of the poor, but the LORD is their **refuge**.

Psalm 16:1
Keep me safe, my God, for in you I take **refuge**.

Psalm 17:7
Show me the wonders of your great love, you who save by your right hand those who take **refuge** in you from their foes.

Psalm 18:2
The LORD is my rock, my fortress and my deliverer; my God is my rock, in whom I take **refuge**, my shield and the horn of my salvation, my stronghold.

Psalm 18:30
As for God, his way is perfect: The LORD's word is flawless; he shields all who take **refuge** in him.

Psalm 25:20
Guard my life and rescue me; do not let me be put to shame, for I take **refuge** in you.

Psalm 31:1
In you, LORD, I have taken **refuge**; let me never be put to shame; deliver me in your righteousness.

Psalm 31:2
Turn your ear to me, come quickly to my rescue; be my rock of **refuge**, a strong fortress to save me.

Psalm 31:4
Keep me free from the trap that is set for me, for you are my **refuge**.

Psalm 31:19
How abundant are the good things that you have stored up for those who fear you, that you bestow in the sight of all, on those who take **refuge** in you.

Psalm 34:8
Taste and see that the LORD is good; blessed is the one who takes **refuge** in him.

Psalm 34:22
The LORD will rescue his servants; no one who takes **refuge** in him will be condemned.

Psalm 36:7
How priceless is your unfailing love, O God! People take **refuge** in the shadow of your wings.

Psalm 37:40
The LORD helps them and delivers them; he delivers them from the wicked and saves them, because they take **refuge** in him.

Psalm 46:1
God is our **refuge** and strength, an ever-present help in trouble.

Psalm 57:1
Have mercy on me, my God, have mercy on me, for in you I take **refuge**. I will take **refuge** in the shadow of your wings until the disaster has passed.

Psalm 59:16
But I will sing of your strength, in the morning I will sing of your love; for you are my fortress, my **refuge** in times of trouble.

Psalm 61:3
For you have been my **refuge**, a strong tower against the foe.

Psalm 61:4
I long to dwell in your tent forever and take **refuge** in the shelter of your wings.

Psalm 62:7
My salvation and my honor depend on God; he is my mighty rock, my **refuge**.

Psalm 62:8
Trust in him at all times, you people; pour out your hearts to him, for God is our **refuge**.

Psalm 64:10
The righteous will rejoice in the LORD and take **refuge** in him;

Psalm 71:1
In you, LORD, I have taken **refuge**; let me never be put to shame.

Psalm 71:3
Be my rock of **refuge**, to which I can always go; give the command to save me, for you are my rock and my fortress.

Psalm 71:7
I have become a sign to many; you are my strong **refuge**.

Psalm 73:28
But as for me, it is good to be near God. I have made the Sovereign LORD my **refuge**;

Psalm 91:2
I will say of the LORD, "He is my **refuge** and my fortress, my God, in whom I trust."

Psalm 91:4
He will cover you with his feathers, and under his wings you will find **refuge**; his faithfulness will be your shield and rampart.

Psalm 91:9
If you say, "The LORD is my **refuge**," and you make the Most High your dwelling,

Psalm 94:22
But the LORD has become my fortress, and my God the rock in whom I take **refuge**.

God Our Refuge

Psalm 118:8
It is better to take **refuge** in the LORD than to trust in humans.

Psalm 118:9
It is better to take **refuge** in the LORD than to trust in princes.

Psalm 119:114
You are my **refuge** and my shield; I have put my hope in your word.

Psalm 141:8
But my eyes are fixed on you, Sovereign LORD; in you I take **refuge**— do not give me over to death.

Psalm 142:5
I cry to you, LORD; I say, "You are my **refuge**, my portion in the land of the living."

Psalm 144:2
He is my loving God and my fortress, my stronghold and my deliverer, my shield, in whom I take **refuge**, who subdues peoples under me.

Proverbs 10:29
The way of the LORD is a **refuge** for the blameless, but it is the ruin of those who do evil.

Proverbs 14:26
Whoever fears the LORD has a secure fortress, and for their children it will be a **refuge**.

Proverbs 14:32
When calamity comes, the wicked are brought down, but even in death the righteous seek **refuge** in God.

Proverbs 30:5
"Every word of God is flawless; he is a shield to those who take **refuge** in him.

Isaiah 4:6
It will be a shelter and shade from the heat of the day, and a **refuge** and hiding place from the storm and rain.

Isaiah 14:32
"The LORD has established Zion, and in her his afflicted people will find **refuge**."

Isaiah 25:4
You have been a **refuge** for the poor, a refuge for the needy in their distress, a shelter from the storm and a shade from the heat.

Isaiah 27:5
Or else let them come to me for **refuge**; let them make peace with me, yes, let them make peace with me."

Isaiah 57:13
But whoever takes **refuge** in me will inherit the land and possess my holy mountain."

Jeremiah 16:19
LORD, my strength and my fortress, my **refuge** in time of distress,

Jeremiah 17:17
Do not be a terror to me; you are my **refuge** in the day of disaster.

Joel 3:16
The LORD will roar from Zion and thunder from Jerusalem; the earth and the heavens will tremble. But the LORD will be a **refuge** for his people, a stronghold for the people of Israel.

Nahum 1:7
The LORD is good, a **refuge** in times of trouble. He cares for those who trust in him,

God is Righteous
Having Righteousness

Righteous:
Someone who does what is morally right.

*The Lord loves **righteousness** and justice; the earth is full of his unfailing love.*

- Psalm 33:5

God is Righteous

1. DEFINE RIGHTEOUS USING YOUR OWN WORDS, SYNONYMS, OR DESCRIPTIONS:

_____

_____

_____

2. THE BIBLE SHOWS GOD AS A RIGHTEOUS JUDGE WHO LOVES JUSTICE AS WELL AS A KING WHO HAS AS THE THE FOUNDATION OF HIS THRONE, RIGHTEOUSNESS AND JUSTICE. FIND THE VERSES THAT SHOW THIS.

_____

_____

_____

_____

_____

3. DO YOU HAVE ANY OBSERVATIONS ABOUT THIS CHARACTER TRAIT OF GOD OR WHY GOD WANTS US TO KNOW THAT HE IS RIGHTEOUS?

_____

_____

_____

_____

_____

NOTES:

God is Righteous

Deuteronomy 33:21
When the heads of the people assembled, he carried out the LORD's **righteous** will, and his judgments concerning Israel."

1 Samuel 12:7
Now then, stand here, because I am going to confront you with evidence before the LORD as to all the **righteous** acts performed by the LORD for you and your ancestors.

Ezra 9:15
LORD, the God of Israel, you are **righteous**!

Nehemiah 9:8
You have kept your promise because you are **righteous**.

Nehemiah 9:33
In all that has happened to us, you have remained **righteous**; you have acted faithfully, while we acted wickedly.

Job 37:23
The Almighty is beyond our reach and exalted in power; in his justice and great **righteousness**,

Psalm 4:1
Answer me when I call to you, my **righteous** God.

Psalm 5:8
Lead me, LORD, in your **righteousness** because of my enemies— make your way straight before me.

Psalm 7:9
Bring to an end the violence of the wicked and make the **righteous** secure— you, the **righteous** God who probes minds and hearts.

Psalm 7:11
God is a **righteous** judge, a God who displays his wrath every day.

Psalm 7:17
I will give thanks to the LORD because of his **righteousness**; I will sing the praises of the name of the LORD Most High.

Psalm 9:4
For you have upheld my right and my cause, sitting enthroned as the **righteous** judge.

Psalm 9:8
He rules the world in **righteousness** and judges the peoples with equity.

Psalm 11:7
For the LORD is **righteous**, he loves justice; the upright will see his face.

Psalm 19:9
The fear of the LORD is pure, enduring forever. The decrees of the LORD are firm, and all of them are **righteous**.

Psalm 22:31
They will proclaim his **righteousness**, declaring to a people yet unborn: He has done it!

Psalm 31:1
In you, LORD, I have taken refuge; let me never be put to shame; deliver me in your **righteousness**.

Psalm 33:5
The LORD loves **righteousness** and justice; the earth is full of his unfailing love.

Psalm 35:24
Vindicate me in your **righteousness**, LORD my God;

Psalm 35:28
My tongue will proclaim your **righteousness**, your praises all day long.

Psalm 36:6
Your **righteousness** is like the highest mountains, your justice like the great deep.

Psalm 36:10
Continue your love to those who know you, your **righteousness** to the upright in heart.

Psalm 40:10
I do not hide your **righteousness** in my heart; I speak of your faithfulness and your saving help.

Psalm 48:10
Like your name, O God, your praise reaches to the ends of the earth; your right hand is filled with **righteousness**.

Psalm 50:6
And the heavens proclaim his **righteousness**, for he is a God of justice.

Psalm 51:14
Deliver me from the guilt of bloodshed, O God, you who are God my Savior, and my tongue will sing of your **righteousness**.

Psalm 65:5
You answer us with awesome and **righteous** deeds, God our Savior, the hope of all the ends of the earth and of the farthest seas,

Psalm 71:2
In your **righteousness**, rescue me and deliver me;

Psalm 71:15
My mouth will tell of your **righteous** deeds, of your saving acts all day long—

Psalm 71:16
I will come and proclaim your mighty acts, Sovereign LORD; I will proclaim your **righteous** deeds, yours alone.

Psalm 71:19
Your **righteousness**, God, reaches to the heavens, you who have done great things. Who is like you, God?

Psalm 71:24
My tongue will tell of your **righteous** acts all day long,

Psalm 72:1
Endow the king with your justice, O God, the royal son with your **righteousness**.

Psalm 85:10
Love and faithfulness meet together; **righteousness** and peace kiss each other.

Psalm 85:11
Faithfulness springs forth from the earth, and **righteousness** looks down from heaven.

Psalm 85:13
Righteousness goes before him and prepares the way for his steps.

Psalm 89:14
Righteousness and justice are the foundation of your throne; love and faithfulness go before you.

Psalm 89:16
They rejoice in your name all day long; they celebrate your **righteousness**.

Psalm 96:13
Let all creation rejoice before the LORD, for he comes, he comes to judge the earth. He will judge the world in **righteousness** and the peoples in his faithfulness.

Psalm 97:2
Clouds and thick darkness surround him; **righteousness** and justice are the foundation of his throne.

God is Righteous

Psalm 97:6
The heavens proclaim his **righteousness**, and all peoples see his glory.

Psalm 98:2
The LORD has made his salvation known and revealed his **righteousness** to the nations.

Psalm 98:9
He will judge the world in **righteousness** and the peoples with equity.

Psalm 103:6
The LORD works **righteousness** and justice for all the oppressed.

Psalm 103:17
But from everlasting to everlasting the LORD's love is with those who fear him, and his **righteousness** with their children's children—

Psalm 111:3
Glorious and majestic are his deeds, and his **righteousness** endures forever.

Psalm 116:5
The LORD is gracious and **righteous**; our God is full of compassion.

Psalm 119:7
I will praise you with an upright heart as I learn your **righteous** laws.

Psalm 119:40
How I long for your precepts! In your **righteousness** preserve my life.

Psalm 119:62
At midnight I rise to give you thanks for your **righteous** laws.

Psalm 119:75
I know, LORD, that your laws are **righteous**,

Psalm 119:106
I have taken an oath and confirmed it, that I will follow your **righteous** laws.

Psalm 119:137
You are **righteous**, LORD, and your laws are right.

Psalm 119:138
The statutes you have laid down are **righteous**; they are fully trustworthy.

Psalm 119:142
Your **righteousness** is everlasting and your law is true.

Psalm 119:144
Your statutes are always **righteous**;

Psalm 119:160
All your words are true; all your **righteous** laws are eternal.

Psalm 119:164
Seven times a day I praise you for your **righteous** laws.

Psalm 119:172
May my tongue sing of your word, for all your commands are **righteous**.

Psalm 129:4
But the LORD is **righteous**; he has cut me free from the cords of the wicked."

Psalm 143:1
LORD, hear my prayer, listen to my cry for mercy; in your faithfulness and **righteousness** come to my relief.

Psalm 143:11
For your name's sake, LORD, preserve my life; in your **righteousness**, bring me out of trouble.

Psalm 145:7
They celebrate your abundant goodness and joyfully sing of your **righteousness**.

Psalm 145:17
The LORD is **righteous** in all his ways and faithful in all he does.

Proverbs 12:28
In the way of **righteousness** there is life; along that path is immortality.

Proverbs 21:12
The **Righteous** One takes note of the house of the wicked and brings the wicked to ruin.

Isaiah 5:16
But the LORD Almighty will be exalted by his justice, and the holy God will be proved holy by his **righteous** acts.

Isaiah 9:7
Of the greatness of his government and peace there will be no end. He will reign on David's throne and over his kingdom, establishing and upholding it with justice and **righteousness** from that time on and forever. The zeal of the LORD Almighty will accomplish this.

Isaiah 11:4
but with **righteousness** he will judge the needy, with justice he will give decisions for the poor of the earth.

Isaiah 11:5
Righteousness will be his belt and faithfulness the sash around his waist.

Isaiah 24:16
From the ends of the earth we hear singing: "Glory to the **Righteous** One."

Isaiah 26:9
When your judgments come upon the earth, the people of the world learn **righteousness**.

Isaiah 28:17
I will make justice the measuring line and **righteousness** the plumb line; hail will sweep away your refuge, the lie, and water will overflow your hiding place.

Isaiah 32:1
See, a king will reign in **righteousness** and rulers will rule with justice.

Isaiah 32:16
The LORD's justice will dwell in the desert, his **righteousness** live in the fertile field.

Isaiah 33:5
The LORD is exalted, for he dwells on high; he will fill Zion with his justice and **righteousness**.

Isaiah 41:10
So do not fear, for I am with you; do not be dismayed, for I am your God. I will strengthen you and help you; I will uphold you with my **righteous** right hand.

Isaiah 42:6
"I, the LORD, have called you in **righteousness**;

Isaiah 42:21
It pleased the LORD for the sake of his **righteousness** to make his law great and glorious.

Isaiah 45:8
"You heavens above, rain down my **righteousness**; let the clouds shower it down. Let the earth open wide, let salvation spring up, let **righteousness** flourish with it; I, the LORD, have created it.

God is Righteous

Isaiah 45:13
I will raise up Cyrus in my **righteousness**: I will make all his ways straight. He will rebuild my city and set my exiles free, but not for a price or reward, says the LORD Almighty."

Isaiah 45:21
And there is no God apart from me, a **righteous** God and a Savior; there is none but me.

Isaiah 46:12
Listen to me, you stubborn-hearted, you who are now far from my **righteousness**.

Isaiah 46:13
I am bringing my **righteousness** near, it is not far away; and my salvation will not be delayed. I will grant salvation to Zion, my splendor to Israel.

Isaiah 51:5
My **righteousness** draws near speedily, my salvation is on the way, and my arm will bring justice to the nations.

Isaiah 51:6
Lift up your eyes to the heavens, look at the earth beneath; the heavens will vanish like smoke, the earth will wear out like a garment and its inhabitants die like flies. But my salvation will last forever, my **righteousness** will never fail.

Isaiah 51:8
For the moth will eat them up like a garment; the worm will devour them like wool. But my **righteousness** will last forever, my salvation through all generations."

Isaiah 56:1
This is what the LORD says: "Maintain justice and do what is right, for my salvation is close at hand and my **righteousness** will soon be revealed.

Isaiah 59:17
He put on **righteousness** as his breastplate, and the helmet of salvation on his head; he put on the garments of vengeance and wrapped himself in zeal as in a cloak.

Isaiah 61:10
I delight greatly in the LORD; my soul rejoices in my God. For he has clothed me with garments of salvation and arrayed me in a robe of his **righteousness**, as a bridegroom adorns his head like a priest, and as a bride adorns herself with her jewels.

Isaiah 61:11
For as the soil makes the sprout come up and a garden causes seeds to grow, so the Sovereign LORD will make **righteousness** and praise spring up before all nations.

Jeremiah 9:24
but let the one who boasts boast about this: that they have the understanding to know me, that I am the LORD, who exercises kindness, justice and **righteousness** on earth, for in these I delight," declares the LORD.

Jeremiah 11:20
But you, LORD Almighty, who judge **righteously** and test the heart and mind, let me see your vengeance on them, for to you I have committed my cause.

Jeremiah 12:1
You are always **righteous**, LORD, when I bring a case before you.

Jeremiah 23:5
"The days are coming," declares the LORD, "when I will raise up for David a **righteous** Branch, a King who will reign wisely and do what is just and right in the land.

Jeremiah 23:6
In his days Judah will be saved and Israel will live in safety. This is the name by which he will be called: The LORD Our **Righteous** Savior.

Jeremiah 33:15
"'In those days and at that time I will make a **righteous** Branch sprout from David's line; he will do what is just and right in the land.

Jeremiah 33:16
This is the name by which it will be called: The LORD Our **Righteous** Savior.'

Lamentations 1:18
"The LORD is **righteous**, yet I rebelled against his command.

Daniel 9:7
"Lord, you are **righteous**,

Daniel 9:14
The LORD did not hesitate to bring the disaster on us, for the LORD our God is **righteous** in everything he does; yet we have not obeyed him.

Daniel 9:16
Lord, in keeping with all your **righteous** acts, turn away your anger and your wrath from Jerusalem, your city, your holy hill.

Hosea 2:19
I will betroth you to me forever; I will betroth you in **righteousness** and justice, in love and compassion.

Micah 6:5
Remember your journey from Shittim to Gilgal, that you may know the **righteous** acts of the LORD."

Micah 7:9
He will bring me out into the light; I will see his **righteousness**.

Zephaniah 3:5
The LORD within her is **righteous**; he does no wrong.

Zechariah 8:8
I will bring them back to live in Jerusalem; they will be my people, and I will be faithful and **righteous** to them as their God."

Zechariah 9:9
Rejoice greatly, Daughter Zion! Shout, Daughter Jerusalem! See, your king comes to you, **righteous** and victorious, lowly and riding on a donkey, on a colt, the foal of a donkey.

Matthew 6:33
But seek first his kingdom and his **righteousness**, and all these things will be given to you as well.

Luke 23:47
[*Jesus' crucifixion*] The centurion, seeing what had happened, praised God and said, "Surely this was a **righteous** man."

John 17:25
"**Righteous** Father, though the world does not know you, I know you, and they know that you have sent me.

Acts 3:14
You disowned the Holy and **Righteous** One and asked that a murderer be released to you.

Acts 7:52
Was there ever a prophet your ancestors did not persecute? They even killed those who predicted the coming of the **Righteous** One.

Acts 22:14
"Then he said: 'The God of our ancestors has chosen you to know his will and to see the **Righteous** One and to hear words from his mouth.

Romans 1:17
For in the gospel the righteousness of God is revealed—a **righteousness** that is by faith from first to last, just as it is written: "The righteous will live by faith."

Romans 1:32
Although they know God's **righteous** decree that those who do such things deserve death, they not only continue to do these very things but also approve of those who practice them.

God is Righteous

Romans 2:5
But because of your stubbornness and your unrepentant heart, you are storing up wrath against yourself for the day of God's wrath, when his **righteous** judgment will be revealed.

Romans 3:5
But if our unrighteousness brings out God's **righteousness** more clearly, what shall we say?

Romans 3:21
[*Righteousness through Faith*] But now apart from the law the **righteousness** of God has been made known, to which the Law and the Prophets testify.

Romans 3:22
This **righteousness** is given through faith in Jesus Christ to all who believe. There is no difference between Jew and Gentile,

Romans 3:25
God presented Christ as a sacrifice of atonement, through the shedding of his blood—to be received by faith. He did this to demonstrate his **righteousness**,

Romans 3:26
he did it to demonstrate his **righteousness** at the present time, so as to be just and the one who justifies those who have faith in Jesus.

Romans 5:17
For if, by the trespass of the one man, death reigned through that one man, how much more will those who receive God's abundant provision of grace and of the gift of **righteousness** reign in life through the one man, Jesus Christ!

Romans 5:18
Consequently, just as one trespass resulted in condemnation for all people, so also one **righteous** act resulted in justification and life for all people.

Romans 5:21
so that, just as sin reigned in death, so also grace might reign through **righteousness** to bring eternal life through Jesus Christ our Lord.

Romans 7:12
So then, the law is holy, and the commandment is holy, **righteous** and good.

Romans 8:10
But if Christ is in you, then even though your body is subject to death because of sin, the Spirit gives life because of **righteousness**.

Romans 10:3
Since they did not know the **righteousness** of God and sought to establish their own, they did not submit to God's **righteousness**.

1 Corinthians 1:30
It is because of him that you are in Christ Jesus, who has become for us wisdom from God—that is, our **righteousness**, holiness and redemption.

2 Corinthians 5:21
God made him who had no sin to be sin for us, so that in him we might become the **righteousness** of God.

Ephesians 4:24
and to put on the new self, created to be like God in true **righteousness** and holiness.

Ephesians 5:9
(for the fruit of the light consists in all goodness, **righteousness** and truth)

Philippians 1:11
filled with the fruit of **righteousness** that comes through Jesus Christ—to the glory and praise of God.

Philippians 3:9
and be found in him, not having a **righteousness** of my own that comes from the law, but that which is through faith in Christ—the **righteousness** that comes from God on the basis of faith.

2 Timothy 4:8
Now there is in store for me the crown of **righteousness**, which the Lord, the righteous Judge, will award to me on that day—and not only to me, but also to all who have longed for his appearing.

2 Peter 1:1
Simon Peter, a servant and apostle of Jesus Christ, To those who through the **righteousness** of our God and Savior Jesus Christ have received a faith as precious as ours:

2 Peter 3:13
But in keeping with his promise we are looking forward to a new heaven and a new earth, where **righteousness** dwells.

1 John 2:1
My dear children, I write this to you so that you will not sin. But if anybody does sin, we have an advocate with the Father-Jesus Christ, the **Righteous** One.

1 John 2:29
If you know that he is **righteous**, you know that everyone who does what is right has been born of him.

1 John 3:7
Dear children, do not let anyone lead you astray. The one who does what is right is righteous, just as he is **righteous**.

Revelation 15:4
Who will not fear you, Lord, and bring glory to your name? For you alone are holy. All nations will come and worship before you, for your **righteous** acts have been revealed."

God Our Rock

Rock:
Something solid and firm.

*He is the **Rock**, his works are perfect, and all his ways are just. A faithful God who does no wrong, upright and just is he.*

- Deuteronomy 32:4

God Our Rock

1. DEFINE ROCK USING YOUR OWN WORDS, SYNONYMS, OR DESCRIPTIONS:

_____

_____

_____

2. THE FIRST MENTION OF GOD AS "THE ROCK OF ISRAEL" IS IN GENESIS 49 WHEN JACOB WAS BLESSING HIS SON, JOSEPH. WHY DO YOU THINK GOD WAS GIVEN THIS NAME?

_____

_____

_____

3. FIND THE VERSES WHERE "ROCK" AND "SAVIOR" ARE MENTIONED TOGETHER. WHAT IS THE CONNECTION?

_____

_____

_____

4. DO YOU HAVE ANY OBSERVATIONS ABOUT THIS CHARACTER TRAIT OF GOD OR WHY GOD WANTS US TO KNOW THAT HE IS OUR ROCK?

_____

_____

_____

_____

_____

NOTES:

God Our Rock

Genesis 49:24
But his bow remained steady, his strong arms stayed limber, because of the hand of the Mighty One of Jacob, because of the Shepherd, the **Rock** of Israel,

Deuteronomy 32:4
He is the **Rock**, his works are perfect, and all his ways are just. A faithful God who does no wrong, upright and just is he.

Deuteronomy 32:15
They abandoned the God who made them and rejected the **Rock** their Savior.

Deuteronomy 32:18
You deserted the **Rock**, who fathered you; you forgot the God who gave you birth.

Deuteronomy 32:30
How could one man chase a thousand, or two put ten thousand to flight, unless their **Rock** had sold them, unless the LORD had given them up?

Deuteronomy 32:31
For their rock is not like our **Rock**, as even our enemies concede.

1 Samuel 2:2
"There is no one holy like the LORD; there is no one besides you; there is no **Rock** like our God.

2 Samuel 22:2
He said: "The LORD is my **rock**, my fortress and my deliverer;

2 Samuel 22:3
my God is my **rock**, in whom I take refuge, my shield and the horn of my salvation. He is my stronghold, my refuge and my savior—

2 Samuel 22:32
For who is God besides the LORD? And who is the **Rock** except our God?

2 Samuel 22:47
"The LORD lives! Praise be to my **Rock**! Exalted be my God, the **Rock,** my Savior!

2 Samuel 23:3
The God of Israel spoke, the **Rock** of Israel said to me: 'When one rules over people in righteousness, when he rules in the fear of God,

Psalm 18:2
The LORD is my **rock**, my fortress and my deliverer; my God is my **rock**, in whom I take refuge, my shield and the horn of my salvation, my stronghold.

Psalm 18:31
For who is God besides the LORD? And who is the **Rock** except our God?

Psalm 18:46
The LORD lives! Praise be to my **Rock**! Exalted be God my Savior!

Psalm 19:14
May these words of my mouth and this meditation of my heart be pleasing in your sight, LORD, my **Rock** and my Redeemer.

Psalm 28:1
To you, LORD, I call; you are my **Rock,**

Psalm 31:2
Turn your ear to me, come quickly to my rescue; be my **rock** of refuge, a strong fortress to save me.

Psalm 31:3
Since you are my **rock** and my fortress, for the sake of your name lead and guide me.

Psalm 40:2
He lifted me out of the slimy pit, out of the mud and mire; he set my feet on a **rock** and gave me a firm place to stand.

Psalm 42:9
I say to God my **Rock**,

Psalm 61:2
From the ends of the earth I call to you, I call as my heart grows faint; lead me to the **rock** that is higher than I.

Psalm 62:2
Truly he is my **rock** and my salvation; he is my fortress, I will never be shaken.

Psalm 62:6
Truly he is my **rock** and my salvation; he is my fortress, I will not be shaken.

Psalm 62:7
My salvation and my honor depend on God ; he is my mighty **rock**, my refuge.

Psalm 71:3
Be my **rock** of refuge, to which I can always go; give the command to save me, for you are my **rock** and my fortress.

Psalm 78:35
They remembered that God was their **Rock**, that God Most High was their Redeemer.

Psalm 89:26
He will call out to me, 'You are my Father, my God, the **Rock** my Savior.'

Psalm 92:15
proclaiming, "The LORD is upright; he is my **Rock**, and there is no wickedness in him."

Psalm 94:22
But the LORD has become my fortress, and my God the **rock** in whom I take refuge.

Psalm 95:1
Come, let us sing for joy to the LORD; let us shout aloud to the **Rock** of our salvation.

Psalm 144:1
Praise be to the LORD my **Rock**, who trains my hands for war, my fingers for battle.

Isaiah 8:14
He will be a holy place; for both Israel and Judah he will be a stone that causes people to stumble and a **rock** that makes them fall.

Isaiah 17:10
You have forgotten God your Savior; you have not remembered the **Rock**, your fortress.

Isaiah 26:4
Trust in the LORD forever, for the LORD, the LORD himself, is the **Rock** eternal.

Isaiah 30:29
And you will sing as on the night you celebrate a holy festival; your hearts will rejoice as when people playing pipes go up to the mountain of the LORD, to the **Rock** of Israel.

Isaiah 44:8
Do not tremble, do not be afraid. Did I not proclaim this and foretell it long ago? You are my witnesses. Is there any God besides me? No, there is no other **Rock**; I know not one."

Habakkuk 1:12
LORD, are you not from everlasting? My God, my Holy One, you will never die. You, LORD, have appointed them to execute judgment; you, my **Rock**, have ordained them to punish.

God Our Rock

Matthew 16:18
And I tell you that you are Peter, and on this **rock** I will build my church, and the gates of Hades will not overcome it.

1 Corinthians 10:4
and drank the same spiritual drink; for they drank from the spiritual **rock** that accompanied them, and that **rock** was Christ.

God Our Savior
Salvation
Able to Save

Savior:
Someone who rescues or delivers from harm, danger or death.

*She will give birth to a son, and you are to give him the name Jesus, because he will **save** his people from their sins.*

- Matthew 1:21

God Our Savior

1. DEFINE SAVIOR USING YOUR OWN WORDS, SYNONYMS, OR DESCRIPTIONS:

_____

_____

_____

2. ISAIAH 45:17, "ISREAL WILL BE SAVED BY THE LORD WITH AN EVERLASTING SALVATION", AND OTHER VERSES SHOW GOD'S SALAVATION AS A THEME THROUGHOUT THE OLD AND NEW TESTAMENTS. LIST SOME OF THESE VERSES AND COMMENT.

_____

_____

_____

3. LUKE 2:11, "TODAY IN THE TOWN OF DAVID A SAVIOR HAS BEEN BORN TO YOU". WHAT A SIMPLE, YET AMAZING STATEMENT! LUKE 19:10, "FOR THE SON OF MAN CAME TO SEEK AND TO SAVE THE LOST." WHAT DOES IT SAY ABOUT GOD THAT JESUS WAS SENT TO BE THE SAVIOR OF THE WORLD?

_____

_____

_____

4. DO YOU HAVE ANY OBSERVATIONS ABOUT THIS CHARACTER TRAIT OF GOD OR WHY GOD WANTS US TO KNOW THAT HE IS OUR SAVIOR, SALVATION AND ABLE TO SAVE?

_____

_____

_____

_____

_____

There are times when I sense such a feeling of peace,
  Like the brooding of wings from above!
There are times when it seems all feeling is gone;
  Then I rest in the fact of His love!
Though kingdoms may crumble,
  His Word is secure, the plan of salvation intact.
Though it's precious to feel His presence is near,
  Our hope is not feeling, but fact!
                    - Alice Hansche Mortenson

NOTES:

God Our Savior

Genesis 45:7
But God sent me ahead of you to preserve for you a remnant on earth and to **save** your lives by a great deliverance.

Exodus 14:30
That day the LORD **saved** Israel from the hands of the Egyptians,

Exodus 15:2
"The LORD is my strength and my defense; he has become my **salvation**.

Exodus 18:4
"My father's God was my helper; he **saved** me from the sword of Pharaoh."

Exodus 18:8
Moses told his father-in-law about everything the LORD had done to Pharaoh and the Egyptians for Israel's sake and about all the hardships they had met along the way and how the LORD had **saved** them.

Deuteronomy 32:15
They abandoned the God who made them and rejected the Rock their **Savior**.

Deuteronomy 33:29
Blessed are you, Israel! Who is like you, a people **saved** by the LORD?

1 Samuel 10:19
But you have now rejected your God, who **saves** you out of all your disasters and calamities.

1 Samuel 14:23
So on that day the LORD **saved** Israel,

2 Samuel 22:3
my God is my rock, in whom I take refuge, my shield and the horn of my **salvation**. He is my stronghold, my refuge and my **savior**—

2 Samuel 22:4
"I called to the LORD, who is worthy of praise, and have been **saved** from my enemies.

2 Samuel 22:28
You **save** the humble,

2 Samuel 22:47
"The LORD lives! Praise be to my Rock! Exalted be my God, the Rock, my **Savior**!

2 Kings 14:27
And since the LORD had not said he would blot out the name of Israel from under heaven, he **saved** them

2 Kings 19:34
I will defend this city and **save** it, for my sake and for the sake of David my servant.'"

1 Chronicles 16:23
Sing to the LORD, all the earth; proclaim his **salvation** day after day.

1 Chronicles 16:35
Cry out, "Save us, God our **Savior**; gather us and deliver us from the nations,

Psalm 6:4
Turn, LORD, and deliver me; **save** me because of your unfailing love.

Psalm 7:1
LORD my God, I take refuge in you; **save** and deliver me from all who pursue me,

Psalm 7:10
My shield is God Most High, who **saves** the upright in heart.

Psalm 9:14
that I may declare your praises in the gates of Daughter Zion, and there rejoice in your **salvatio**n.

Psalm 13:5
But I trust in your unfailing love; my heart rejoices in your **salvation**.

Psalm 17:7
Show me the wonders of your great love, you who **save** by your right hand those who take refuge in you from their foes.

Psalm 18:2
The LORD is my rock, my fortress and my deliverer; my God is my rock, in whom I take refuge, my shield and the horn of my **salvation**, my stronghold.

Psalm 18:3
I called to the LORD, who is worthy of praise, and I have been **saved** from my enemies.

Psalm 18:27
You **save** the humble but bring low those whose eyes are haughty.

Psalm 18:46
The LORD lives! Praise be to my Rock! Exalted be God my **Savior**!

Psalm 22:5
To you they cried out and were **saved**; in you they trusted and were not put to shame.

Psalm 24:5
They will receive blessing from the LORD and vindication from God their **Savior**.

Psalm 25:5
Guide me in your truth and teach me, for you are God my **Savior**, and my hope is in you all day long.

Psalm 27:1
The LORD is my light and my **salvation**— whom shall I fear?

Psalm 27:9
Do not hide your face from me, do not turn your servant away in anger; you have been my helper. Do not reject me or forsake me, God my **Savior**.

Psalm 28:8
The LORD is the strength of his people, a fortress of **salvation** for his anointed one.

Psalm 31:2
be my rock of refuge, a strong fortress to **save** me.

Psalm 31:16
Let your face shine on your servant; **save** me in your unfailing love.

Psalm 34:6
This poor man called, and the LORD heard him; he **saved** him out of all his troubles.

Psalm 34:18
The LORD is close to the brokenhearted and **saves** those who are crushed in spirit.

Psalm 35:9
Then my soul will rejoice in the LORD and delight in his **salvation**.

Psalm 37:39
The **salvation** of the righteous comes from the LORD; he is their stronghold in time of trouble.

Psalm 37:40
The LORD helps them and delivers them; he delivers them from the wicked and **saves** them, because they take refuge in him.

God Our Savior

Psalm 38:22
Come quickly to help me, my Lord and my **Savior**.

Psalm 39:8
Save me from all my transgressions;

Psalm 40:13
Be pleased to **save** me, LORD; come quickly, LORD, to help me.

Psalm 42:5, 11 and 43:5
Put your hope in God, for I will yet praise him, my **Savior** and my God.

Psalm 50:23
Those who sacrifice thank offerings honor me, and to the blameless I will show my **salvation**."

Psalm 51:14
Deliver me from the guilt of bloodshed, O God, you who are God my **Savior**,

Psalm 54:1
Save me, O God, by your name; vindicate me by your might.

Psalm 55:16
As for me, I call to God, and the LORD **saves** me.

Psalm 57:3
He sends from heaven and **saves** me, rebuking those who hotly pursue me— God sends forth his love and his faithfulness.

Psalm 60:5
Save us and help us with your right hand, that those you love may be delivered.

Psalm 62:1
Truly my soul finds rest in God; my **salvation** comes from him.

Psalm 62:2
Truly he is my rock and my **salvation**; he is my fortress, I will never be shaken.

Psalm 62:6
Truly he is my rock and my **salvation**; he is my fortress, I will not be shaken.

Psalm 62:7
My **salvation** and my honor depend on God; he is my mighty rock, my refuge.

Psalm 65:5
You answer us with awesome and righteous deeds, God our **Savior**, the hope of all the ends of the earth and of the farthest seas,

Psalm 67:2
so that your ways may be known on earth, your **salvation** among all nations.

Psalm 68:19
Praise be to the Lord, to God our **Savior**, who daily bears our burdens.

Psalm 68:20
Our God is a God who **saves**; from the Sovereign LORD comes escape from death.

Psalm 69:1
Save me, O God, for the waters have come up to my neck.

Psalm 69:13
But I pray to you, LORD, in the time of your favor; in your great love, O God, answer me with your sure **salvation**.

Psalm 69:29
But as for me, afflicted and in pain— may your **salvation**, God, protect me.

Psalm 69:35
for God will **save** Zion and rebuild the cities of Judah.

Psalm 70:1
Hasten, O God, to **save** me; come quickly, LORD, to help me.

Psalm 71:2
In your righteousness, rescue me and deliver me; turn your ear to me and **save** me.

Psalm 71:3
Be my rock of refuge, to which I can always go; give the command to **save** me, for you are my rock and my fortress.

Psalm 72:13
He will take pity on the weak and the needy and **save** the needy from death.

Psalm 74:12
But God is my King from long ago; he brings **salvation** on the earth.

Psalm 76:9
when you, God, rose up to judge, to **save** all the afflicted of the land.

Psalm 79:9
Help us, God our **Savior**, for the glory of your name; deliver us and forgive our sins for your name's sake.

Psalm 80:7
Restore us, God Almighty; make your face shine on us, that we may be **saved**.

Psalm 80:19
Restore us, LORD God Almighty; make your face shine on us, that we may be **saved**.

Psalm 85:4
Restore us again, God our **Savior**, and put away your displeasure toward us.

Psalm 85:7
Show us your unfailing love, LORD, and grant us your **salvation**.

Psalm 85:9
Surely his **salvation** is near those who fear him,

Psalm 86:2
Guard my life, for I am faithful to you; **save** your servant who trusts in you. You are my God;

Psalm 88:1
LORD, you are the God who **saves** me; day and night I cry out to you.

Psalm 89:26
'You are my Father, my God, the Rock my **Savior**.'

Psalm 91:3
Surely he will **save** you from the fowler's snare and from the deadly pestilence.

Psalm 91:16
With long life I will satisfy him and show him my **salvation**."

Psalm 95:1
Come, let us sing for joy to the LORD; let us shout aloud to the Rock of our **salvation**.

Psalm 96:2
Sing to the LORD, praise his name; proclaim his **salvation** day after day.

God Our Savior

Psalm 98:1
Sing to the LORD a new song, for he has done marvelous things; his right hand and his holy arm have worked **salvation** for him.

Psalm 98:2
The LORD has made his **salvation** known and revealed his righteousness to the nations.

Psalm 98:3
He has remembered his love and his faithfulness to Israel; all the ends of the earth have seen the **salvation** of our God.

Psalm 106:4
Remember me, LORD, when you show favor to your people, come to my aid when you **save** them,

Psalm 106:8
Yet he **saved** them for his name's sake, to make his mighty power known.

Psalm 106:10
He **saved** them from the hand of the foe; from the hand of the enemy he redeemed them.

Psalm 106:21
They forgot the God who **saved** them, who had done great things in Egypt,

Psalm 106:47
Save us, LORD our God,

Psalm 107:13, 19
Then they cried to the LORD in their trouble, and he **saved** them from their distress.

Psalm 108:6
Save us and help us with your right hand, that those you love may be delivered.

Psalm 109:26
Help me, LORD my God; **save** me according to your unfailing love.

Psalm 109:31
For he stands at the right hand of the needy, to **save** their lives from those who would condemn them.

Psalm 116:4
Then I called on the name of the LORD: "LORD, **save** me!"

Psalm 116:6
The LORD protects the unwary; when I was brought low, he **saved** me.

Psalm 118:14
The LORD is my strength and my defense; he has become my **salvation**.

Psalm 118:21
I will give you thanks, for you answered me; you have become my **salvation**.

Psalm 118:25
LORD, **save** us! LORD, grant us success!

Psalm 119:41
May your unfailing love come to me, LORD, your **salvation**, according to your promise;

Psalm 119:81
My soul faints with longing for your **salvation**, but I have put my hope in your word.

Psalm 119:94
Save me, for I am yours; I have sought out your precepts.

Psalm 119:123
My eyes fail, looking for your **salvation**, looking for your righteous promise.

Psalm 119:146
I call out to you; **save** me and I will keep your statutes.

Psalm 119:166
I wait for your **salvation**, LORD, and I follow your commands.

Psalm 119:174
I long for your **salvation**, LORD, and your law gives me delight.

Psalm 138:7
Though I walk in the midst of trouble, you preserve my life. You stretch out your hand against the anger of my foes; with your right hand you **save** me.

Psalm 145:19
He fulfills the desires of those who fear him; he hears their cry and **saves** them.

Isaiah 12:2
Surely God is my **salvation**; I will trust and not be afraid. The LORD, the LORD himself, is my strength and my defense; he has become my **salvation**."

Isaiah 17:10
You have forgotten God your **Savior**; you have not remembered the Rock, your fortress.

Isaiah 25:9
In that day they will say, "Surely this is our God; we trusted in him, and he **saved** us. This is the LORD, we trusted in him; let us rejoice and be glad in his **salvation**."

Isaiah 33:2
LORD, be gracious to us; we long for you. Be our strength every morning, our **salvation** in time of distress.

Isaiah 33:6
He will be the sure foundation for your times, a rich store of **salvation** and wisdom and knowledge; the fear of the LORD is the key to this treasure.

Isaiah 33:22
For the LORD is our judge, the LORD is our lawgiver, the LORD is our king; it is he who will **save** us.

Isaiah 35:4
say to those with fearful hearts, "Be strong, do not fear; your God will come, he will come with vengeance; with divine retribution he will come to **save** you."

Isaiah 37:35
"I will defend this city and **save** it, for my sake and for the sake of David my servant!"

Isaiah 38:20
The LORD will **save** me,

Isaiah 43:3
For I am the LORD your God, the Holy One of Israel, your **Savior**;

Isaiah 43:11
I, even I, am the LORD, and apart from me there is no **savior**.

Isaiah 45:8
"You heavens above, rain down my righteousness; let the clouds shower it down. Let the earth open wide, let **salvation** spring up, let righteousness flourish with it; I, the LORD, have created it.

Isaiah 45:15
Truly you are a God who has been hiding himself, the God and **Savior** of Israel.

God Our Savior

Isaiah 45:17
But Israel will be **saved** by the LORD with an everlasting **salvation**;

Isaiah 45:21
Declare what is to be, present it— let them take counsel together. Who foretold this long ago, who declared it from the distant past? Was it not I, the LORD? And there is no God apart from me, a righteous God and a **Savior**; there is none but me.

Isaiah 45:22
"Turn to me and be **saved**, all you ends of the earth; for I am God, and there is no other.

Isaiah 46:13
I am bringing my righteousness near, it is not far away; and my **salvation** will not be delayed. I will grant **salvation** to Zion, my splendor to Israel.

Isaiah 49:6
I will also make you a light for the Gentiles, that my **salvation** may reach to the ends of the earth."

Isaiah 49:8
This is what the LORD says: "In the time of my favor I will answer you, and in the day of **salvation** I will help you;

Isaiah 49:26
Then all mankind will know that I, the LORD, am your **Savior**, your Redeemer, the Mighty One of Jacob."

Isaiah 51:5
My righteousness draws near speedily, my **salvation** is on the way, and my arm will bring justice to the nations.

Isaiah 51:6
Lift up your eyes to the heavens, look at the earth beneath; the heavens will vanish like smoke, the earth will wear out like a garment and its inhabitants die like flies. But my **salvation** will last forever, my righteousness will never fail.

Isaiah 51:8
But my righteousness will last forever, my **salvation** through all generations."

Isaiah 52:10
The LORD will lay bare his holy arm in the sight of all the nations, and all the ends of the earth will see the **salvation** of our God.

Isaiah 56:1
This is what the LORD says: "Maintain justice and do what is right, for my **salvation** is close at hand and my righteousness will soon be revealed.

Isaiah 59:1
Surely the arm of the LORD is not too short to **save**, nor his ear too dull to hear.

Isaiah 59:16
He saw that there was no one, he was appalled that there was no one to intervene; so his own arm achieved **salvation** for him, and his own righteousness sustained him.

Isaiah 59:17
He put on righteousness as his breastplate, and the helmet of **salvation** on his head;

Isaiah 60:16
Then you will know that I, the LORD, am your **Savior**, your Redeemer, the Mighty One of Jacob.

Isaiah 61:10
I delight greatly in the LORD; my soul rejoices in my God. For he has clothed me with garments of **salvation** and arrayed me in a robe of his righteousness, as a bridegroom adorns his head like a priest, and as a bride adorns herself with her jewels.

Isaiah 62:1
For Zion's sake I will not keep silent, for Jerusalem's sake I will not remain quiet, till her vindication shines out like the dawn, her **salvation** like a blazing torch.

Isaiah 62:11
The LORD has made proclamation to the ends of the earth: "Say to Daughter Zion, 'See, your **Savior** comes! See, his reward is with him, and his recompense accompanies him.'"

Isaiah 63:1
Who is this, robed in splendor, striding forward in the greatness of his strength? "It is I, proclaiming victory, mighty to **save**."

Isaiah 63:5
I looked, but there was no one to help, I was appalled that no one gave support; so my own arm achieved **salvation** for me, and my own wrath sustained me.

Isaiah 63:8
He said, "Surely they are my people, children who will be true to me"; and so he became their **Savior**.

Jeremiah 3:23
surely in the LORD our God is the **salvation** of Israel.

Jeremiah 4:14
Jerusalem, wash the evil from your heart and be **saved**.

Jeremiah 14:8
You who are the hope of Israel, its **Savior** in times of distress,

Jeremiah 15:20
they will fight against you but will not overcome you, for I am with you to rescue and **save** you," declares the LORD.

Jeremiah 15:21
"I will **save** you from the hands of the wicked and deliver you from the grasp of the cruel."

Jeremiah 17:14
Heal me, LORD, and I will be healed; **save** me and I will be **saved**, for you are the one I praise.

Jeremiah 23:6
In his days Judah will be saved and Israel will live in safety. This is the name by which he will be called: The LORD Our Righteous **Savior**.

Jeremiah 30:11
I am with you and will **save** you,' declares the LORD.

Jeremiah 33:16
In those days Judah will be **saved** and Jerusalem will live in safety. This is the name by which it will be called: The LORD Our Righteous **Savior**.'

Jeremiah 39:18
I will **save** you; you will not fall by the sword but will escape with your life, because you trust in me, declares the LORD.'"

Jeremiah 42:11
Do not be afraid of him, declares the LORD, for I am with you and will **save** you and deliver you from his hands.

Ezekiel 13:23
I will **save** my people from your hands. And then you will know that I am the LORD.'"

Ezekiel 34:22
I will **save** my flock, and they will no longer be plundered.

Ezekiel 36:29
I will **save** you from all your uncleanness.

Ezekiel 37:23
for I will **save** them from all their sinful backsliding, and I will cleanse them. They will be my people, and I will be their God.

God Our Savior

Daniel 6:27
He rescues and he **saves**; he performs signs and wonders in the heavens and on the earth.

Lamentations 3:26
it is good to wait quietly for the **salvation** of the LORD.

Hosea 1:7
Yet I will show love to Judah; and I will **save** them—not by bow, sword or battle, or by horses and horsemen, but I, the LORD their God, will **save** them."

Hosea 13:4
"But I have been the LORD your God ever since you came out of Egypt. You shall acknowledge no God but me, no **Savior** except me.

Joel 2:32
And everyone who calls on the name of the LORD will be **saved**;

Jonah 2:9
What I have vowed I will make good. I will say, '**Salvation** comes from the LORD.'"

Micah 7:7
But as for me, I watch in hope for the LORD, I wait for God my **Savior**; my God will hear me.

Zephaniah 3:17
The LORD your God is with you, the Mighty Warrior who **saves**.

Zechariah 9:16
The LORD their God will **save** his people on that day as a shepherd saves his flock.

Matthew 1:21
She will give birth to a son, and you are to give him the name Jesus, because he will **save** his people from their sins."

Matthew 10:22
You will be hated by everyone because of me, but the one who stands firm to the end will be **saved**.

Luke 1:47
and my spirit rejoices in God my **Savior**,

Luke 1:69
He has raised up a horn of **salvation** for us in the house of his servant David

Luke 1:77
to give his people the knowledge of **salvation** through the forgiveness of their sins,

Luke 2:11
Today in the town of David a **Savior** has been born to you; he is the Messiah, the Lord.

Luke 2:30
For my eyes have seen your **salvation**,

Luke 3:6
And all people will see God's **salvation**.'"

Luke 19:10
For the Son of Man came to seek and to **save** the lost."

John 3:17
For God did not send his Son into the world to condemn the world, but to **save** the world through him.

John 4:42
"We no longer believe just because of what you said; now we have heard for ourselves, and we know that this man really is the **Savior** of the world."

John 10:9
I am the gate; whoever enters through me will be **saved**.

John 12:47
For I did not come to judge the world, but to **save** the world.

Acts 2:21
And everyone who calls on the name of the Lord will be **saved**.'

Acts 4:12
Salvation is found in no one else, for there is no other name under heaven given to mankind by which we must be **saved**."

Acts 5:31
God exalted him to his own right hand as Prince and **Savior** that he might bring Israel to repentance and forgive their sins.

Acts 13:23
"From this man's descendants God has brought to Israel the **Savior** Jesus, as he promised.

Acts 15:11
We believe it is through the grace of our Lord Jesus that we are **saved**,

Acts 16:31
They replied, "Believe in the Lord Jesus, and you will be **saved**—you and your household."

Romans 1:16
For I am not ashamed of the gospel, because it is the power of God that brings **salvation** to everyone who believes: first to the Jew, then to the Gentile.

Romans 5:10
For if, while we were God's enemies, we were reconciled to him through the death of his Son, how much more, having been reconciled, shall we be **saved** through his life!

Romans 10:9
If you declare with your mouth, "Jesus is Lord," and believe in your heart that God raised him from the dead, you will be **saved**.

Romans 10:13
for, "Everyone who calls on the name of the Lord will be **saved**."

2 Corinthians 6:2
For he says, "In the time of my favor I heard you, and in the day of **salvation** I helped you." I tell you, now is the time of God's favor, now is the day of **salvation**.

Ephesians 1:13
And you also were included in Christ when you heard the message of truth, the gospel of your **salvation**.

Ephesians 2:5
made us alive with Christ even when we were dead in transgressions—it is by grace you have been **saved**.

Ephesians 2:8
For it is by grace you have been **saved**, through faith—and this is not from yourselves, it is the gift of God—

Ephesians 5:23
For the husband is the head of the wife as Christ is the head of the church, his body, of which he is the **Savior**.

Philippians 3:20
But our citizenship is in heaven. And we eagerly await a **Savior** from there, the Lord Jesus Christ,

1 Thessalonians 5:9
For God did not appoint us to suffer wrath but to receive **salvation** through our Lord Jesus Christ.

God Our Savior

1 Timothy 1:1
Paul, an apostle of Christ Jesus by the command of God our **Savior** and of Christ Jesus our hope,

1 Timothy 1:15
Christ Jesus came into the world to **save** sinners—of whom I am the worst.

1 Timothy 2:3
This is good, and pleases God our **Savior**,

1 Timothy 2:4
who wants all people to be **saved** and to come to a knowledge of the truth.

1 Timothy 4:10
because we have put our hope in the living God, who is the **Savior** of all people, and especially of those who believe.

2 Timothy 1:9
He has **saved** us and called us to a holy life—not because of anything we have done but because of his own purpose and grace. This grace was given us in Christ Jesus before the beginning of time,

2 Timothy 1:10
but it has now been revealed through the appearing of our **Savior**, Christ Jesus, who has destroyed death and has brought life and immortality to light through the gospel.

2 Timothy 2:10
Therefore I endure everything for the sake of the elect, that they too may obtain the **salvation** that is in Christ Jesus, with eternal glory.

2 Timothy 3:15
and how from infancy you have known the Holy Scriptures, which are able to make you wise for **salvation** through faith in Christ Jesus.

Titus 1:3
and which now at his appointed season he has brought to light through the preaching entrusted to me by the command of God our **Savior**,

Titus 1:4
Grace and peace from God the Father and Christ Jesus our **Savior**.

Titus 2:10
so that in every way they will make the teaching about God our **Savior** attractive.

Titus 2:11
For the grace of God has appeared that offers **salvation** to all people.

Titus 2:13
while we wait for the blessed hope—the appearing of the glory of our great God and **Savior**, Jesus Christ,

Titus 3:4
But when the kindness and love of God our **Savior** appeared,

Titus 3:5
he **saved** us, not because of righteous things we had done, but because of his mercy. He saved us through the washing of rebirth and renewal by the Holy Spirit,

Titus 3:6
whom he poured out on us generously through Jesus Christ our **Savior**,

Hebrews 2:3
how shall we escape if we ignore so great a **salvation**? This **salvation**, which was first announced by the Lord,

Hebrews 2:10
it was fitting that God, for whom and through whom everything exists, should make the pioneer of their **salvation** perfect through what he suffered.

Hebrews 5:7
During the days of Jesus' life on earth, he offered up prayers and petitions with fervent cries and tears to the one who could **save** him from death, and he was heard because of his reverent submission.

Hebrews 5:9
and, once made perfect, he became the source of eternal **salvation** for all who obey him

Hebrews 7:25
Therefore he is able to **save** completely those who come to God through him, because he always lives to intercede for them.

Hebrews 9:28
so Christ was sacrificed once to take away the sins of many; and he will appear a second time, not to bear sin, but to bring **salvation** to those who are waiting for him.

James 4:12
There is only one Lawgiver and Judge, the one who is able to **save** and destroy.

1 Peter 1:5
who through faith are shielded by God's power until the coming of the **salvation** that is ready to be revealed in the last time.

1 Peter 1:9-11
for you are receiving the end result of your faith, the **salvation** of your souls. Concerning this **salvation**, the prophets, who spoke of the grace that was to come to you, searched intently and with the greatest care, trying to find out the time and circumstances to which the Spirit of Christ in them was pointing when he predicted the sufferings of the Messiah and the glories that would follow.

1 Peter 3:21
and this water symbolizes baptism that now **saves** you also—not the removal of dirt from the body but the pledge of a clear conscience toward God. It **saves** you by the resurrection of Jesus Christ,

2 Peter 1:1
To those who through the righteousness of our God and **Savior** Jesus Christ have received a faith as precious as ours:

2 Peter 1:11
and you will receive a rich welcome into the eternal kingdom of our Lord and **Savior** Jesus Christ.

2 Peter 2:20
If they have escaped the corruption of the world by knowing our Lord and **Savior** Jesus Christ

2 Peter 3:2
I want you to recall the words spoken in the past by the holy prophets and the command given by our Lord and **Savior** through your apostles.

2 Peter 3:15
Bear in mind that our Lord's patience means **salvation**,

2 Peter 3:18
But grow in the grace and knowledge of our Lord and **Savior** Jesus Christ.

1 John 4:14
And we have seen and testify that the Father has sent his Son to be the **Savior** of the world.

Jude 1:25
to the only God our **Savior** be glory, majesty, power and authority, through Jesus Christ our Lord, before all ages, now and forevermore!

God Our Savior

Revelation 7:10
And they cried out in a loud voice: "**Salvation** belongs to our God, who sits on the throne, and to the Lamb."

Revelation 12:10
Then I heard a loud voice in heaven say: "Now have come the **salvation** and the power and the kingdom of our God, and the authority of his Messiah. For the accuser of our brothers and sisters, who accuses them before our God day and night, has been hurled down.

Revelation 19:1
After this I heard what sounded like the roar of a great multitude in heaven shouting: "Hallelujah! **Salvation** and glory and power belong to our God,

God Our Shepherd

Shepherd:
Someone who tends a flock of sheep;
A caretaker of sheep.

*For "you were like sheep going astray," but now you have returned to the **Shepherd** and Overseer of your souls.*

- I Peter 2:25

God Our Shepherd

1. DEFINE SHEPHERD USING YOUR OWN WORDS, SYNONYMS, OR DESCRIPTIONS:

_____

_____

_____

2. GOD, LIKE A SHEPHERD, IS VERY PROTECTIVE OF HIS FLOCK. HE SEEMS TO TAKE TO TASK OTHER SHEPHERDS (OR SPIRITUAL LEADERS) WHO LEAD HIS FLOCK IN A WRONG OR DANGEROUS DIRECTION. FIND THESE VERSES AND SEE HIS WARNINGS TO THOSE WHO WOULD CAUSE HIS SHEEP HARM.

_____

_____

_____

3. DO YOU HAVE ANY OBSERVATIONS ABOUT THIS CHARACTER TRAIT OF GOD OR WHY GOD WANTS US TO KNOW THAT HE IS OUR SHEPHERD?

_____

_____

_____

_____

_____

NOTES:

God Our Shepherd

Genesis 48:15
Then he blessed Joseph and said, "May the God before whom my fathers Abraham and Isaac walked faithfully, the God who has been my **shepherd** all my life to this day,

Genesis 49:24
But his bow remained steady, his strong arms stayed limber, because of the hand of the Mighty One of Jacob, because of the **Shepherd**, the Rock of Israel,

Psalm 23:1
The LORD is my **shepherd**, I lack nothing.

Psalm 28:9
Save your people and bless your inheritance; be their **shepherd** and carry them forever.

Psalm 80:1
Hear us, **Shepherd** of Israel, you who lead Joseph like a flock.

Isaiah 40:11
He tends his flock like a **shepherd**: He gathers the lambs in his arms and carries them close to his heart; he gently leads those that have young.

Jeremiah 23:1
"Woe to the shepherds who are destroying and scattering the **sheep of my pasture**!" declares the LORD.

Jeremiah 23:2
Therefore this is what the LORD, the God of Israel, says to the shepherds who tend my people: "Because you have scattered **my flock** and driven them away and

Jeremiah 31:10
"Hear the word of the LORD, you nations; proclaim it in distant coastlands: 'He who scattered Israel will gather them and will watch over his flock like a **shepherd**.'

Ezekiel 34:8
As surely as I live, declares the Sovereign LORD, because my flock lacks a shepherd and so has been plundered and has become food for all the wild animals, and because my shepherds did not search for **my flock** but cared for themselves rather than for **my flock**,

Ezekiel 34:10
This is what the Sovereign LORD says: I am against the shepherds and will hold them accountable for my flock. I will remove them from tending the flock so that the shepherds can no longer feed themselves. I will rescue **my flock** from their mouths, and it will no longer be food for them.

Ezekiel 34:12
As a **shepherd** looks after his scattered flock when he is with them, so will I look after my sheep. I will rescue them from all the places where they were scattered on a day of clouds and darkness.

Ezekiel 34:16
I will search for the lost and bring back the strays. I will bind up the injured and strengthen the weak, but the sleek and the strong I will destroy. I will **shepherd** the flock with justice.

Amos 3:12
This is what the LORD says: "As a **shepherd** rescues from the lion's mouth only two leg bones or a piece of an ear, so will the Israelites living in Samaria be rescued,

Zechariah 10:3
"My anger burns against the shepherds, and I will punish the leaders; for the LORD Almighty will care for **his flock**, the people of Judah, and make them like a proud horse in battle.

Matthew 2:6
"'But you, Bethlehem, in the land of Judah, are by no means least among the rulers of Judah; for out of you will come a ruler who will **shepherd** my people Israel.'"

Matthew 25:32
All the nations will be gathered before him, and he will separate the people one from another as a **shepherd** separates the sheep from the goats.

Matthew 26:31
[*Jesus Predicts Peter's Denial*] Then Jesus told them, "This very night you will all fall away on account of me, for it is written: "'I will strike the **shepherd**, and the sheep of the flock will be scattered.'

John 10:11
"I am the good **shepherd**. The good **shepherd** lays down his life for the sheep.

John 10:14
"I am the good **shepherd**; I know my sheep and my sheep know me—

John 10:16
I have other sheep that are not of this sheep pen. I must bring them also. They too will listen to my voice, and there shall be one flock and one **shepherd**.

Hebrews 13:20
Now may the God of peace, who through the blood of the eternal covenant brought back from the dead our Lord Jesus, that great **Shepherd** of the sheep,

1 Peter 2:25
For "you were like sheep going astray," but now you have returned to the **Shepherd** and Overseer of your souls.

1 Peter 5:2
Be shepherds of **God's flock** that is under your care, watching over them—

1 Peter 5:4
And when the Chief **Shepherd** appears, you will receive the crown of glory that will never fade away.

Revelation 7:17
For the Lamb at the center of the throne will be their **shepherd**; 'he will lead them to springs of living water.' 'And God will wipe away every tear from their eyes.' "

God Our Shield
Able to Shield Against Attack

Shield:
Something that covers or protects against a direct attack.

*Blessed are you, Israel! Who is like you, a people saved by the Lord? He is your **shield** and helper and your glorious sword.*

- Deuteronomy 33:29

God Our Shield

1. DEFINE SHIELD USING YOUR OWN WORDS, SYNONYMS, OR DESCRIPTIONS:

_____

_____

_____

2. A SHIELD IS A DEFENSIVE WEAPON, UNLIKE A SWORD WHICH IS PRIMARILY AN OFFENSIVE WEAPON. WHAT DO YOU THINK GOD IS TRYING TO CONVEY BY SAYING HE IS OUR SHIELD?

_____

_____

_____

3. DO YOU HAVE ANY OBSERVATIONS ABOUT THIS CHARACTER TRAIT OF GOD OR WHY GOD WANTS US TO KNOW THAT HE IS OUR SHIELD AND ABLE TO SHIELD AGAINST ATTACK?

_____

_____

_____

_____

_____

_____

You are my strength, O God; You are my help, O God;
You are the One on whom I call.
You are my shield, O God; my life I yield, O God;
For You will ever be my all in all.

NOTES:

God Our Shield

Genesis 15:1
[*The LORD's Covenant With Abram*] After this, the word of the LORD came to Abram in a vision: "Do not be afraid, Abram. I am your **shield**, your very great reward. "

Deuteronomy 32:10
In a desert land he found him, in a barren and howling waste. He **shielded** him and cared for him; he guarded him as the apple of his eye,

Deuteronomy 33:12
About Benjamin he said: "Let the beloved of the LORD rest secure in him, for he **shields** him all day long, and the one the LORD loves rests between his shoulders."

Deuteronomy 33:29
Blessed are you, Israel! Who is like you, a people saved by the LORD? He is your **shield** and helper and your glorious sword.

2 Samuel 22:3
my God is my rock, in whom I take refuge, my **shield** and the horn of my salvation. He is my stronghold, my refuge and my savior— from violent people you save me.

2 Samuel 22:31
"As for God, his way is perfect: The LORD's word is flawless; he **shields** all who take refuge in him.

2 Samuel 22:36
You make your saving help my **shield**; your help has made me great.

Psalm 3:3
But you, LORD, are a **shield** around me, my glory, the One who lifts my head high.

Psalm 5:12
Surely, LORD, you bless the righteous; you surround them with your favor as with a **shield**.

Psalm 7:10
My **shield** is God Most High, who saves the upright in heart.

Psalm 18:2
The LORD is my rock, my fortress and my deliverer; my God is my rock, in whom I take refuge, my **shield** and the horn of my salvation, my stronghold.

Psalm 18:30
As for God, his way is perfect: The LORD's word is flawless; he **shields** all who take refuge in him.

Psalm 18:35
You make your saving help my **shield**, and your right hand sustains me; your help has made me great.

Psalm 28:7
The LORD is my strength and my **shield**; my heart trusts in him, and he helps me. My heart leaps for joy, and with my song I praise him.

Psalm 33:20
We wait in hope for the LORD; he is our help and our **shield**.

Psalm 35:2
Take up **shield** and armor; arise and come to my aid.

Psalm 59:11
But do not kill them, Lord our **shield**, or my people will forget.

Psalm 84:11
For the LORD God is a sun and **shield**; the LORD bestows favor and honor; no good thing does he withhold from those whose walk is blameless.

Psalm 91:4
He will cover you with his feathers, and under his wings you will find refuge; his faithfulness will be your **shield** and rampart.

Psalm 115:9
All you Israelites, trust in the LORD— he is their help and **shield**.

Psalm 115:10
House of Aaron, trust in the LORD— he is their help and **shield**.

Psalm 115:11
You who fear him, trust in the LORD— he is their help and **shield**.

Psalm 119:114
You are my refuge and my **shield**; I have put my hope in your word.

Psalm 140:7
Sovereign LORD, my strong deliverer, you **shield** my head in the day of battle.

Psalm 144:2
He is my loving God and my fortress, my stronghold and my deliverer, my **shield**, in whom I take refuge, who subdues peoples under me.

Proverbs 2:7
He holds success in store for the upright, he is a **shield** to those whose walk is blameless,

Proverbs 30:5
"Every word of God is flawless; he is a **shield** to those who take refuge in him.

Isaiah 31:5
Like birds hovering overhead, the LORD Almighty will **shield** Jerusalem; he will shield it and deliver it, he will 'pass over' it and will rescue it."

Zechariah 9:15
and the LORD Almighty will **shield** them.

Zechariah 12:8
On that day the LORD will **shield** those who live in Jerusalem, so that the feeblest among them will be like David, and the house of David will be like God, like the angel of the LORD going before them.

1 Peter 1:5
who through faith are **shielded** by God's power until the coming of the salvation that is ready to be revealed in the last time.

God is Terrible
Causing Terror
Consuming Fire
Fear of the Lord

Terrible:
One who causes extreme fear or dread.

Fear of the Lord:
Great reverence and respect given the One worthy of it; Honor given to the Most Powerful.

Serve the Lord with fear and celebrate his rule with trembling.

- Psalm 2:11

God is Terrible

1. DEFINE TERRIBLE USING YOUR OWN WORDS, SYNONYMS, OR DESCRIPTIONS:

_____

_____

_____

2. WHILE ON EARTH, ONE OF JESUS' CLOSEST FRIENDS WAS THE DISCIPLE JOHN WHOM IT WAS SAID WAS "THE DISCIPLE WHOM JESUS LOVED" (JOHN 13:23; 19:26). YET, LATER WHEN JESUS IN HIS GLORY APPEARED TO JOHN (REVELATION 1:12-18), JOHN SAID HE WAS TERRIFIED AND "FELL AT HIS FEET AS THOUGH DEAD." ALTHOUGH GOD EXTENDS HIS FRIENDSHIP AND HIS LOVE TO US, WE SHOULD MAINTAIN A HEALTHY RESPECT AND FEAR OF GOD IN OUR LIVES -- IT IS HIS DUE. FIND VERSES THAT SPEAK TO THIS AND COMMENT.

_____

_____

_____

3. THE "FEAR OF THE LORD" IS A REOCCURING THEME OF THE PROVERBS. LIST SOME OF THE THINGS PROVERBS TELLS US ABOUT THE FEAR OF THE LORD.

_____

_____

_____

_____

_____

4. DO YOU HAVE ANY OBSERVATIONS ABOUT THIS CHARACTER TRAIT OF GOD OR WHY GOD WANTS US TO KNOW THAT HE IS TERRIBLE AND ABLE TO CAUSE TERROR, A CONSUMING FIRE, AND DESERVING OF FEAR?

_____

_____

_____

_____

_____

There is a hard and terrifying side of God that is as much a part of the Bible as God's gentleness and kindness. We dare not neglect it because we cannot fit it into our theology. Above all, we dare not misrepresent the character of God to those who must one day meet Him face to face.
- Monty Ledford

NOTES:

God is Terrible

Genesis 35:5
Then they set out, and the **terror** of God fell on the towns all around them so that no one pursued them.

Exodus 9:20
Those officials of Pharaoh who **feared the word of the LORD** hurried to bring their slaves and their livestock inside.

Exodus 14:31
And when the Israelites saw the mighty hand of the LORD displayed against the Egyptians, the people **feared the LORD** and put their trust in him and in Moses his servant.

Exodus 15:16
terror and dread will fall on them. By the power of your arm they will be as still as a stone— until your people pass by, LORD, until the people you bought pass by.

Exodus 23:27
"I will send my **terror** ahead of you and throw into confusion every nation you encounter. I will make all your enemies turn their backs and run.

Exodus 24:17
To the Israelites the glory of the LORD looked like a **consuming fire** on top of the mountain.

Leviticus 19:14
"'Do not curse the deaf or put a stumbling block in front of the blind, but **fear your God**. I am the LORD.

Leviticus 25:17
Do not take advantage of each other, but **fear your God**. I am the LORD your God.

Leviticus 26:16
then I will do this to you: I will bring on you sudden **terror**, wasting diseases and fever that will destroy your sight and sap your strength.

Deuteronomy 2:25
This very day I will begin to put the **terror** and fear of you on all the nations under heaven. They will hear reports of you and will tremble and be in anguish because of you."

Deuteronomy 4:24
For the LORD your God is a **consuming fire**, a jealous God.

Deuteronomy 6:2
so that you, your children and their children after them may **fear the LORD** your God as long as you live by keeping all his decrees and commands that I give you, and so that you may enjoy long life.

Deuteronomy 6:13
Fear the LORD your God, serve him only and take your oaths in his name.

Deuteronomy 6:24
The LORD commanded us to obey all these decrees and to **fear the LORD** our God, so that we might always prosper and be kept alive,

Deuteronomy 9:19
I feared the anger and wrath of the LORD, for he was angry enough with you to destroy you. But again the LORD listened to me.

Deuteronomy 10:12
And now, Israel, what does the LORD your God ask of you but to **fear the LORD your God**, to walk in obedience to him, to love him, to serve the LORD your God with all your heart and with all your soul,

Deuteronomy 10:20
Fear the LORD your God and serve him.

Deuteronomy 11:25
No one will be able to stand against you. The LORD your God, as he promised you, will put the **terror** and fear of you on the whole land, wherever you go.

Deuteronomy 26:8
So the LORD brought us out of Egypt with a mighty hand and an outstretched arm, with great **terror** and with signs and wonders.

Deuteronomy 31:12
Assemble the people—men, women and children, and the foreigners residing in your towns—so they can listen and learn to **fear the LORD your God** and follow carefully all the words of this law.

Deuteronomy 31:13
Their children, who do not know this law, must hear it and learn to **fear the LORD your God**

Joshua 2:11
When we heard of it, our **hearts melted in fear** and everyone's courage failed because of you, for the LORD your God is God in heaven above and on the earth below.

Joshua 4:24
He did this so that all the peoples of the earth might know that the hand of the LORD is powerful and so that you might always **fear the LORD your God.**"

Joshua 24:14
"Now **fear the LORD** and serve him with all faithfulness.

1 Samuel 11:7
Then the **terror** of the LORD fell on the people, and they came out together as one.

1 Samuel 12:14
If you **fear the LORD** and serve and obey him and do not rebel against his commands, and if both you and the king who reigns over you follow the LORD your God—good!

1 Samuel 12:24
But be sure to **fear the LORD** and serve him faithfully with all your heart; consider what great things he has done for you.

2 Samuel 22:9
Smoke rose from his nostrils; **consuming fire** came from his mouth, burning coals blazed out of it.

1 Chronicles 14:17
So David's fame spread throughout every land, and the LORD made all the nations **fear** him.

1 Chronicles 16:25
For great is the LORD and most worthy of praise; **he is to be feared above all gods**.

2 Chronicles 14:14
They destroyed all the villages around Gerar, for the **terror of the LORD** had fallen on them.

2 Chronicles 19:7
Now let the **fear of the LORD** be on you. Judge carefully, for with the LORD our God there is no injustice or partiality or bribery."

2 Chronicles 26:5
He sought God during the days of Zechariah, who instructed him in the **fear of God**. As long as he sought the LORD, God gave him success.

Job 1:8
Then the LORD said to Satan, "Have you considered my servant Job? There is no one on earth like him; he is blameless and upright, a man who **fears God** and shuns evil."

God is Terrible

Job 2:3
Then the LORD said to Satan, "Have you considered my servant Job? There is no one on earth like him; he is blameless and upright, a man who **fears God** and shuns evil. And he still maintains his integrity, though you incited me against him to ruin him without any reason."

Job 28:28
And he said to the human race, "The **fear of the Lord**—that is wisdom, and to shun evil is understanding."

Psalm 2:11
Serve the LORD with fear and celebrate his rule with **trembling**.

Psalm 9:20
Strike them with **terror**, LORD; let the nations know they are only mortal.

Psalm 18:8
Smoke rose from his nostrils; **consuming fire** came from his mouth, burning coals blazed out of it.

Psalm 25:14
The LORD confides in those who **fear him**; he makes his covenant known to them.

Psalm 33:8
Let all the earth **fear the LORD**; let all the people of the world revere him.

Psalm 33:18
But the eyes of the LORD are on those who **fear him**, on those whose hope is in his unfailing love,

Psalm 34:9
Fear the LORD, you his holy people, for those who **fear him** lack nothing.

Psalm 76:11
Make vows to the LORD your God and fulfill them; let all the neighboring lands bring gifts to the **One to be feared**.

Psalm 88:16
Your wrath has swept over me; your **terrors** have destroyed me.

Psalm 90:11
If only we knew the power of your anger! Your wrath is as great as **the fear that is your due**.

Psalm 96:4
For great is the LORD and most worthy of praise; **he is to be feared** above all gods.

Psalm 102:15
The nations will **fear the name of the LORD**, all the kings of the earth will revere your glory.

Psalm 103:13
As a father has compassion on his children, so the LORD has compassion on those who **fear him**;

Psalm 103:17
But from everlasting to everlasting the LORD's love is with those who **fear him**, and his righteousness with their children's children—

Psalm 111:10
The **fear of the LORD** is the beginning of wisdom; all who follow his precepts have good understanding.

Psalm 115:11
You who **fear him**, trust in the LORD— he is their help and shield.

Psalm 115:13
he will bless those who **fear the LORD**— small and great alike.

Psalm 128:1
Blessed are all who **fear the LORD**, who walk in obedience to him.

Psalm 147:11
the LORD delights in those who **fear him**, who put their hope in his unfailing love.

Proverbs 1:7
The **fear of the LORD** is the beginning of knowledge, but fools despise wisdom and instruction.

Proverbs 2:5
then you will understand the **fear of the LORD** and find the knowledge of God.

Proverbs 3:7
Do not be wise in your own eyes; **fear the LORD** and shun evil.

Proverbs 8:13
To **fear the LORD** is to hate evil; I hate pride and arrogance, evil behavior and perverse speech.

Proverbs 9:10
The **fear of the LORD** is the beginning of wisdom, and knowledge of the Holy One is understanding.

Proverbs 14:2
Whoever **fears the LORD** walks uprightly, but those who despise him are devious in their ways.

Proverbs 14:16
The wise **fear the LORD** and shun evil, but a fool is hotheaded and yet feels secure.

Proverbs 14:26
Whoever **fears the LORD** has a secure fortress, and for their children it will be a refuge.

Proverbs 14:27
The **fear of the LORD** is a fountain of life, turning a person from the snares of death.

Proverbs 15:16
Better a little with the **fear of the LORD** than great wealth with turmoil.

Proverbs 15:33
Wisdom's instruction is to **fear the LORD**, and humility comes before honor.

Proverbs 16:6
Through love and faithfulness sin is atoned for; through the **fear of the LORD** evil is avoided.

Proverbs 19:23
The **fear of the LORD** leads to life;

Proverbs 22:4
Humility is the **fear of the LORD**;

Isaiah 2:10
Go into the rocks, hide in the ground from the **fearful presence of the LORD** and the splendor of his majesty!

Isaiah 2:19
People will flee to caves in the rocks and to holes in the ground from the **fearful presence of the LORD** and the splendor of his majesty, when he rises to shake the earth.

Isaiah 2:21
They will flee to caverns in the rocks and to the overhanging crags from the **fearful presence of the LORD** and the splendor of his majesty, when he rises to shake the earth.

Isaiah 8:13
The LORD Almighty is the one you are to regard as holy, **he is the one you are to fear**, he is the one you are to dread.

God is Terrible

Isaiah 22:5
The Lord, the LORD Almighty, has a day of tumult and trampling and **terror**

Isaiah 30:27
See, the Name of the LORD comes from afar, with burning anger and dense clouds of smoke; his lips are full of wrath, and his tongue is a **consuming fire**.

Isaiah 30:30
The LORD will cause people to hear his majestic voice and will make them see his arm coming down with raging anger and **consuming fire**, with cloudburst, thunderstorm and hail.

Isaiah 59:19
From the west, people will **fear the name of the LORD**, and from the rising of the sun, they will revere his glory.

Jeremiah 5:22
Should you not fear me?" declares the LORD. "Should you not tremble in my presence? I made the sand a boundary for the sea, an everlasting barrier it cannot cross. The waves may roll, but they cannot prevail; they may roar, but they cannot cross it.

Jeremiah 32:21
You brought your people Israel out of Egypt with signs and wonders, by a mighty hand and an outstretched arm and with great **terror**.

Jeremiah 49:5
I will bring **terror** on you from all those around you," declares the Lord, the LORD Almighty.

Ezekiel 30:13
"'This is what the Sovereign LORD says: "'I will destroy the idols and put an end to the images in Memphis. No longer will there be a prince in Egypt, and I will spread **fear** throughout the land.

Ezekiel 32:32
Although I had him spread **terror** in the land of the living, Pharaoh and all his hordes will be laid among the uncircumcised, with those killed by the sword, declares the Sovereign LORD."

Malachi 1:14
"For I am a great king," says the LORD Almighty, "and **my name is to be feared** among the nations.

Malachi 3:16
[*The Faithful Remnant*] Then those who **feared the LORD** talked with each other, and the LORD listened and heard. A scroll of remembrance was written in his presence concerning those who feared the LORD and honored his name.

Hebrews 10:28-31
Anyone who rejected the law of Moses died without mercy on the testimony of two or three witnesses. How much more severely do you think someone deserves to be punished who has trampled the Son of God underfoot, who has treated as an unholy thing the blood of the covenant that sanctified them, and who has insulted the Spirit of grace? For we know him who said, "It is mine to avenge; I will repay," and again, "The Lord will judge his people." **It is a dreadful thing** to fall into the hands of the living God.

Hebrews 12:29
for our "God is a **consuming fire**."

Revelation 6:16
They called to the mountains and the rocks, "Fall on us and **hide us from the face of him who sits on the throne** and from the wrath of the Lamb!

Revelation 15:4
Who will not fear you, Lord, and bring glory to your name? For you alone are holy. All nations will come and worship before you, for your righteous acts have been revealed."

God is Trustworthy

Trustworthy:
Someone worthy of trust; reliable.

The works of his hands are faithful and just; all his precepts are **trustworthy**.

- *Psalm 111:7*

God is Trustworthy

1. DEFINE TRUSTWORTHY USING YOUR OWN WORDS, SYNONYMS, OR DESCRIPTIONS:

_____

_____

_____

2. THE BIBLE SHOWS THAT GOD IS TRUSTWORTHY -- OR WORTHY OF OUR TRUST. IT STATES THE FOLLOWING ARE ALSO TRUSTWORTHY: HIS COVENANT, HIS STATUTES, HIS PRECEPTS, HIS COMMANDS, HIS PROMISES AND HIS WORDS. COMMENT ON WHAT THIS REVEALS ABOUT GOD.

_____

_____

_____

3. DO YOU HAVE ANY OBSERVATIONS ABOUT THIS CHARACTER TRAIT OF GOD OR WHY GOD WANTS US TO KNOW THAT HE IS TRUSTWORTHY?

_____

_____

_____

_____

_____

My religious belifs teach me to feel as safe in battle as in bed.
                                        - Thomas (Stonewall) Jackson

Job didn't get an immediate answer to his questions. He had to accept the fact that a relationship with the One who knows the answers is better than the answers themselves.
                                        - David W. Dyke

NOTES:

God is Trustworthy

2 Samuel 7:28
Sovereign LORD, you are God! Your covenant is **trustworthy**, and you have promised these good things to your servant.

Psalm 19:7
The law of the LORD is perfect, refreshing the soul. The statutes of the LORD are **trustworthy**, making wise the simple.

Psalm 111:7
The works of his hands are faithful and just; all his precepts are **trustworthy**.

Psalm 119:86
All your commands are **trustworthy**;

Psalm 119:138
The statutes you have laid down are righteous; they are fully **trustworthy**.

Psalm 145:13
The LORD is **trustworthy** in all he promises and faithful in all he does.

Revelation 21:5
He who was seated on the throne said, "I am making everything new!" Then he said, "Write this down, for these words are **trustworthy** and true."

God is Truth
He and His Words are True

Truth:
Possessing the quality of being true or in accordance with fact; Genuine and not false; Accurate.

*But the Lord is the **true** God; he is the living God, the eternal King.*

- Jeremiah 10:10

God is Truth

1. DEFINE TRUTH USING YOUR OWN WORDS, SYNONYMS, OR DESCRIPTIONS:

_____

_____

_____

2. JOHN 14: 6, "JESUS ANSWERED, 'I AM THE WAY AND THE TRUTH AND THE LIFE. NO ONE COME TO THE FATHER EXCEPT THROUGH ME.'" THIS WAS JUST ANOTHER WAY OF STATING WHAT WAS SAID IN JEREMIAH 10:10, "THE LORD IS THE TRUE GOD; HE IS THE LIVING GOD AND ETERNAL KING." EXPLAIN.

_____

_____

_____

3. DO YOU HAVE ANY OBSERVATIONS ABOUT THIS CHARACTER TRAIT OF GOD OR WHY GOD WANTS US TO KNOW THAT HE IS TRUTH AND THAT HE AND HIS WORDS ARE TRUE?

_____

_____

_____

_____

_____

Let us be true to truth, loving it not because it is pleasant or picturesque or anient, but because it is true and divine.

— Horatius Bonar

"I know not the way!" despairing, I cried.
  "I am the Way" Jesus kindly replied.
"I'm searching for truth!" was my heart's plaintive cry.
  "I am the Truth," was his gentle reply.
"I am longing for life! Oh, where can it be?"
  "I am the Life. Thou shalt find it in Me!"

— Flora Smith

NOTES:

God is Truth

Isaiah 65:16
Whoever invokes a blessing in the land will do so by the one **true** God; whoever takes an oath in the land will swear by the one **true** God.

Jeremiah 10:10
But the LORD is the **true** God; he is the living God, the eternal King.

Psalm 33:4
For the word of the LORD is right and **true**; he is faithful in all he does.

Psalm 119:142
Your righteousness is everlasting and your law is **true**.

Psalm 119:151
Yet you are near, LORD, and all your commands are **true**.

Psalm 119:160
All your words are **true**;

John 3:33
Whoever has accepted it has certified that God is **truthful**.

John 7:28
Then Jesus, still teaching in the temple courts, cried out, "Yes, you know me, and you know where I am from. I am not here on my own authority, but he who sent me is **true**.

John 8:16
But if I do judge, my decisions are **true**, because I am not alone. I stand with the Father, who sent me.

John 14:6
Jesus answered, "I am the way and the **truth** and the life. No one comes to the Father except through me.

John 17:3
Now this is eternal life: that they know you, the only **true** God, and Jesus Christ, whom you have sent.

Romans 3:4
Let God be **true**, and every human being a liar.

Romans 3:7
Someone might argue, "If my falsehood enhances God's **truthfulness** and so increases his glory, why am I still condemned as a sinner?"

1 Thessalonians 1:9
They tell how you turned to God from idols to serve the living and **true** God,

1 John 5:20
We know also that the Son of God has come and has given us understanding, so that we may know him who is **true**. And we are in him who is **true** by being in his Son Jesus Christ. He is the **true** God and eternal life.

Revelation 3:7
These are the words of him who is holy and **true**, who holds the key of David.

Revelation 6:10
They called out in a loud voice, "How long, Sovereign Lord, holy and **true**, until you judge the inhabitants of the earth and avenge our blood?"

Revelation 15:3
"Great and marvelous are your deeds, Lord God Almighty. Just and **true** are your ways, King of the nations.

Revelation 16:7
And I heard the altar respond: "Yes, Lord God Almighty, **true** and just are your judgments."

Revelation 19:2
for **true** and just are his judgments.

Revelation 19:9
Then the angel said to me, "Write this: Blessed are those who are invited to the wedding supper of the Lamb!" And he added, "These are the **true** words of God."

Revelation 19:11
I saw heaven standing open and there before me was a white horse, whose rider is called Faithful and **True**. With justice he judges and wages war.

Revelation 21:5
He who was seated on the throne said, "I am making everything new!" Then he said, "Write this down, for these words are trustworthy and **true**."

God Our Warrior

Warrior:
One who fights in a battle; having a mission of war.

*The Lord your God is with you, the Mighty **Warrior** who saves.*

- Zephaniah 3:17

God Our Warrior

1. DEFINE WARRIOR USING YOUR OWN WORDS, SYNONYMS, OR DESCRIPTIONS:

_____

_____

_____

2. ZEPHANIAH 3:17, "THE LORD YOUR GOD IS WITH YOU, THE MIGHTY WARRIOR WHO SAVES." IT CERTAINLY SOUNDS LIKE GOD IS NOT ONE TO RUN FROM BATTLE -- AND "MIGHTY WARRIOR" IMPLIES ONE WHO HAS BEEN WAR TESTED AND PROVEN VICTORIOUS ON THE BATTLEFIELD. TAKE TIME TO FIND SOME OF THE BATTLES IN THE BIBLE THAT GOD HAS FOUGHT AND WON FOR HIS PEOPLE (THERE ARE A LOT OF GOOD WAR STORIES).

_____

_____

_____

3. DO YOU HAVE ANY OBSERVATIONS ABOUT THIS CHARACTER TRAIT OF GOD OR WHY GOD WANTS US TO KNOW THAT HE IS OUR WARRIOR?

_____

_____

_____

_____

_____

NOTES:

God Our Warrior

Exodus 15:3
The LORD is a **warrior**; the LORD is his name.

Isaiah 42:13
The LORD will march out like a champion, like a **warrior** he will stir up his zeal; with a shout he will raise the battle cry and will triumph over his enemies.

Jeremiah 20:11
But the LORD is with me like a mighty **warrior**;

Zephaniah 3:17
The LORD your God is with you, the Mighty **Warrior** who saves.

God is Wonderful
Able To Do Wonderful Things
Awesome; Amazing

Wonderful:
Marvelous, surprisingly excellent, remarkable, an admiration almost beyond words.

Now therefore, our God, the great God, mighty and ***awesome****, who keeps his covenant of love,*
- Nehemiah 9:32

God is Wonderful

1. DEFINE WONDERFUL AND AWESOME USING YOUR OWN WORDS, SYNONYMS, OR DESCRIPTIONS:

_____

_____

_____

2. THE VERSES CONCERNING GOD AS AWESOME AND WONDERFUL REFER MOSTLY TO HIS WORKS, DEEDS AND ACTS. THEY SPEAK OF THE AMAZING AND REMARKABLE THINGS GOD HAS DONE FOR HIS PEOPLE. LIST SOME OF THESE WONDERFUL DEEDS AND AWESOME WORKS.

_____

_____

_____

3. DO YOU HAVE ANY OBSERVATIONS ABOUT THIS CHARACTER TRAIT OF GOD OR WHY GOD WANTS US TO KNOW THAT HE IS AWESOME, AMAZING, WONDERFUL AND ABLE TO DO WONDERFUL THINGS?

_____

_____

_____

_____

_____

NOTES:

God is Wonderful

Genesis 28:17
He was afraid and said, "How **awesome** is this place! This is none other than the house of God; this is the gate of heaven."

Exodus 15:11
Who among the gods is like you, LORD? Who is like you— majestic in holiness, **awesome** in glory, working wonders?

Exodus 34:10
Then the LORD said: "I am making a covenant with you. Before all your people I will do wonders never before done in any nation in all the world. The people you live among will see how **awesome** is the work that I, the LORD, will do for you.

Deuteronomy 4:34
or by great and **awesome** deeds, like all the things the LORD your God did for you in Egypt before your very eyes?

Deuteronomy 7:21
Do not be terrified by them, for the LORD your God, who is among you, is a great and **awesome** God.

Deuteronomy 10:17
For the LORD your God is God of gods and Lord of lords, the great God, mighty and **awesome**,

Deuteronomy 10:21
He is the one you praise; he is your God, who performed for you those great and **awesome** wonders you saw with your own eyes.

Deuteronomy 28:58
If you do not carefully follow all the words of this law, which are written in this book, and do not revere this glorious and **awesome** name—the LORD your God—

Joshua 3:5
Joshua told the people, "Consecrate yourselves, for tomorrow the LORD will do **amazing** things among you."

Judges 13:19
Then Manoah took a young goat, together with the grain offering, and sacrificed it on a rock to the LORD. And the LORD did an **amazing** thing while Manoah and his wife watched:

2 Samuel 7:23
And who is like your people Israel—the one nation on earth that God went out to redeem as a people for himself, and to make a name for himself, and to perform great and **awesome** wonders

1 Chronicles 16:9
Sing to him, sing praise to him; tell of all his **wonderful** acts.

1 Chronicles 17:21
And who is like your people Israel—the one nation on earth whose God went out to redeem a people for himself, and to make a name for yourself, and to perform great and **awesome** wonders

Nehemiah 1:5
Then I said: "LORD, the God of heaven, the great and **awesome** God, who keeps his covenant of love with those who love him and keep his commandments,

Nehemiah 4:14
"Don't be afraid of them. Remember the Lord, who is great and **awesome**,

Nehemiah 9:32
"Now therefore, our God, the great God, mighty and **awesome**, who keeps his covenant of love,

Job 37:22
Out of the north he comes in golden splendor; God comes in **awesome** majesty.

Psalm 9:1
I will give thanks to you, LORD, with all my heart; I will tell of all your **wonderful** deeds.

Psalm 26:7
proclaiming aloud your praise and telling of all your **wonderful** deeds.

Psalm 45:4
In your majesty ride forth victoriously in the cause of truth, humility and justice; let your right hand achieve **awesome** deeds.

Psalm 47:2
For the LORD Most High is **awesome**, the great King over all the earth.

Psalm 65:5
You answer us with **awesome** and righteous deeds, God our Savior,

Psalm 66:3
Say to God, "How **awesome** are your deeds! So great is your power that your enemies cringe before you.

Psalm 66:5
Come and see what God has done, his **awesome** deeds for mankind!

Psalm 68:35
You, God, are **awesome** in your sanctuary;

Psalm 75:1
We praise you, God, we praise you, for your Name is near; people tell of your **wonderful** deeds.

Psalm 89:7
In the council of the holy ones God is greatly feared; he is more **awesome** than all who surround him.

Psalm 99:3
Let them praise your great and **awesome** name— he is holy.

Psalm 105:2
Sing to him, sing praise to him; tell of all his **wonderful** acts.

Psalm 106:22
miracles in the land of Ham and **awesome** deeds by the Red Sea.

Psalm 107:8, 15, 21, 31
Let them give thanks to the LORD for his unfailing love and his **wonderful** deeds for mankind,

Psalm 107:24
They saw the works of the LORD, his **wonderful** deeds in the deep.

Psalm 111:9
He provided redemption for his people; he ordained his covenant forever— holy and **awesome** is his name.

Psalm 119:18
Open my eyes that I may see **wonderful** things in your law.

Psalm 119:27
Cause me to understand the way of your precepts, that I may meditate on your **wonderful** deeds.

Psalm 119:129
Your statutes are **wonderful**; therefore I obey them.

Psalm 139:6
Such knowledge is too **wonderful** for me, too lofty for me to attain.

Psalm 139:14
I praise you because I am fearfully and **wonderfully** made; your works are **wonderful**,

God is Wonderful

Psalm 145:5
They speak of the glorious splendor of your majesty— and I will meditate on your **wonderful** works.

Psalm 145:6
They tell of the power of your **awesome** works— and I will proclaim your great deeds.

Isaiah 9:6
For to us a child is born, to us a son is given, and the government will be on his shoulders. And he will be called **Wonderful** Counselor, Mighty God, Everlasting Father, Prince of Peace.

Isaiah 25:1
LORD, you are my God; I will exalt you and praise your name, for in perfect faithfulness you have done **wonderful** things, things planned long ago.

Isaiah 28:29
All this also comes from the LORD Almighty, whose plan is **wonderful**, whose wisdom is magnificent.

Isaiah 64:3
For when you did **awesome** things that we did not expect, you came down, and the mountains trembled before you. Since ancient times no one has heard, no ear has perceived, no eye has seen any God besides you, who acts on behalf of those who wait for him.

Daniel 9:4
I prayed to the LORD my God and confessed: "Lord, the great and **awesome** God, who keeps his covenant of love with those who love him and keep his commandments,

Zephaniah 2:11
The LORD will be **awesome** to them when he destroys all the gods of the earth. Distant nations will bow down to him, all of them in their own lands.

Matthew 21:15
But when the chief priests and the teachers of the law saw the **wonderful** things he did and the children shouting in the temple courts, "Hosanna to the Son of David,"

Luke 13:17
people were delighted with all the **wonderful** things he was doing.

1 Peter 2:9
But you are a chosen people, a royal priesthood, a holy nation, God's special possession, that you may declare the praises of him who called you out of darkness into his **wonderful** light.